FAVORITE PLAYS
for
CLASSROOM READING

Favorite Plays
for
Classroom Reading

by

DONALD D. DURRELL

Professor of Elementary Education,
Boston University

and

B. ALICE CROSSLEY

Professor of Elementary Education,
Boston University

Publishers   PLAYS, INC.   *Boston*

FAVORITE PLAYS FOR CLASSROOM READING

Library of Congress Card Catalog Number: 65-18596

ISBN: 0-8238-0130-6

Preface to the New Edition

For several years, teachers throughout the United States and Canada have found many uses for *Favorite Plays for Classroom Reading*. With the publication of this new edition, the authors feel that some attempt should be made to aid teachers in recognizing the place of this book in today's curriculum.

Current educational philosophy is based on the concept of the open school and the open classroom. This means much more self-direction on the part of the pupils, more choice of activities, and more individual and small-group work centered around children's interests. Teachers and consultants are clamoring for materials which children can use with little or no teacher direction.

Favorite Plays for Classroom Reading can readily be used in open classroom situations. In the middle grades, the teacher should find it necessary to assist the children with only one play. From that time on, a group of children should work alone under the direction of a chairman who has had careful instructions as to his duties.

This book is one of the few in the reading field to emphasize oral reading. All of the material is in the field of drama, and the reading of it must stress the use of the child's voice, developing an awareness of accent, stress, and juncture. Without these, the dialogue is stilted and unreal. Some general teaching will be necessary to make the children aware that skill of this type is hard-earned and the result of intelligent practice.

It is our hope that through the use of this book, your students not only become self-sufficient, but also excellent oral readers who can hold the attention of the audience.

B. ALICE CROSSLEY
DONALD D. DURRELL

TABLE OF

CONTENTS

Introduction

FAVORITE PLAYS FOR CLASSROOM READING is designed to be an essential part of the reading program. The plays themselves will possess appeal for the older child, and have been chosen to represent a wide variety of interests. This collection includes mysteries, comedies, historical plays, legends, holiday plays, and adaptations from the classics.

The primary purpose of this book is to develop an understanding of the use of voice in the oral reading process. A great deal of practice material is concerned with imparting a knowledge of intonation—pitch, stress, and pause—as important in conveying meaning to the listener.

Whenever possible, attention is also given to certain characteristics of plays and play reading. The child is introduced to dialogue, the purpose of the narrator's part, and a recognition of climax.

In the intermediate grades the basic reading program stresses silent reading and the skills of study. Emphasis is placed on various types of reading, speed of reading and comprehension. While it is not our purpose to minimize the need for such emphasis, it is suggested that plays provide an excellent source of material for developing oral reading and will help to overcome some of the weaknesses which result from too much silent reading.

When the play is performed for the class, the true audience situation prevails. Varying shades of meaning, fine vocal characterizations —in fact, the success of the performance—will depend on ability to project meaning to the listener through good oral reading.

FAVORITE PLAYS FOR CLASSROOM READING should be used as a regular part of the reading program. A set of seven books should be adequate for class needs since two children may use the same book. After one or two sessions with the teacher, children should be able to prepare the play under the leadership of a chairman. Suggestions in the text help them to go through the steps required to prepare for reading to the class. No staging or properties are needed. The narrator's part is written into the play and provides necessary changes of scene as well as detailed descriptions of action.

The introduction to *Thirty Plays for Classroom Reading*[1] contains a great deal of material on the values of play reading. This section is repeated on the following pages for the benefit of those who are not acquainted with our first book of plays.

Values in Play Reading

Imagination plays a large part in the lives of children. They have spent countless hours in imaginative play as mother, father, baby, doctor, nurse, teacher, policeman, robber, cowboy, Indian, sheriff, airplane pilot, spaceman, athlete, princess, king, or President. Their reveries include such dramatization even when they are not engaged in social play. Television, radio, movies, and books of fiction employ dramatization to catch the interests of millions of people.

The classroom teacher may use this force to enrich the reading program, increasing reading interests and adding to the importance of the reading skills program. All children enjoy the reading of plays; the dramatized situation is a familiar one to them—they have spent so many voluntary enjoyable hours in it. Play reading provides an outlet for the imagination.

Play Reading a Natural Bridge to the Reading of Fiction

Children who have not learned to enjoy the reading of fiction find play reading a natural bridge from imaginative play to imaginative reading. Most children enjoy having stories read to them, but some cannot find pleasure in reading to themselves. They can create vivid imagery while listening, getting "lost" in the seeming reality of the situation. In silent reading, however, some children fail to make these rich images and find reading dull. Yet these same children engage eagerly in dramatic play. Play reading combines the imagery-producing qualities of listening and self-dramatization. Play reading encourages imagery in reading, leading the child to the enjoyment of fiction and giving practice in translating words into images.

Social and Personal Values in Play Reading

Play reading is inherently sociable, with every person adding to the creation of the whole, and all enjoying the contributions of the others. The "social caste" system of a two- or three-level class is broken down;

[1] Durrell, Donald, and Crossley, B. Alice, *Thirty Plays for Classroom Reading.* Boston, Mass.: Plays, Inc., 1957.

children at all reading levels may be cast in the same play, since each child learns to read his lines in the preparatory period. Undesirable competition is avoided, because every child reads a different part and each part is important to the whole play. A classroom becomes more closely knit socially when the pupils engage in mutual tasks that are enjoyed by everyone.

Undiscovered personality qualities are often brought out in play reading. When a child is "someone else" while reading a play, new and delightful aspects of his personality are often revealed. Plays are good for bringing out timid children, for finding sympathetic qualities in aggressive ones. By suitable casting, children can gain confidence in themselves and learn their own possibilities for improving social habits.

Plays allow discussion of personal qualities, manners, bad habits, and ethical choices without self-consciousness on the part of pupils or "moralizing" by the teacher. They can talk about the actions of the characters objectively, since the parts they take are only imaginary.

Play reading requires disciplines not encountered in other reading. Alertness to timing of speeches, coming in at the right time, keeping one's place on the page, correct reading of words and phrases, good expression—these and other factors are recognized by the child as important to the success of the play. He cannot be inattentive or careless in his reading, or the desired effect is spoiled. Standards of craftsmanship in reading are important to him, and the voluntary disciplines he encounters in play reading help him in other situations.

Enhancing Reading Skills Through Play Reading

The motivating power of the true audience situation is always found in play reading. Comprehension is assured; the child cannot interpret his lines unless he understands them. Careless and inattentive reading is seldom encountered in play reading, because each child realizes the importance of his particular part; if he reads it inaccurately the listener is confused.

Attention to new words or unfamiliar phrases is equally important to interpretation of the lines of the play. While most of the words in the plays are within the oral vocabularies of children, there was no attempt to limit the words to the reading vocabulary of a particular level. As the child has the opportunity to learn the words in advance of presentation, and as no one part contains many difficult words, even the slower learner can read the parts successfully. Vocabulary enrichment is an essential part of play reading, and children enjoy displaying new words in the dramatized situation. Even the words of an unfamiliar period, words in dialect, or even parts in colloquial English are relished by children. If they are playing the parts of "stuffy" adults, they enjoy using very large words or stilted expressions.

Improvement of expression in reading, is, of course, the main outcome of play reading. Teachers who have used these plays comment favorably on the noticeable improvement in expression. The desire to read with good expression carries over into other reading. Superior silent reading does not assure good oral reading. Even pupils in advanced reading groups will profit by play reading, and the reluctant reader who resists descriptive or narrative passages will take readily to reading dialogue.

Phrase reading is always improved by play reading. The child who is inclined to read a word at a time or to ignore commas and periods in oral reading, will strive voluntarily to make good phrases and to pay attention to punctuation when he reads plays.

Improving Speech Skills Through Play Reading

Because the listeners need to understand the play, poor enunciation and pronunciation are unacceptable in play reading. The child who is careless in speech habits finds that he *must* improve if people are to understand and enjoy his part in the play. The social pressure of one's classmates has greater effect than any amount of adult admonition.

The increase of oral vocabulary is a natural outcome of play reading. The child who has used new words to express ideas is more likely to venture into such words in his regular speech. Many expressions used in plays become a normal part of the child's speech pattern.

Values in Expressive Oral Reading

It is high time that oral reading resume some of its former importance in the reading program. The delights of much imaginative reading simply cannot be discovered by lonely silent reading. The increasing amount of oral reading in modern life requires that it be served in school. Almost every parent reads bedtime stories to children. More and more people appear before television and radio; there are frequent business and professional meetings at which papers are read; clubs and organizations in school and community life often require oral reading; almost anyone in an executive position finds some oral reading necessary. An inquiry among any group of adults will reveal that all would like to be better oral readers. Expressive oral reading should be given a significant place in the reading program, especially among children who will later have high responsibility.

Use of FAVORITE PLAYS FOR CLASSROOM READING in Remedial Reading Classes

Remedial reading is usually concerned with systematic development of basic reading skills. It requires carefully graded exercises in various vocabulary abilities, in comprehension and recall, in speeded skills and various thinking skills related to interpretation of reading. Although FAVORITE PLAYS FOR CLASSROOM READING is not primarily a remedial reading book, it serves well some of the needs commonly found among children who have reading difficulty.

As the child approaches fifth grade reading ability, he will be able to get much enjoyment from FAVORITE PLAYS FOR CLASSROOM READING. He can learn the lines of a particular part and share the pleasure of reading with others of higher reading ability. He may require several days of advance preparation, mastering his part and learning to follow the cues for his lines, but the reward for successful reading is highly motivating. Variety of reading is essential to high interest, and the preparation of a play for reading adds zest to the learning.

The reading of plays is especially helpful in phrase reading and for observing the importance of punctuation in reading. Word-by-word reading and awkward phrasing are helped by play reading. The analytical task of word perception is lightened by the reward of a meaningful sentence in a play. The poor reader is encouraged by successful handling of new vocabulary found in the lines of the play. He may need separate practice on words and phrases which appear in his part, but this task is lightened by his anticipation of taking part in a play.

Since the burden of word learning often distracts the slow learner from the imagery contained in the reading material, the alternate listening and reading helps to keep the imagery alive. The child with reading difficulty often needs an unusual amount of help in preserving attention to imagery and meaning in reading. Plays help him greatly in both of these needs.

Values in the Content of the Plays

Although the values of play reading have been given much emphasis here, the plays themselves are desirable additions to the literature of the classroom. In content and spirit, they offer enrichment of ideas, aesthetics, literary values. Some are historical, some are highly imaginative, some nonsensical; many are humorous, some are regional, some present dialect—all reveal delightful aspects of character. The authors of the plays are experienced in writing plays for children. To keep a play moving, to bring out values in lines, to fit lines to normal speech patterns, and to write materials which appeal to children, require particular experience and talent. These authors have accomplished their objectives well.

A study of the titles in the Table of Contents reveals the great variety of materials.

Suggestions for Teachers

Successful use of these plays depends in the final analysis on the teacher. Her delight, enthusiasm, and interest will be shared by the children. This book should provide fun and give zest to the reading program.

Ultimate enjoyment for the listener is dependent on the skill of the performers. Such skill is hard-earned, and the result of intelligent practice. Only the teacher can help the children to see the need for following the directions outlined for each play.

In the beginning it is suggested that the children work with the teacher in order to develop an understanding of the procedures and a recognition of the level of reading required for a good performance. In a short time it should be possible to have a group of children work alone. When the chairman of the group is chosen, the teacher should emphasize the need for him to follow the directions preceding each play.

The remainder of this section is organized under three major headings: *Use of Voice, Characteristics of Plays*, and *Techniques of Evaluation*. Sample materials are given under each of the three headings. It is suggested that teachers prepare multiple materials of this type for *Articulation, Pitch, Stress*, and *Pause*, based on excerpts from the plays which the children are going to read. These exercises should be so constructed that children can practice them alone.

If some of the plays seem very long for a single performance, do not hesitate to break them into two acts. This can be done by choosing a natural break just before the entrance of the Narrator.

Use of Voice

Formal training in use of voice is an intricate and scientific procedure which does not fit the purposes of this book. There are, however, a few simple techniques to which children can be introduced, that will prove both interesting and effective.

Articulation

A clear and distinct utterance of the syllables within words is very important to good reading. It has often been said that good articulation is to the ear what clear open type is to the eye.

Rapid and slovenly speech coupled with lack of opportunities for oral practice often result in a monotonous, slurred, inarticulate oral performance in reading.

The following is a short list of tongue-twisters which can be practiced to advantage by most youngsters. Use of the teeth, tongue and lips is essential to keep the articulation clear and clean-cut.

He sawed six, sleek, slim saplings for sale.
The slim, strong masts stood still in the midst of the stays.
I thrust three thousand thistles through the thick of my thumb.

"And the flung spray and the blown spume, and sea gulls crying." (*Sea Fever* by John Masefield)
"To the gull's way and the whale's way, where the wind's like a whetted knife." (*Sea Fever*)

Pitch

Children associate pitch with music more than with reading and speaking. Essentially it deals with the highness or lowness of a tone.

All good reading and speaking utilize variety of pitch. Nothing is more deadly or conducive to sleep than a complete monotone from speaker or reader.

Change of pitch is often very natural when one is speaking with emotion. Excitement or anger not only make the voice louder but they also make the pitch rise. In contrast, as one feels sadness, deep seriousness, or fatigue, the voice is apt to lower in pitch and become softer.

Many exercises in pitch can be done in a choral situation.

Place the voice on a comfortable low middle range and call the tone low *do*. Practice the scale ascending and descending using the speaking voice. Do not attempt accurate scale tones. Use the scale as an approximation to move the pitch up or down.

$$\begin{array}{llllllll} & & & & & & & \text{do} \\ & & & & & & \text{ti} & \\ & & & & & \text{la} & & \\ & & & & \text{sol} & & & \\ & & & \text{fa} & & & & \\ & & \text{mi} & & & & & \\ & \text{re} & & & & & & \\ \text{do} & & & & & & & \end{array}$$

When the children can use their voices in unison to speak a scale, try varying the pitch of a sentence. Repeat "May I go to a movie?" for every single note of the scale, starting with low *do*. Then use the same sentence for a *do-mi-sol-do* sequence.

Vary your sentences and practice in like manner at different times. This type of exercise will help to vary the pitch of the reading voice and result in a more effective interpretation of the play.

Stress

Increasing the force or accent on a word in a sentence can bring about changes in meaning both subtle and obvious. Children enjoy choral reading of simple sentences, placing the stress on different words.

Try the following with your class or a small group:

Will you ride to town today? (Merely asking)
Will *you* ride to town today? (Designating a person)
Will you *ride* to town today? (Ride, not walk)
Will you ride to *town* today? (Place is now important)
Will you ride to town *today?* (Time is now important)

or

You sound as if you didn't believe in magic.
You sound as if *you* didn't believe in magic.
You *sound* as if you didn't believe in magic.
You sound as if you didn't *believe* in magic.
You sound as if you didn't believe in *magic.*
You *sound* as if you didn't believe in *magic.*

Try a combination of pitch and stress:

Mary is going to the party tomorrow.

w?
o
r
r
o
m
o

Mary is going to the party *t*

y
t
r
a

Mary is going to the *p*   tomorrow?

```
                          g
                    n
                  i
              o
Mary is g                    to the party tomorrow?
          y
       r
     a
M              is going to the party tomorrow?
```

Pause

If children could be taught to understand the value of the pause there would be less unintelligible reading and fewer incorrect pauses which obscure meaning.

Good oral reading is in part dependent on knowing when to pause and take a breath. Reading over to oneself to understand the meaning is essential in deciding where one should pause.

The following practices are taken from plays presented in this book:

"My passenger is angry beyond belief; / he has stalked off to the Blake farm / calling down curses on my head."

"Elijah is beside himself with worry / and perhaps doesn't mean / what he says."

"We have called you here / to relay a special message / from His Majesty / the King."

"Word has reached him / that there is talk in the palace / that the Prince has gone mad."

Practices of this type can be made from speeches within the various plays.

Emphasis

Emphasis can be gained by employing any one or a combination of the following.

1. Change of pitch.
2. Change of stress.
3. Use of the pause.

In the final analysis good oral reading is dependent on a clear understanding of the material to be shared with the listener. Given this, the children can employ any of the uses of voice described above to the mutual satisfaction of both reader and listener.

Characteristics of Plays

The following points should be clarified in connection with play practice and reading.

Comparison of Stories and Plays

Stories are written to be read aloud or silently. Plays are written to be acted and spoken. Stories have the opportunity to make detailed descriptions of places and action. Plays depend upon the scenery and the limited action possible on the stage. Everything else is brought out in the conversation.

Dialogue

The conversation among those who are characters in the play makes the listener aware of what is happening. This conversation is supported by some action. The dialogue may also bring out things that have happened previously or will happen later.

Climax

The climax is that point in the play or story where there must be a turning point. Everything up to this time has led to this point, step by step. Everything from the climax on will lead to an ending.

Climax is most important to a play. It often occurs at the end of a scene or an act. Events are then rapidly brought to a close in the next scene or act.

Narrator

When plays are read instead of acted on the stage, one is limited to dialogue. Since no scenery, props, or action are employed, the narrator keeps the listener aware of changes of place or action which are important to understanding.

While discussing these points, use the plays in this book to illustrate and clarify.

Techniques of Evaluation

Constant evaluation of a child's reading performance is encouraged throughout this book. Lists of questions similar to the following are included in the text:

1. Did you speak clearly and distinctly?
2. Did you match your voice to the character you are playing?
3. Did you come in on time with your part?
4. Did your voice change pitch often enough to hold interest?
5. Did you pay attention to commas and periods?

It is hoped that this type of self-evaluation will enable the child to work for improvement in specific areas prior to class performance.

Evaluation of the same type by members of the group is encouraged through using the tape recorder for the first reading. The tape is then played back to the group and the children evaluate each other as well as themselves.

Occasionally the class is asked to rate a performance. This type of rating can be made on mimeographed slips of paper which are given to each child. After listening to the play, each question is rated as "Excellent," "Good," "Fair," "Poor." The slips are collected and handed to the group leader. Later the teacher can work with the group to identify strong and weak areas.

Example of rating sheet:

1. Did the children speak clearly and distinctly?
2. Did the voices fit the characters?
3. Did the children come in on time with their parts?
4. Did the voices change pitch or were they monotonous and sing-song?

Use such evaluation only often enough to keep children alert. Remember, enjoy these plays and help the children to enjoy them also. Over-emphasis and drill on these skills will defeat the purpose of this book. Casual reading with no understanding of how to improve can be equally devastating. Seek some happy medium which keeps interest high and encourages the best possible reading.

FAVORITE PLAYS
for
CLASSROOM READING

The Prince and the Pauper

This play is adapted from a book written by Mark Twain.

Do you know any other books by this author?

Mark Twain was the author's pen name. See if you can find his *real* name. Use your encyclopedia.

Because this story is written about old England some of the language is very different from our own. Below are some phrases that may cause trouble. Practice them until you read them smoothly and easily.

He's always had a fancy for royalty!

Mind your manners, you young beggar!

'Tis an odd name.

I salute your gracious Highness!

You crazy rubbish!

Seems it not to you that his manner and speech differ in some trifles from what they were before?

Peace, my lord, you utter treasonous words.

Do all you can to hide your doubts.

Let none listen to this false and foolish matter, nor carry it abroad.

I crave your help.

Methinks I have forgotten about that, too.

'Tis ill breeding in such as you to command me to speak.

Call back your wandering memory.

Do you mark the resemblance?

Read the entire play to yourself. Can you answer these questions?

1. How did the boys change places?
2. What did the people in the palace believe had happened?

3. What did Tom's family believe had happened?
4. How did the true prince convince the Court of his identity?

Although the boys looked alike, there was one important thing they did not change when they changed clothes—
The way in which they spoke!

It was because Tom continued to speak in a common fashion and Edward continued to speak like a prince that people believed they were mad.

This must show clearly when you are reading the play. The person who takes the part of Edward must act and speak like a prince throughout the entire play.

The person who is Tom must continue to talk like an ordinary boy even after people believe him to be the prince.

Try two or three boys for the part of Edward. Choose the one whose voice seems most like that of a prince.

Choose someone for each part.

Read to yourself to become familiar with your part.

Practice reading the play aloud. Be careful not to have long pauses between speeches.

Work together until you feel that this play is good enough to read for an audience. When you are sure it is, find time to read it to the rest of your class.

THE PRINCE AND THE PAUPER

by Mark Twain
adapted by Elizabeth Brenner

Characters

(16 boys, 5 girls, and the narrator)
NARRATOR
TOM CANTY, *a poor boy who looks like the prince*
PRINCE EDWARD, *a young English prince*

LORD ST. JOHN ⎱ *advisors to the king and prince*
EARL OF HERTFORD ⎰

JOHN CANTY, *Tom's father*

MOTHER, *Tom's mother*

GAMMER CANTY, *Tom's grandmother*

HUGO ⎱ *friends of John Canty*
RUFFLER ⎰

TWO GUARDS, *palace guards*

TWO WOMEN ⎱ *part of crowd*
TWO MEN ⎰

PAGE ⎫
COOK ⎪
GROOM ⎬ *Attendants of the Court*
BUTLER ⎪
LORD ⎪
LADY ⎭

NARRATOR: This play takes place in the early sixteenth century. The setting is outside the gate of Westminster Palace. Two guards march to their stations while a crowd moves in on both sides. The crowd is talking about the royal family.

1ST WOMAN: Perhaps the King himself will come outside today.

2ND WOMAN: You hope for too much. If only I could get a glimpse of the young Prince! They say he is very handsome.

1ST MAN: I hear the King is ill. He'll not show himself this afternoon.

1ST WOMAN: I saw the royal Princess only last Sunday. She grows more beautiful every day.

2ND MAN: Look out, young fellow. Standing there is not a safe occupation for the likes of you.

TOM (*Excitedly*): The Prince! I can see the Prince!

1ST GUARD: Mind your manners, you young beggar!

TOM: Let me go! Let me go!

1ST MAN (*Quickly*): Look, the Prince is here!

2ND MAN: The Prince has come out of the palace grounds!

PRINCE (*Indignantly*): Guards! How dare you treat a poor lad like that! How dare you use my father's lowest subject so! Release him! Open the gates and let him in. Away with you! (*In a kindly voice*) Lad, you look tired and hungry; you have been ill-treated. Come with me.

NARRATOR: A few minutes later, we find ourselves in the chamber of the Prince. Tom is sitting at a table spread with all kinds of food. He looks at it with awe as he eats. The Prince walks about the room, talking to Tom.

PRINCE: Good. Now that I've dismissed my attendants, we can talk. What is your name?

TOM: Tom Canty, if it please you, sir.

PRINCE: 'Tis an odd name. Where do you live?

TOM: Offal Court, in the city, sir.

PRINCE: Offal Court! Another odd name. Have you parents?

TOM: I have two parents and Gammer Canty, my grandmother, besides; but I do not care so much for her, if I may say so, sir. I also have sisters, Nan and Bet.

PRINCE: Is your grandmother not kind to you?

TOM: She has, I fear, a wicked heart, and is not kind to me or to anyone else.

PRINCE: Does she mistreat you?

TOM: There are times when she beats me, sir.

PRINCE: Beats you—and you so frail and small. To the Tower with her!

TOM: Sir, you forget our low station. The Tower is only for great criminals.

PRINCE: So it is. I shall have to think of some other punishment for her. Is your father kind to you?

TOM: No worse than my grandmother, sir, but my mother is good to me, as are my sisters.

PRINCE: Well, that is better! Tell me more about your life at Offal Court. What do you do for fun there?

TOM: Oh, we do have a good time there, except when we are

hungry. There are Punch and Judy shows, and dancing monkeys!

PRINCE: Yes, yes, go on!

TOM: We boys of Offal Court have sparring matches and races, and in the summer we wade and swim in the canals and the river.

PRINCE: It would be worth my father's kingdom to enjoy that just once!

TOM: We dance and sing around the Maypole, and roll in the mud sometimes, too.

PRINCE: Oh, say no more! If only I could wear clothes like yours just once and run barefoot through mud—I think I would give up my crown for that!

TOM: If I could wear such fine clothes as yours just once—

PRINCE (*Quickly*): Would you really like that? Then it shall be. I'll call the servants to clear away the table. While they do that, you and I shall go into the next room and exchange clothing. (*Calls*) Page!

PAGE: Yes, Your Highness?

PRINCE: Tell the First Groom of the Chamber, the Lord Chief Butler, and the Lord Head Cook to come and clear away this table.

PAGE: Yes, Your Highness.

PRINCE: Quickly, lad, follow me. Now's our chance. My attendants will be occupied and will not find us.

NARRATOR: A moment later, the royal servants enter and clear the dining table. While they are busy, Tom and the Prince leave the room. When the boys re-enter, they have exchanged clothing. They run over and stare first into the mirror, then at each other.

PRINCE: What do you make of this, Tom Canty?

TOM: Your worship, do not make me answer. It is not right that a person of my station say such a thing.

PRINCE: Then *I* will say it. You have the same hair, the same eyes, the same voice and manner, the same stature, the same face as I. Now that we have exchanged clothing, there's no one who could tell us apart. Where did you get that bruise on your hand?

TOM: It is nothing, sir. The poor guard at the gate—

PRINCE: That was a cruel thing to do. I'll speak to him at once. Do not move until I return. That is a command.

NARRATOR: The Prince, in Tom's clothing, goes to the main gate. The guards, thinking he is Tom, laugh and push him into the street.

1ST GUARD: Away with you, beggar!

2ND GUARD: That's what you get for making trouble for us with the Prince, you pauper.

PRINCE: I am the Prince of Wales, and you will be hanged for laying a hand on me.

1ST GUARD (*Mockingly*): I salute your gracious Highness. (*Angrily*) Be off, you crazy rubbish! And you too, old man! What do you want?

JOHN CANTY: I want the lad. So there you are, Tom, out gawking at royalty and haven't begged a farthing for me, I warrant. If it be so, I'll break all the bones in your body, or I'm not John Canty.

PRINCE: So you're his father. Then you will fetch him away and restore me to the palace.

JOHN: *His* father? I am *your* father, and I'll pound that lesson into you, I will.

PRINCE: Do not joke or delay any longer. Take me to the King, my father, and he shall make you rich. Believe me—I am indeed the Prince of Wales.

JOHN (*Astonished*): He's always had a fancy for royalty, and now he's gone stark mad. But mad or not, Gammer Canty and I will cure the likes of you.

NARRATOR: John Canty drags the boy to his home, believing the Prince is his son Tom. The next day, at the palace, several lords come into the Prince's room, where a table is elaborately spread for dinner. Listen as the men talk together.

ST. JOHN: What do you think, Lord Hertford?

HERTFORD: It worries me, Lord St. John. The King is near his end and my nephew is mad; mad he will mount the throne, and mad he will remain. God protect England. She will need it!

ST. JOHN: But—have you no doubts as to—as to—

HERTFORD: Speak on—doubts as to what?

ST. JOHN: I am loath to say what is on my mind, and you so closely related to him, my lord. Beg pardon if I offend you, then, but seems it not to you that his manner and speech differ in some trifles from what they were before? He did not recognize his own father and he insists that he is not the Prince!

HERTFORD: Peace, my lord, you utter treasonous words. Remember the King's command.

ST. JOHN (*Concerned*): True, true, I did forget myself. Yes, he must be the Prince. There could not be two in the land who look so much alike.

HERTFORD (*A little doubtfully*): An impostor would claim to be the Prince. Has there ever been an impostor who would deny this? No, this must be the Prince gone mad. We must help him all we can. Ah, it is the Lord Head Cook.

COOK: Everything is ready for the Prince's dinner.

ST. JOHN: Good. Call in the other attendants. Lord Hertford and I have a message from the King.

COOK: Yes, my lord.

HERTFORD: Lord St. John, I understand your questioning, but you must do all you can to hide your doubts. It is up to us to see him through this.

ST. JOHN: I'm sorry, my lord. I should not have even mentioned such thoughts.

HERTFORD: Lord Head Cook, are the others coming?

COOK: Yes, my lord.

NARRATOR: Three court attendants enter the room: the butler, the groom and the page. They bow to Hertford and St. John.

HERTFORD: Good afternoon, gentlemen. We have called you

here to relay a special message from His Majesty, the King. Word has reached him that there is talk in the palace that the Prince has gone mad. Lord St. John will read to you the declaration of the King. I shall fetch His Highness, the Prince.

ST. JOHN (*Reading*): "In the name of the King. Let none listen to this false and foolish matter, upon pain of death, nor discuss the same, nor carry it abroad. In the name of the King."

NARRATOR: Hertford and Tom enter. Tom sits at the table, awkward and ill at ease. He picks up the napkin and looks at it curiously, for he has never seen one before.

TOM: Please take this away. I am afraid it might get soiled.

HERTFORD: Your Highness had best retire early this evening, so you will not be tired for the city's banquet tomorrow.

TOM (*Surprised*): Banquet?

ST. JOHN: Your memory plays tricks on you, Your Highness. The King did promise a banquet in the city in your honor. Do you not recall?

TOM (*Still puzzled*): Yes, yes. I recall it now.

GROOM: What is the trouble, Your Highness?

TOM: I crave your help. My nose itches terribly. Pray, tell me —what is the royal custom in such a matter? I cannot bear it much longer.

GROOM: Lord Head Butler, what do you think? There has never been a case like this in all of England's history!

BUTLER: Alas, there is no hereditary Nose Scratcher!

COOK: What shall we do?

GROOM: What's to be done?

TOM: I hope I do not offend you, gentlemen, but I can wait no longer. I *must* scratch my nose.

HERTFORD: Ah, here comes the page.

PAGE: Your Highness.

HERTFORD: Tell the page to rise, Your Highness.

TOM: Yes, Page. Rise and come forward.

PAGE: Your Highness, His Majesty the King requests the Great Seal. He says that it is most urgent.

Tom (*Bewildered*): The Great Seal? Methinks I have forgotten about that, too!

Hertford: The Great Seal which, during his illness, the King gave to you as a symbol of your approaching responsibilities.

Tom: Oh, yes, the Seal. Tell my father I have forgotten where I put it, but shall think upon it most carefully.

Page (*Hesitantly*): Yes, Your Majesty.

Tom: I am finished with my meal, my lord, and am in need of a rest.

Hertford: Lord Head Butler, pray clear away the table.

St. John: We shall leave you now, Your Highness, but shall return to remind you of your duties at the city's banquet.

Tom: Good, my lord. (*Pause*) I miss my mother, Nan, and Bet, though I cannot speak the same for my father and Gammer Canty. A city banquet in my honor! If I'm reminded of enough of the manners I've forgotten, I might begin to like it here. Ah! What book is this? "The E-ti-quette of the English Court." (*Happily*) This should be of great help!

Narrator: A few weeks pass. Now we go to the Cantys' room in Offal Court. John Canty enters dragging the Prince with him.

John (*Angrily*): Enough of your nonsense! This is your last chance to say who you really are or suffer the same beating as you had yesterday, and the day before, and the day before that one, too.

Prince: 'Tis ill breeding in such as you to command me to speak. I tell you now, as I told you before, I am Edward, Prince of Wales, and none other.

Gammer (*Cackling*): So, 'tis still the Prince he is. Still too fancy for his own Gammer and his father, I warrant. 'Tis my turn to help him realize who he is. (*She laughs wickedly.*)

Mother: Oh, please do not hurt him today, husband. He is near ill with fatigue and hunger. My poor boy! Your foolish ideas have taken your wits away and are breaking my heart.

Prince: I tell you, your son is well and has not lost his wits, good dame. If you would let me go to the palace where he is, the King, my father, will return him to you.

MOTHER: The King your father! My child, do not say such things. They might mean death for you and the ruin of all of us. Call back your wandering memory and look upon me. Am I not your mother?

PRINCE (*Reluctantly*): I do not like to grieve you, kind madam, but you are not my mother.

GAMMER: 'Tis royalty he still is—too fine for his own family.

JOHN (*Sarcastically*): How dare you ladies stand in the Prince's presence? Upon your knees and do him reverence!

MOTHER: More rest and food will cure his madness. I'll fix him some soup with what scraps I can find. Come, Gammer, please help me.

GAMMER: I'll help you, but the soup will be for me and his father first.

JOHN: There'll be little rest for any of us unless you lower your royal self to begging soon. The rent is due tomorrow and you have not yet begged a single penny.

PRINCE: Offend me not with your sordid matters. I tell you again, I am the King's son. Oh—who are these men?

JOHN: Ah, Hugo and Ruffler. Where have you been these many months? It is long since I have seen you.

HUGO: We've been in prison, that's where we've been. We were suspected of stealing a deer from the King's park. They kept us in prison a few months, but could not prove us guilty. They gave us a good whipping for causing them so much trouble, then set us free.

PRINCE: But why would they whip you if you were innocent? That is not just!

RUFFLER (*Laughing*): You young ones have such strange ideas. As if justice mattered in dear old England! We were lucky to escape with our lives; many innocents there be in prison, waiting to be hanged or burned as witches.

MOTHER: Here's some soup, Tom. 'Twill do you good to drink it.

PRINCE: Thank you, good madam. Your kindness will be remembered.

MOTHER: Oh, Tom, you talk as if your wits had left you. Please have the soup; perhaps it will restore your health and your memory.

JOHN: After you're finished bothering with "His Royal Highness," what about some food for the rest of your family?

MOTHER: Forgive me. I'll fix some for you now.

JOHN: Well, "Your Majesty," I hope that soup pleases your royal tongue.

PRINCE: I do not mean to offend your kind wife, sir, but I cannot eat this without the proper service.

JOHN: Is that so? Then you'll be starving, you will, before you find any "service" around here.

HUGO: The boy is ill, John Canty. Here's how you do it, Tom.

NARRATOR: Hugo takes the bowl in his hands and drinks a large portion of the soup.

PRINCE: I command you to stop!

RUFFLER: Come, Hugo, leave "His Majesty" to his dinner.

HUGO: But there is big news, John Canty. Word has got about that the King is dead!

NARRATOR: The Prince looks up, startled, then buries his head in his arms. His shoulders are shaking with sobs. John Canty looks at the Prince, shakes his head and smiles.

JOHN: Little meaning that has for me. The new King is probably no better than his father.

RUFFLER: 'Tis heard that the young Prince will be crowned King before long. Then we shall see how much he cares for justice.

PRINCE (*Explosively*): Enough of this treason! I shall see that justice be done to you and to all the others who were illtreated.

HUGO: Why, Tom Canty, who be you to talk such?

PRINCE (*Solemnly*): I am Edward the Sixth, King of England.

JOHN: Mates, my son is a dreamer, a fool, and stark mad. Mind him not. He thinks he is the King.

PRINCE (*Turning toward him*): I am the King, and as justice will be done these two men for their suffering, so will you be punished for treating me as you have.

JOHN: So you threaten me now! I shall go out with my friends here for a while and when I return, you'd best have begged the pennies for the rent or we'll see who's punishing whom around here. Come, Hugo, come, Ruffler, we'll tell the others you've returned. (*Mockingly*) Good day, Your Majesty.

HUGO *and* RUFFLER: Good day, Your Majesty.

PRINCE: My father is dead and the pauper is an impostor. He must be more clever than I thought, or surely his rude manners would have betrayed him by now. I must get back to the palace, and I will.

NARRATOR: It is the day of the Coronation. At Westminster Abbey, Tom Canty is to be crowned King of England.

HERTFORD: A glorious day for all of England it is today, Lord St. John.

ST. JOHN: That it is, my lord—a day that will be long remembered.

HERTFORD: Did you mark how well the young King has been feeling and behaving of late?

ST. JOHN: Yes, I did. Perhaps his madness has left him at last.

NARRATOR: The sound of trumpets and drums is heard. The King is announced. Tom Canty, looking downcast, slowly approaches the throne.

HERTFORD: My liege, people see your downcast head and take it for a bad omen. Lift up your head and smile upon your subjects.

TOM: I am sorry, my lord, but as I came here, I saw my poor mother in the crowd. She recognized me, but I did not speak to her. I betrayed my own mother.

ST. JOHN: He has gone mad again!

HERTFORD: Your Majesty, we must proceed with the Coronation. Where is your kingly bearing?

Tom: I do not feel very kingly now, but let the ceremony begin.

Narrator: At this moment, the real prince forces his way into the room. He is dressed in Tom Canty's poor clothes but he holds up his hand and speaks with authority.

Prince: Stop the ceremony at once!

Lord: Look there!

Lady: How did that pauper get in here?

Lord: I think he looks like the Prince.

Prince: I forbid you to set the crown of England upon that head. I am the King!

Narrator: Guards rush forward and seize the real prince for they do not recognize him. Tom steps down from the throne and speaks.

Tom (*Imperiously*): Let him go! He is the King!

Hertford: Mind not His Majesty. His malady is touching him again. Seize the pauper.

Tom: On your peril! Touch him not. He is the King! Your Majesty, let poor Tom Canty be first to swear his loyalty to you.

St. John: My lord, do you mark the resemblance between them?

Hertford: 'Tis an astonishing likeness! By your favor, sir, I desire to ask certain questions.

Prince: I will answer them, my lord.

Hertford: If you are the true King, tell me how many servants were there at the palace when you left?

Prince (*Quickly*): Four hundred and nineteen.

Hertford: What was the color of the curtains in the late King's bedchamber?

Prince (*Quickly*): Royal blue, of course.

Hertford: The answers are correct, but they prove nothing.

St. John: Wait! I have a question on which hangs the throne. Where is the Great Seal? Only he who truly was the Prince of Wales can answer that.

PRINCE (*Confidently*): There is nothing difficult about that. Lord St. John, go to my room in the palace. In the left-hand corner farthest from the door, you will find in the wall a brazen nailhead. Press on it and a little jewel chest will fly open. No one else in the world knows about that chest. The first thing you will see will be the Great Seal. Bring it here.

TOM: Why do you hesitate? Haven't you heard the King's command? Go!

PRINCE: Tom, you are indeed loyal to help me this way. I have suffered much these past weeks.

TOM: And I, though I like the comforts of royalty, dearly miss my mother and my friends at Offal Court. I have been most concerned about your welfare.

PRINCE: I have seen much unhappiness and injustice, but when I rule England, I hope what I've seen will help me. I shall give my people the justice they deserve.

TOM: I hope Your Majesty will not mind, but I have already released and pardoned many prisoners.

PRINCE: I do not mind at all, and you shall be rewarded for your generosity and loyalty to me.

NARRATOR: Lord St. John returns carrying the Great Seal.

ST. JOHN: The Great Seal of England!

TOM: Now, my King, take back these regal clothes and give poor Tom, thy servant, his rags again.

LADY: Arrest the impostor!

LORD: To the tower! Hang him.

PRINCE: I will not have this. Were it not for him, I would not have my crown again. Hear my first proclamation as Edward the Sixth: Whereas Tom Canty has been a king, he shall continue to wear royal clothes and all will pay him reverence. He will have the protection of the throne and the support of the crown. He shall be known by the honorable title of the King's Ward.

ALL: Long live the King! Long live the King's Ward! Hurrah!

THE END

Too Many Kittens

This is a long play about three children who were trying very hard to find good homes for their kittens.

Read the play silently. Be sure you know the answers to these questions:

1. Why did the children have to give the kittens away?
2. Why couldn't some of the other children take them?
3. What made them dislike the idea of the Animal Shelter?
4. How did Samantha protect her kittens?
5. How did Miss Anderson solve the problem?

Because this play is long you must read it very well if you wish to hold the attention of your audience.

Father must be tired, bored, stern, and angry at different times.

Mother must be impatient, stern, angry, and sometimes sympathetic.

The children are discouraged, frightened, pleading, even crying.

You have only your voice to show all these different feelings.

Talk the play over together and choose your part.
Study your part silently. Get help if you need it.
Practice reading the play aloud.
Evaluate your reading. Help each other.

1. Did your voice show how you felt?
2. Did you all come in on time?
3. Were you all awake or did some of you need a nudge or two?

Keep practicing until you are sure you are ready to read for others.

Have your chairman consult the teacher and arrange for a time to read to the class.

TOO MANY KITTENS

by Mildred Hark and Noel McQueen

Characters

(2 boys, 6 girls, and the narrator)

NARRATOR
JANET, *a twelve-year-old girl*
GAIL, *her sister, who is ten*
PETE, *their eight-year-old brother*
MOTHER ⎱ *their parents*
FATHER ⎰
SUE ⎱ *school friends*
ANNABELLE ⎰
MISS ANDERSON, *Pete's teacher*

NARRATOR: The time is late afternoon. In the living room, Janet is curled up in a chair frowning at the sheet of paper she is reading. Gail is sitting on the sofa, and Pete is sprawled in an easy chair.

GAIL: Janet, can't you think of anyone else we can call who might want a kitten?

JANET: That's what I'm trying to do. This is the list of people we've asked already. The Joneses, and the man at the cleaner's and the mailman, and Aunt Amy and—oh, what's the use? We've asked dozens of people.

GAIL: Poor Samantha. Nobody wants her four beautiful kittens.

PETE: We do. I don't see why we can't keep all of them.

JANET: You know very well why we can't. Dad says five cats are too many.

PETE: I suppose. But gee, why is it so hard to find homes for kittens? I saw in the paper where they get as much as fifty dollars for some kittens. And we're giving ours away!

JANET: Oh, those fifty-dollar ones are fancy kittens with fancy mammas and papas. Poor Samantha is just an old alley cat.

PETE (*Hotly*): Samantha is just as good as any other cat.

JANET: Of course she is, Pete, and we all love her but that doesn't seem to be much help. Have you tried all the kids in your class?

PETE: Have I tried? Didn't I tell you I almost had to stay after school today because I was telling Danny Foley about the kittens? Miss Anderson said that if I didn't pay attention and stop talking about our kittens, she'd have to speak to Mom.

GAIL: Oh, I hope she doesn't. Mom's upset enough about the kittens as it is.

JANET: Yes, she says this is positively the last day. The kittens have to go.

PETE: Well, Danny may take one.

JANET: Why, Pete, that's wonderful.

GAIL: I've told all the kids in my class. They all said they wanted to see the kittens, but they haven't come to look yet.

NARRATOR: The doorbell rings and Pete gets up.

PETE: I'll bet that's Danny. I'll go.

JANET: If that's Danny, let's try to get him to take two kittens.

GAIL: Sure—tell him how cute they are when they play together.

NARRATOR: Pete goes out. A moment later, he comes back into the living room with Sue and Annabelle.

PETE: It's not Danny. It's Sue and Annabelle.

SUE: We've come to see the kittens.

GAIL: Hello, Sue.

JANET: Hello, Annabelle.

ANNABELLE: Where are the kittens?

PETE: In the back hall, in our old picnic basket. Come on, I'll show you.

NARRATOR: Pete, Sue, and Annabelle go to the back hall to see the kittens.

GAIL: Oh, I hope they take two. Maybe I'd better go along and help them choose.

JANET: No, stay here, Gail. The kittens get frightened if there are too many people.

GAIL: Janet, do you think Mom really means it this time?

JANET: I know she does. She put her foot down after Whitey tore the sofa last night.

GAIL: Yes, I know. That's a bad rip. I tried to tell Mom that the kittens won't always be like that. Samantha's well-trained and she'll train her kittens.

JANET: Well, maybe, but Mom says by that time the whole house would be torn apart.

GAIL: But suppose—suppose we don't find homes for them today?

JANET: Well, you know what Dad says. He'll take them to the Animal Shelter.

GAIL: But Janet, we can't do that. You know what they do.

JANET: What do you mean?

GAIL: If they can't find homes for them, they—they just put them to sleep.

JANET: But Gail, we're not sure of that.

GAIL: Yes, we are, Janet. Don't you remember that time Samantha wouldn't come down from the tree and the nice man came from the Animal Shelter?

JANET: Yes.

GAIL: Well, I asked him what they did with all their kittens and he said that sometimes if no one wanted a kitten, they —they just had to put—

JANET: Don't say it again. I can't bear it. And for goodness' sakes, Gail, don't mention it to Pete. He's too little to hear a tragic thing like that.

GAIL: Well, we just can't let it happen.

JANET: No.

NARRATOR: Sue, Annabelle, and Pete return to the living room. Sue and Annabelle are arguing.

SUE: I want the black one!

ANNABELLE: No, *I* want the black one.

PETE: Well, gee, you both can't have him.

JANET: Wait, girls. They're all just as cute as can be. I just love the white one—she's so sweet and gentle.

NARRATOR: Before the girls can see the tear in the sofa, Gail covers it with a soft pillow.

GAIL: Yes, she is.

ANNABELLE: I want the black one.

PETE: But Annabelle, what about the yellow one? He can turn somersaults.

GAIL: Or the gray one. She's got black feet.

ANNABELLE: No, I want all black.

SUE: I'm going to have the black one. I said it first and it isn't fair.

JANET: Now, listen, Sue and Annabelle, I'm sure we can talk this over.

ANNABELLE: No! If I can't have the black one, I don't want any! You can keep your old kittens!

NARRATOR: Annabelle is very angry because she can't have the black kitten. She leaves, slamming the door after her.

SUE: So there. I'm going to have the black one.

PETE: Yeah, I guess you are.

SUE: I'll go home and ask my mother and come right back for him. Goodbye.

PETE: Girls! What did they have to fight for?

JANET: Oh, I don't know. Well, we have a home for one, anyway.

GAIL: But we might have had two. And it's getting later and later.

JANET: Wait—I just thought of someone. What about Miss

Hopkins at the bookstore? She grows flowers in her window. Maybe she likes animals, too.

PETE: That's a good idea. I'll run right over and ask her, and I'll take the white kitten.

GAIL: No, it's no use.

JANET: Why not, Gail?

GAIL: She has a cat. Last time I was in there, she told me she'd been having trouble with mice and that she'd bought a cat.

JANET: *Bought* a cat? And we can't give ours away.

NARRATOR: Mother's voice is heard, coming from the kitchen.

MOTHER: Oh, my goodness, oh, my goodness! Get off of there. Scat, scat, all of you! Oh, my poor fern!

JANET: The kittens! Pete, you must have left the basket open.

PETE: I—guess I did. The girls were arguing and—and I—

NARRATOR: Mother enters the room. She looks very disturbed.

MOTHER: This is the end. The kittens have to go. All four of them were up on the buffet chewing and clawing at my best fern. It's ruined.

GAIL: Oh, Mom, we're sorry.

MOTHER: Sorry? I should think so. Who let them out of their basket?

PETE: I guess I did, Mom.

MOTHER: Well, you hurry and put them back in again and close the cover before anything else happens.

PETE: O. K.

JANET: Mom, it really wasn't all Pete's fault. Sue and Annabelle were here and had a fight.

MOTHER: I don't care whose fault it was or who was here. I've been very lenient about those kittens, but now they have to go.

GAIL: But they *are* going. We're giving them away.

MOTHER: Well, they're still here. And another thing, I can't have children tramping through the house all day long. There have been five or six or seven here every day, not counting the field trip from school when Miss Anderson brought the whole class.

JANET: But Mom, that was part of their nature study. We ought to be glad to let them see Samantha's kittens.

GAIL: And they all loved the kittens.

MOTHER: Maybe they did, but nobody took any of them.

GAIL: There was always some reason they couldn't. Charlie wanted one, but he has a dog.

MOTHER: Yes, and the little girl who wanted one was afraid it would eat up her goldfish.

NARRATOR: Pete comes back into the room and speaks to Mother.

PETE: It's all right now, Mom. They're all back in the basket.

MOTHER: All right, indeed! Did you see my fern?

PETE: Yeah. Say, they sure did chew it up. You know, I was thinking, Mom—

MOTHER: What about? Getting me a new fern?

PETE: Well, not exactly, but you know how you're always telling me to eat my salad.

MOTHER: Peter, if you are just trying to change the subject, you are not going to. I'm not through about those kittens. What does your eating salad have to do with it?

PETE: I just thought maybe the kittens needed vitamins.

GAIL: Gee, Mom, maybe Pete's right. Maybe we haven't been feeding them enough green things.

MOTHER: Whether we have or not doesn't make much difference because someone else is going to be doing it from now on. If you children can't give them away, we'll have to—

JANET: But Mom, we have given one away. Sue is taking the black one.

MOTHER: Well, he's still here. He was with the rest of them on the buffet.

GAIL: She went home, but she's coming right back for him, Mom.

NARRATOR: The telephone rings, and Mother answers it. Pete goes and stands beside her.

MOTHER: Hello? . . . . Oh, yes, Grace, the children were just telling me Sue wants the black kitten. . . .

GAIL: It's Sue's mother.

PETE: Yeah, maybe she wants us to take it over. Mom, Mom, tell her I can run over with him.

MOTHER: Quiet, Peter. Excuse me, Grace, Peter was interrupting. . . . Yes. . . . Yes. . . . Of course I understand. Goodbye, Grace. (*Pause*) Well, now, you still have four kittens.

JANET: But—but what happened?

MOTHER: They have a parakeet that flies around the house, and the kitten would chase it. Sue hadn't thought of that.

GAIL: Oh dear, it's always something.

JANET: And—and here comes Dad.

FATHER (*Cheerfully*): Hello, family. Well, how's the cat business? How many do we have left now?

MOTHER (*Disgustedly*): Five, John. They haven't been able to find a home for one of them.

JANET: Oh, it's terrible, Dad. We thought Sue was going to take one, but her mother just called and said she can't.

GAIL: We've tried and tried but all our prospects seem to fall through.

FATHER: Well, prospects have a way of doing that.

MOTHER: And that's not all. The kittens just chewed up my best fern.

FATHER: Not the big one? That's too bad.

NARRATOR: Father settles into his easy chair and begins to read his newspaper.

FATHER: Well, you know what I said, children. I'm afraid it's the Animal Shelter for those kittens.

GAIL: Oh, no. After all, we've still got some prospects. Or one anyhow. Pete, what about Danny? You said he was a prospect.

PETE: I don't know.

JANET: But if we could get him to take two—or even one. Call him up, Pete, and find out.

FATHER (*Sighing*): You mean we're going to have cat calls all evening again?

MOTHER: John, you make it sound like a jungle.

FATHER: Well, it's been going on for weeks.

GAIL: But, Dad, how can we find homes if we don't call people? Hurry and try, Pete. Their number is Oak 7401.

PETE: O. K., I'll try. Oak 7401. . . . Hello, is Danny there? This is Pete. . . .

JANET: Tell him we have to know right away.

PETE: O. K. . . . (*Pause*) Hello, Danny. I thought you were coming over to look at the kittens. . . . You what? . . . . It did? . . . . Just this morning? . . . . Six of them? . . . . Gee, Danny, that's kind of disgusting . . . . Yeah, six. . . . Well, all right, so long, Danny.

JANET: What is it, Pete? Doesn't he want one?

PETE: No.

GAIL: Why not? And what's so disgusting?

PETE: That old tabby cat of the Burgesses. She had six kittens and they're all tabbies and Danny's pop says tabbies are good luck so he's going to have two of them.

JANET: Oh, my.

PETE (*Disgustedly*): Wouldn't you know? That old cat would have to have kittens right now—just when Samantha's got hers.

FATHER: Son, all cats have kittens. In fact, there are too many kittens in this world.

PETE: But Dad, there can't be too many.

GAIL: They're so cute.

MOTHER: Cute, indeed! Well, that was your last prospect, children. Something has to be done.

GAIL: Just give us a little more time.

MOTHER: I've given you long enough. And in the meantime, my best fern gets eaten and the sofa gets torn. Oh, John, did you find out about the sofa?

FATHER: Yes, Margaret, I went to the upholsterer's and explained what had happened.

MOTHER: Well, can it be fixed?

FATHER: Yes, but he tells me with a slit that long, it wouldn't cost much more to recover the whole sofa.

MOTHER: The whole sofa. . . . Well, John, we've needed a new cover on that sofa for ages.

FATHER: That's what I thought, so I told him to come over. He'll be here tomorrow with samples.

MOTHER: That's wonderful. Did he say how long it will take?

FATHER: Yes, if he picks it up tomorrow, you can have it back by the end of the week.

MOTHER: Fine. My, it'll really add a lot to this room. It'll be just like having a new sofa.

PETE: Say, I guess the kittens aren't so bad after all. They're going to get Mom a new sofa.

MOTHER: Now don't exaggerate. It's not a new sofa—just a new cover. And that's just another reason why those kittens will have to go. We're not going to have the new cover ruined.

JANET: But Mom, this gives us more time.

MOTHER: More time? What do you mean?

JANET: Well, don't you see? The sofa won't be back till the end of the week.

MOTHER: I don't see how this changes anything.

GAIL: But of course it does, Mom. You were worrying about the new cover. And there's no need to worry till the end of the week now. By that time we can find homes for the kittens.

JANET: And I just thought, Gail. We have another prospect. We forgot Annabelle.

GAIL: Of course. Now that Sue didn't take the black one, she will.

MOTHER: Children, I'm not sure we should wait.

FATHER: Margaret, let them have a little more time. But remember, children, I don't want to hear any more about kittens tonight. I want to relax, read my paper. Where's my pipe?

MOTHER: I think you left it in the dining room.

NARRATOR: Father starts to go out of the room. He stops at the door to talk to the children.

FATHER: Very well. . . . Pete, Janet, Gail, lend me your ears. If you have any more to say about kittens, prepare to say it now—while I'm out of the room.

PETE: Gee, what did he mean about lending him our ears?

MOTHER: He was joking, Peter. It's something Shakespeare said. But he wasn't joking about the kittens. Now, not another word in front of your father.

JANET: O. K. Pete, you'd better run over and see Annabelle.

GAIL: Maybe I'd better do it.

JANET: All right. Tell her she can have the black one.

PETE: Gee, that'll be one, and now that we have till the end of the week, I know we can find homes for them.

FATHER: Margaret! Margaret!

MOTHER: Sh-h, not another word.

NARRATOR: Father's angry voice can be heard as he comes into the room holding a small headless statue in one hand, and the head of the statue in the other hand. He tries to speak calmly, but his voice becomes angry again.

FATHER: Margaret, look at this.

MOTHER: Why, John, your golf trophy. It's broken.

FATHER: Exactly! My hole-in-one golf trophy. Everyone knows how I prize this trophy. I'm the only resident of this town who ever shot a hole in one. (*Raising his voice*) What I want to know is—how did it happen?

MOTHER: Why, I—I don't know, John. I remember dusting it this morning. It was on the buffet.

FATHER: Well, that wasn't where I found it. It was on the dining room floor. The head had rolled under the table. Will someone please tell me how this happened?

CHILDREN: Oh . . . oh dear!

MOTHER: John, it must have been the kittens—while they were playing with my fern. I was so anxious about my fern, I didn't notice.

FATHER: Kittens—of course it was the kittens! My hole-in-one golf trophy decapitated by kittens. Well, they have to go —and now!

JANET: Oh, Dad.

GAIL: You mean right away?

FATHER: Yes, right away, immediately—at once! I'll drive them over to the Animal Shelter.

PETE: Oh, gee, Dad—please, no.

FATHER: They'll go now. Get the basket ready.

JANET: Oh, Dad.

FATHER: I'll get the car out of the garage and wait out front. Hurry now.

MOTHER: Children, please, it can't be helped. We knew the kittens might have to go to the Animal Shelter.

GAIL (*Almost crying*): We can't let them go alone!

MOTHER: Your father will take care of them.

JANET: But one of us ought to go along—to hold the basket.

GAIL: I think we all ought to go. I'll get our coats.

MOTHER (*Comfortingly*): Now, children, try not to be too upset. The people will be kind at the Animal Shelter.

JANET: I know, Mother.

NARRATOR: Gail goes to the closet and brings back the hats and coats.

GAIL: I—I guess we'd better hurry. Who's—who's going to get the kittens?

PETE: I don't want to.

GAIL: I—I don't know if I can.

JANET: No, you are both too little. I'm the eldest. I'll have to do it.

PETE: Gee, what's Samantha going to think when Janet takes the kittens away from her?

MOTHER: Well, dear, you were going to find homes for them.

PETE: I know. Just this morning I explained that to Samantha and she rubbed her head against my knee the way she always does—as if she understood.

MOTHER (*Sympathetically*): Did she, dear?

PETE: Yes, but I didn't say anything about the Animal Shelter. That's different.

NARRATOR: Janet appears in the door of the living room. She is crying.

MOTHER: Janet, what on earth is the matter?

JANET: I—I can't do it, Mom. I can't do it. Samantha won't let me.

MOTHER: What do you mean? Did she try to scratch you?

JANET: Of course not. Samantha never scratches. But when I went to pick up the basket, she jumped on it and just sat there. I tried to make her get off but she kept looking at me so accusingly with those big eyes. Oh, I just couldn't, Mom!

MOTHER: But Janet, your father is waiting.

JANET: I know—but Mom, how would you feel if someone was trying to take all of us away from you?

MOTHER: Dear, that's different. You were going to give the kittens away anyhow.

JANET: Yes, but to homes where they were wanted. Samantha knows this is different, and I just can't take them!

MOTHER: Oh, dear, it is sad.

JANET: Yes. Samantha had her kittens and now—I ask you, why have kittens when nobody wants them? Oh, Mom, the world is all mixed up!

MOTHER: Now, Janet, it's not the whole world.

JANET: Yes, it is. We take care of sick people, we take care of criminals. We find a place for all kinds of members of society.

MOTHER: My dear, where have you been learning all these things?

JANET: In social studies, Mom. And—and it's all true, but still there's no place for four innocent little kittens.

GAIL (*Crying*): Janet's right. It's not fair!

PETE (*Starting to cry*): I—I guess Samantha's kittens are just as good as anybody else.

JANET (*Crying*): They're homeless, Mom. We can't cast them out.

MOTHER: Oh, the poor little things. I don't know. I just don't know. (*She starts to cry, too.*)

FATHER: Well, well, what's the matter? I've been waiting in the car. For goodness' sakes, what's all the crying about?

MOTHER (*Crying*): The kittens, John.

FATHER: You, too?

MOTHER: Yes, John. Samantha is sitting on top of the basket. There is a place for everything in the world but her kittens and—we can't cast them out.

FATHER: Oh—oh, so that's it. You mean we are to keep them all?

MOTHER: Yes, John. Suppose someone asked us to give up our children?

FATHER: But no one has asked us.

MOTHER: I know, but we're asking Samantha to give up her kittens.

FATHER: Well—well—you gave up your fern. I gave up my trophy.

MOTHER: The fern will grow again, your trophy can be mended, but Samantha's kittens—they need a good home.

FATHER: I see what you mean.

NARRATOR: Father takes off his hat and coat, and slumps into his chair.

JANET: Dad, you mean that—that—

FATHER: If your mother says so.

GAIL: Mom?

MOTHER: Yes, children, you needn't take them to the Animal Shelter. Take off your coats.

PETE: Oh boy, let's tell Samantha.

MOTHER: John, can you blame me?

FATHER: No, my dear. I was beginning to weaken, too. I'm resigned to it. Four kittens and a cat. Soon they'll grow up. There will be five cats.

MOTHER: Yes, I know.

FATHER: And each cat has nine lives. That's equal to forty-five cats.

MOTHER: Oh, John!

FATHER: And if each cat has four kittens, let me see. That will be 225 cats.

MOTHER: Now, John, you know it won't be as bad as that.

FATHER: Perhaps not, but don't you think we'd better call a tinsmith instead of an upholsterer and have a sheet metal cover put on that sofa?

JANET: Oh, Mom, you ought to see Samantha. She's purring and swishing her tail.

NARRATOR: At this moment the doorbell rings.

MOTHER: Dear me, company. Please answer the door, one of you.

JANET: I'll go.

FATHER: Janet, if it should happen to be someone wanting to give us a cat, politely but firmly refuse.

PETE: Gosh, Dad, why would anyone want to give us a cat? We have five.

MOTHER: Your father was joking, Peter.

PETE: Oh.

NARRATOR: Janet returns with Miss Anderson, Pete's teacher.

JANET: Miss Anderson is here.

MOTHER: Good afternoon, Miss Anderson. Won't you come in and sit down?

MISS ANDERSON: Thank you, but I really can't stay more than a minute. I heard Peter talking about the kittens during class.

PETE: Oh, Miss Anderson, I was just trying to get some of the kids to take our kittens. Honest, Mom, that's all I was doing.

FATHER: Peter, you interrupted Miss Anderson.

MISS ANDERSON: That's all right. I was just going to say that if you had any of those darling kittens left, I'd like one.

PETE: You, Miss Anderson?

MISS ANDERSON: Yes, I wanted one the day we all came here on the field trip, but I didn't want to deprive the children.

FATHER: Deprive? Miss Anderson, you wouldn't be depriving anyone. And I'm sure that Samantha would approve of a teacher having one of her kittens.

PETE: I didn't know you liked kittens, Miss Anderson.

MISS ANDERSON: Oh, I like all animals. My folks live on a farm and now that I'm in town I miss having animals around. But if I can have one of the kittens to keep me company, it will be wonderful!

GAIL: Oh, Mom, somebody really wants one of Samantha's kittens!

PETE: Maybe she'd want all four of them.

MISS ANDERSON (*Laughing*): No, I'm afraid I wouldn't have room for four, but my father's farm would make a wonderful home for the rest of them.

PETE: It—it would?

MISS ANDERSON: Yes, the kittens will love it. Why, they'll get fresh milk to drink. They can roll and play in the hay all day. Can't you just see them? I'm going home this weekend, and I can take them.

MOTHER: Why, Miss Anderson, that's very kind of you.

JANET: Yes, thanks, Miss Anderson. Oh, just think, we've finally found homes for all of them.

GAIL: Yes, but—I guess we'll miss them.

FATHER: Now, now, Gail, think of how happy they are going to be. And besides, you'll still have Samantha.

MOTHER: That's right. Well, children, are you satisfied?

JANET *and* GAIL: Sure, Mom. We'll still have Samantha.

MOTHER: Peter?

PETE: Why not? We'll still have Samantha—and next year she'll have more kittens!

THE END

The Swiss Mystery

This is a story about an American family visiting in Switzerland. It is a simple mystery with not too much excitement or suspense, but it does have a surprise ending.

Read the play to yourself.

1. List four things that you learned about Switzerland from reading this play.
2. What device do the authors use to give you the above information?
3. What is the mystery part of the play?
4. What do the authors do to center your attention on the doll?

Talk the story over together. Decide who should play each character.

Read your part silently. Be sure you understand and can pronounce every word in your part. Ask for help if you need it.

Read the entire play aloud together.

Remember these things:

1. Read smoothly and fluently as if you were talking.
2. Speak clearly and distinctly.
3. Be ready with your part—do not wait until someone has to remind you.
4. Try to speak in the kind of voice you believe this character would have.

Reread the play together. Practice those parts that need improvement.

Ask your teacher if she can find time for your group to read the play to the entire class.

Let the class tell you whether you read well and why.

THE SWISS MYSTERY

by Esther MacLellan and Catherine V. Schroll

Characters

(3 boys, 4 girls, and the narrator)
NARRATOR
MRS. ROBINSON, *who runs a Swiss inn*
ANNA, *her daughter*
WALTER, *her son*
MR. EDWARDS, *an American staying with the Robinsons*
MRS. EDWARDS, *his wife*
SUSAN, *their daughter*
JIM, *their son*

NARRATOR: The story takes place on a summer afternoon in the living room of the Robinson home in Switzerland. Mrs. Edwards, a guest in the home, is seated beside a table, turning the pages of a large book. She looks up and sees her daughter Susan come in, carrying a doll.

MRS. EDWARDS: Hello, Susan. Where have you been?

SUSAN: To the store with Anna. Mother, I love Switzerland! I'm so glad we could come with Daddy. Wasn't it lucky for us, too, that we found Mrs. Robinson so we could live with her and not have to stay at an old hotel?

MRS. EDWARDS: I thought you liked hotels.

SUSAN: I do, usually, but it's better here where Jim and I have friends of our own age. Anna is lots of fun, Mother.

MRS. EDWARDS: She's a nice girl. I like her very much.

SUSAN: She's always wanting to do something for me, Mother. Today she let me play with her doll.

MRS. EDWARDS: You don't enjoy playing with dolls now, do you, dear?

SUSAN: Not much. I'm getting too old, but I wouldn't tell Anna.

MRS. EDWARDS: Of course not.

NARRATOR: Susan puts the doll on her mother's lap.

SUSAN: This is a very special doll to Anna. It's been handed down in the Robinson family for years and years. Isn't it odd? Look at the eyes, Mother. They're not like eyes at all.

MRS. EDWARDS: They look like two black stones. Aren't they funny?

SUSAN: Sh! You mustn't laugh, Mother. Anna's coming any minute. You'll hurt her feelings.

MRS. EDWARDS: I'm sorry, Susan, but her eyes *are* funny. Two stones. And a wig of horse's hair!

NARRATOR: Susan picks up the doll and fondles it as she speaks.

SUSAN: Never mind, Dolly. Pay no attention to unkind remarks. Anna loves you. What are you reading, Mother?

MRS. EDWARDS: A book on Switzerland. We want to see as much of the country as we can. If your father isn't too busy, perhaps we can visit Geneva this weekend.

SUSAN: Is this a picture of Lake Geneva?

MRS. EDWARDS: Yes. Isn't it lovely? The lofty, snowy peak is Mont Blanc.

SUSAN: How beautiful! What does it mean?

MRS. EDWARDS: Mont Blanc means white mountain in French.

SUSAN: So Geneva is near France?

MRS. EDWARDS: That's right.

SUSAN: If we go to Geneva, the Swiss will be talking French, while here they speak German.

MRS. EDWARDS: And in Ticino, still another tongue—Italian.

SUSAN: Anna learns two languages at school, German and French; and she knows some Italian, too. She can speak English as well as we do. I wish I knew another language.

MRS. EDWARDS: You must learn as much from Anna as you can.

JIM: Hi, Mother! Hello, Sue. When do we eat?

MRS. EDWARDS: Jim Edwards! You simply can't be hungry after that enormous breakfast you ate.

JIM: I am. It's the brisk air sweeping down from the Alps, I suppose. The food tastes wonderful. I want three big cheese sandwiches. Boy! Do I love Swiss cheese!

SUSAN: I was reading in the guide book that Swiss cheese is so good because of the grass the cows eat. The grass has extra vitamins or extra flavor, I forget which.

JIM: Who cares? Maybe both. Swiss cheese is good. No wonder it's famous.

SUSAN: I like the chocolate. I could eat six pounds of Swiss chocolate right this minute.

JIM: Only six? I could eat ten. Maybe twenty, if I tried.

MRS. EDWARDS: Please don't try!

JIM: Shall I call Mrs. Robinson? Shall I tell her we're hungry?

MRS. EDWARDS: Indeed you won't. We'll have lunch when Mrs. Robinson is ready. While you're waiting you can write a letter to Aunt Edna.

JIM: Me? Write a letter now? I'm half starved. I might faint.

MRS. EDWARDS: We'll take that chance. Aunt Edna gave you five dollars before you left and it's time you thanked her. There's paper and pen on the table.

JIM: I know I'd do a better job if I had something inside me.

NARRATOR: Jim sits down and begins to write. There is a pause. Susan plays with the doll. Walter and Anna enter the room and start to talk to Mrs. Edwards.

MRS. EDWARDS: Hello, Walter.

JIM: Hi!

MRS. EDWARDS: Jim! Letter!

JIM: It's finished, Mom. All I have to do is write "Your loving nephew." Here it is! Done! Ended! Completed! Ready to mail!

MRS. EDWARDS: How could you write a letter so fast? Let's hear it.

JIM: Yes, ma'am. "Dear Aunt Edna. Thank you for the five dollars. I haven't spent it yet. I'd like to buy a watch. You know the Swiss are wonderful watchmakers. However, I can't find the watch I want for five dollars. I'm still looking. Your loving nephew, Jim."

MRS. EDWARDS: Jim Edwards! You don't call that a letter, do you?

JIM: Sure. It tells everything. Thanks for the money. Swiss watches are terrific. They are, Mother. You never saw such watches.

SUSAN: French Switzerland is the center of the watch industry. If we go to Geneva this weekend, you can look for one there.

MRS. EDWARDS: First you'll write a real letter. Throw that letter away, and in your next don't mention wanting a watch or not having enough money. It isn't polite.

JIM: What shall I say?

MRS. EDWARDS: Read this guide book. Find some interesting facts about Switzerland. Show Aunt Edna you're learning something. Not a word out of you till you're finished.

NARRATOR: Jim throws the letter into the wastebasket, gets another piece of paper from the table, sits and writes again.

WALTER: Did you know we have an aunt in America, Mrs. Edwards? In Grover, New York.

SUSAN: Grover! That's right near Crestview where we live.

ANNA: Really? Grover is near your town?

JIM: Sure. If you could come to America, we'd be almost neighbors.

MRS. EDWARDS: Jim! The letter!

JIM: Yes, ma'am.

WALTER: My aunt wants us to come to America. We're her only relatives.

SUSAN: Why don't you? We'd have lots of fun together.

ANNA: Because we don't have the money. We're not as rich as you Americans.

SUSAN: We're not rich, Anna. We were able to come to Switzerland because Daddy's an importer.

ANNA: Importer?

JIM: Dad buys things in Switzerland and then sells them again in America. I think he's looking at cameras today.

MRS. EDWARDS: Jim! For the last time!

NARRATOR: Jim starts to write furiously.

JIM: I'm sorry, Mother, I forgot.

ANNA: We were rich once, our family.

WALTER: Oh, Anna! That was long ago. Don't bring up that old story again.

ANNA: It's interesting. A mystery always is.

SUSAN: A mystery! Tell us, Anna, please.

NARRATOR: Mrs. Robinson comes in.

MRS. ROBINSON: Would you like to have lunch now?

SUSAN: Not yet, Mrs. Robinson. Anna is going to tell us the mystery.

MRS. ROBINSON: The story of the lost treasure?

SUSAN: Lost treasure! It sounds better and better. Is it really true?

MRS. ROBINSON: Who knows? It's a story that has been handed down in our family for generations.

SUSAN: Please tell us.

ANNA: Go ahead, Mother.

MRS. EDWARDS: Sit down, Mrs. Robinson, and be comfortable. You'll have to tell the story now. You have made us all excited.

MRS. ROBINSON: Dear me! There's very little to tell. My ancestor, Hans Robinson, who built this house, was a wealthy man, wealthy at least for the times in which he lived. The room we're sitting in was his business office.

SUSAN: How exciting to live in an old, old house! Ours doesn't have any treasures or mysteries or anything.

ANNA: An electric dishwasher! A color television set! Those would be treasures enough for me.

JIM: Quiet, you girls! Go on, Mrs. Robinson.

MRS. ROBINSON: As Hans grew older and wealthier, the strong-box where he kept his gold no longer seemed safe to him. The fear of being robbed preyed on his mind. One morning he sent his whole family to the mountains for the day. When they returned every scrap of gold had been removed from the strongbox. And well—that's all.

SUSAN: All! A story has to have an end.

WALTER: This one doesn't. No one knows what old Hans did with the money.

JIM: He must have hidden the gold somewhere in the house or the garden.

ANNA: Our grandmother said that each room in the house was searched thoroughly. Even the floors were taken up.

WALTER: Every inch of the garden was searched. The vegetables were uprooted and the flower beds were dug up.

MRS. ROBINSON: Who knows whether there really was a treasure?

SUSAN: Of course there was.

JIM: Why didn't old Hans tell his sons where he put the treasure?

MRS. ROBINSON: One son went away to war—and the other was a spendthrift. Hans wanted the treasure for his little granddaughter, Marguerite, whom he dearly loved. He was strong and healthy. He did not guess he would die suddenly.

ANNA: This doll belonged to Marguerite. Old Hans gave it to her.

SUSAN: No wonder you take such good care of the doll, Anna. She's been in your family for ages.

ANNA: Yes, I've had her since I was little. She was Mama's doll, and Grandma's, and I love her.

SUSAN: I love her because she's yours, Anna.

JIM: Oh, boy! What silly talk over an old doll. Do you love her, Walter? If you love her, I'll love her. Mother, will you love her if Dad loves her?

MRS. EDWARDS (*Laughing*): Jim, behave yourself. Is that letter finished? Remember you weren't to talk until it was.

JIM: You can treat me like a human being again. The letter is done and I don't mind saying that it's a masterpiece.

MRS. ROBINSON: I'll go now and bring luncheon. Come, Anna, you may help.

JIM: Don't go, Mrs. Robinson. You'll miss a real treat—hearing me read my letter.

MRS. ROBINSON: Perhaps you will let me read it later.

JIM: Two of my audience gone. Alas!

MRS. EDWARDS: No more of your joking now. Let's hear the letter.

JIM: "Dear Aunt Edna, We are all enjoying our visit to Switzerland, which is a small country situated in central Europe. The area is 15,944 square miles, of which 22.6% is unproductive, that is, bare mountain, plateau slopes, lakes and rivers; 24.8% is occupied by forests, 24.3% consists of Alpine pastures, and only 28.3% is agricultural land. The largest cities of Switzerland are Zurich, Basle, Berne, Geneva, and Lausanne. Berne is the capital. Tourism is a big business as are watch-making and the manufacture of machinery and textiles. The Swiss are very clean, intelligent and hard working." Hear that, Walter? You're clean, intelligent, and hard working.

WALTER: Thank you.

JIM: "Many Swiss winter resorts in the high Alps are famous for—"

MRS. EDWARDS: Jim!

JIM: Good, isn't it?

MRS. EDWARDS: That letter will not do, and you know it.

JIM: I think it's interesting.

SUSAN: It's full of information, Mother. Aunt Edna will learn a lot. Switzerland is a small country in central Europe consisting of about 16,000 square miles . . .

JIM: The largest cities are Zurich, Basle, Berne, Geneva, and Lausanne.

WALTER: Berne is the capital. Tourism is a big business.

JIM: Look how much we all know, Mother. My letter is just like a book.

MRS. EDWARDS: That's the trouble. You might as well send the book; you've copied it word for word. No, Jim, you'll have to write another letter, but I'll give you a rest. You may do it tonight.

JIM: Couldn't I send a postcard? Aunt Edna loves me. She wouldn't want me to suffer.

MRS. EDWARDS: No.

SUSAN: I'll help set the table. Anna, let's look for the treasure this afternoon. Maybe we can find it.

NARRATOR: Jim taps the walls.

JIM: If the treasure's going to be found, Walt and I will do it. This should be the best place to search. It was old Hans' office, where he spent most of his time. Shall we start, Walt, old man, by looking for a secret hiding place or a hidden room?

WALTER: Sorry, Jim, but there's no hidden room or secret hiding place. My great-grandfather found that out.

JIM: Too bad. Too bad. I was counting on a hidden room. Every old house should have at least one hidden room.

MR. EDWARDS: Hello! Am I in time for lunch?

SUSAN: Just in time, Daddy. Anna and I were setting the table. Did you buy any cameras?

MR. EDWARDS: No, I didn't have time. I was buying wood carvings.

JIM: The Swiss are famous for wood carving. See page 7 in my book.

MRS. EDWARDS: And rightly so. Good Swiss wood carvings are lovely. Anna, please tell your mother that Mr. Edwards will be here for lunch, too.

MR. EDWARDS: What did I hear about a hidden room? Is there a mystery in the house?

SUSAN: Yes, a mystery and a lost treasure.

MR. EDWARDS: Splendid.

MRS. EDWARDS: For once you're home early. I want you to see Mrs. Robinson's beautiful flowers. We can stroll through the garden while I tell you the story.

MR. EDWARDS: A good idea.

JIM: Now, Walter, while we're waiting for lunch we'll start on the treasure hunt. First we'll think.

SUSAN: We'll all think.

NARRATOR: Jim gets the doll and hands it to Susan.

JIM: Treasure hunting is a man's work. You'd better get Anna and play with the doll.

SUSAN: Well!

JIM: Quiet, please! Now, Walter, you say that there is positively no secret room or hiding place. Right?

WALTER: Right.

JIM: Ceilings have been thoroughly inspected and floors torn up. Right?

WALTER: Right.

JIM: In my opinion, then, it would be a waste of time to search this room any further.

WALTER: Right, I agree. Now what?

JIM: We consider the rest of the house. Are there any parts as old as this?

WALTER: My room was old Hans' bedroom.

NARRATOR: Jim excitedly strikes his fist against his palm.

JIM: The very place. Let's go, Walter.

SUSAN: Don't you want Anna and me to help?

JIM: No, no, little sister. Walter and I can handle this treasure hunt very nicely.

SUSAN: Little sister! I'm a year younger, and Jim acts as though I belong in a baby carriage.

ANNA: Walter is the same.

SUSAN: Let's show those two, Anna. We can find the treasure as well as they.

ANNA: How? My grandfather and my great-grandfather looked everywhere.

SUSAN: They couldn't have looked everywhere. They didn't

find it. Let's think, Anna. Did Hans keep a diary? Do you have any of his old letters?

ANNA: No, nothing.

SUSAN: I'm beginning to dislike old Hans. Didn't he leave any clue?

ANNA: Well, there were his dying words.

SUSAN: Dying words? They're always important. What were they?

ANNA: Before he collapsed, he had time only to murmur weakly, "The stones! The stones!"

SUSAN: "The stones! The stones!" That's a clue all right. The treasure must be diamonds or something like that.

ANNA: My grandparents looked for jewels all their lives.

SUSAN: Where?

ANNA: Everywhere.

SUSAN: Stones! Stones! Who was talking about stones? Anna! I have it! I know where the treasure is!

ANNA: You do?

SUSAN: It's the doll. Don't you see it's the doll?

ANNA: What about the doll?

SUSAN: You've had her all your life. You're used to her looks. But when I showed her to Mother she said right away, "Her eyes are like stones." *Stones*. Get it?

ANNA: No.

SUSAN: Have you ever heard of black pearls?

ANNA: Yes. They're frightfully expensive.

SUSAN: Have you ever seen black pearls?

ANNA: No.

SUSAN: Naturally, then, you wouldn't recognize black pearls. Why couldn't her eyes be black pearls? Or brilliant diamonds covered with tar?

ANNA: Do you believe it?

SUSAN: Sure.

JIM: We're back. Isn't lunch ready?

SUSAN: Did you boys find the treasure?

WALTER: Jim was too hungry.

JIM: We'll find it after lunch.

SUSAN: You don't need to bother.

ANNA: Susan's found it.

WALTER: Where? Where?

JIM: Honest, Susan? You really found it?

MR. EDWARDS: What's all the excitement?

ANNA: Susan found the treasure.

SUSAN: It's the doll. Remember, Mother, how you said her eyes were like stones? Anna just told me that old Hans' dying words were, "The stones! The stones!" He meant her eyes. Couldn't they be black pearls or diamonds covered with tar?

MRS. EDWARDS: The doll does have strange eyes. Like none that I have ever seen.

MRS. ROBINSON: Lunch is ready.

ANNA: Not now, Mama! Not now! Susan's found the treasure.

MR. EDWARDS: Let me see the doll. I'm no expert, but I believe I can tell you if the stones are precious ones.

MRS. ROBINSON: Stones! Did Susan find some precious stones?

MR. EDWARDS: No, I'm afraid not.

SUSAN: They're not black pearls or diamonds?

MR. EDWARDS: The doll's eyes are black stones. Plain ordinary black stones. Nothing more.

SUSAN: Oh, dear! I'm so sorry, Anna. I was sure we'd found the treasure.

JIM: Maybe you have, Susan, maybe you have.

SUSAN: No. The eyes are only stones.

JIM: Never mind the eyes. It's the doll. The insides. Aren't dolls like this stuffed with sawdust? Hans gave the doll to Marguerite. He wanted her to have the jewels. Maybe he hid them here. Did anybody look inside the doll?

MRS. ROBINSON: No, I don't believe so. When the cloth on the doll became worn, we just re-covered her for Anna. The doll had been stored in an old trunk. I took her out and sewed on a new cover, a new skin, and made her new clothes.

MRS. EDWARDS: Are you willing to rip out the stitches in the doll's body, Mrs. Robinson? Perhaps the children are right.

MRS. ROBINSON: Why not? Anna, get my scissors, please.

NARRATOR: Anna runs out to the kitchen and returns with the scissors.

WALTER: Hurry up, Mother.

MRS. ROBINSON: Dear me! My hands are shaking. Will you finish, Mrs. Edwards?

MRS. EDWARDS: Certainly.

JIM: Yippee! There's a stone! Is it glass or is it—

SUSAN: Examine it, Daddy.

NARRATOR: Mr. Edwards holds the stone to the light.

MR. EDWARDS: Ah, this is better. Now you've found something!

ANNA: What is it? What is it, please?

MR. EDWARDS: It's a diamond, all right.

WALTER: Here's another.

NARRATOR: Susan hands the stones to Mr. Edwards.

SUSAN: And another! And another!

MRS. EDWARDS: That's all.

MR. EDWARDS: Four diamonds. A very nice treasure.

JIM: The mystery is solved.

MRS. ROBINSON: How much are the diamonds worth, Mr. Edwards?

MR. EDWARDS: I couldn't tell you exactly.

MRS. ROBINSON: Do you think if we sold them we could get enough money to go to America?

MR. EDWARDS: I certainly think there'd be enough for that. After lunch, we'll take the diamonds to a good jeweler. He'll know their value.

MRS. ROBINSON: Lunch! That reminds me. Come, sit down, everyone.

SUSAN: After finding diamonds who could think of lunch?

JIM: I could.

WALTER: I could.

MR. EDWARDS: I won't say no.

MRS. EDWARDS: Come, girls. The treasure has been waiting to be found for a long, long time.

MR. EDWARDS: It can wait a little longer before going to the jeweler's.

SUSAN: We might as well give up, Anna.

NARRATOR: As the play ends, the children are sitting at the table talking excitedly about the treasure.

THE END

The Reluctant Ghost

Here is an amusing ghost story with a happy ending. Read it to yourself and find the answers to the following questions:

1. Why did the girls wish to haunt the house?
2. How did they choose Emily for the ghost?
3. Who was the ghost that caught the girls?
4. Was there any foundation for the rumor that the house was haunted by a "Green Lady"?
   Explain.
5. How did the girls help Mrs. Allen?

Discuss the answers to the questions. Choose parts with the help of your leader.

Read your part to yourself. Be sure you are thoroughly familiar with it. Understand the character you are playing. Decide just how you are going to use your voice.

Practice reading the play aloud together.

Try to determine which places need to be improved. Help each other.

Now read the play aloud again.

Evaluate your reading:

1. Did you pay attention to periods, commas, question marks?
2. Did you use your voice to show how you felt?
3. Did you vary the pitch of your voice?
4. Did you stress certain words to make the meaning clear?

If you are sure everyone is ready, arrange to read for your class.

THE RELUCTANT GHOST

by Margaret Wylie Brydon and Esther Ziegler

Characters

(10 girls and the narrator)

NARRATOR
JANE, *the leader of the group*
MIMI, *a girl who likes to act slightly superior*
MELANIE, *a girl from the South*
EMILY, *a timid girl*

JULIA
GINNY } *other members of the group*
CAROL } *who plan to haunt the house*
JACKY

MRS. ALLEN, *the owner of the house*
MISS BLAKE, *Mrs. Allen's guest*

NARRATOR: It is ten o'clock on a Friday night. Eight girls climb a tall tree and enter the attic of a darkened house. The last girl, dressed as a ghost, is following along reluctantly. Jane, who is already in the attic, goes to the window and calls back to her.

JANE: Emily, hurry up before someone sees us.

EMILY: Stop shaking the limb. I'm all wound up in this sheet.

JANE: Shh-h-h! There! See how easy it was?

EMILY: Easy for you maybe! You didn't have to bring your bed along.

JULIA: Well, why didn't you cut the sheet off then? You look more like a mummy than a ghost in that.

EMILY: Cut it off? My mother will murder me if I even so much as tear one of her sheets.

MIMI: Then you can be a real ghost!

MELANIE: Ooooooh! What a spooky-looking place this is!

MIMI (*With a superior laugh*): What did you expect in a haunted house?

JANE: Now let's get started. Emily, as soon as I give the word, you open that door over there and creep downstairs.

EMILY: In the dark?

CAROL: Of course, silly. Do you think ghosts turn on all the lights before they begin haunting?

MELANIE: You're beginning to look like a ghost now, Emily.

EMILY (*With a little moan*): I feel like one, too . . . all empty inside.

JULIA: I'll bet it's the first time you've felt empty in years.

EMILY: I think this idea of yours is awful, Jane. Especially making me the ghost. *Me*, a ghost! I don't care if I did draw the short straw, it isn't fair. Anybody else would make a better ghost. Why I . . . I'm too fat, for one thing!

JULIA: She admits it!

CAROL: Tell us a little more about this friend of yours, Jane. The nice old lady who gives you cookies, I mean.

JANE: I *told* you. She is having trouble, money trouble—you know, the kind our fathers have—and now she has to sell this house. It's real old, and someone is coming to look at it, and stay overnight, and I thought if the house turned out to be haunted, no one would want to buy it. People are awfully scared of ghosts.

JACKY: Horses aren't.

JULIA: That's 'cause they have horse sense, I guess.

GINNY: Maybe ghosts are scared of people, too.

JANE: So I thought if one of us would dress up in a sheet, and hide in the attic, and scare these people, they will go away, and Mrs. Allen can keep her home.

MELANIE: But if she needs the money—

JANE: Her daughter-in-law can easily afford to give her the money. Mrs. Allen has always wanted to spend her last days in her own home, and we are going to see that she does!

CAROL: Yes, and there may really be a ghost in this house. Some of the high school girls told me that the spirit of a Green Lady haunts this place. She was a beautiful young girl who died of grief when her lover didn't return from the Civil War, and she comes back every ten years on the anniversary of his death to search for him.

EMILY: That settles it! I'm going home! Two ghosts in one house is just one too many, especially if the other ghost is me.

MIMI: Be quiet, Emily, and stop being so childish. Why do they call her the Green Lady?

CAROL: I don't know. She wears green, I guess.

JULIA: Oh, I don't believe such a silly story. It's just childish nonsense.

MELANIE: I believe in ghosts. We have lots of them in the South and I believe in them, especially at night.

EMILY: Well, anyway, I know my mother won't approve of my being a ghost. And how do I start haunting?

MIMI: How do you expect to do it? Walk up to the front door and say: "Good evening, ma'am. I've come to haunt your house."

EMILY: It may be funny to you, Mimi, but it isn't to me. If only I hadn't drawn the short straw!

JULIA: My dad is always talking about being "caught short." I wonder if that's what he means?

GINNY: It seems to me we are talking a lot, and doing nothing. Why don't we get started? There's a grand moon.

JULIA: The better to haunt you with, my dear.

EMILY: Listen! What's that noise?

JULIA: Only a mouse, silly.

JACKY: I could have brought Black Beauty. He wouldn't have made any noise, and if we needed a quick getaway. . . .

MIMI: How childish! Quick getaway! You sound like a comic book, Jacky. Who wants to get away? This is rather fun.

CAROL: I'm glad you're pleased, for once.

MIMI: Oh, anything to break the monotony of small-town life.

It's deadly here, after New York.

JULIA: She heard her mother say that.

MELANIE: I don't blame Emily for being scared. This old house does look haunted.

JANE: Do your wail now . . . real soft, Emily.

EMILY (*Weakly*): Oooooooooo!

JULIA: That's awful. You sound as if you have a stomach-ache. It should have a scream at the end, like this. (*Screams softly*)

EMILY: Don't do that! You scared the daylights out of me!

MIMI: And if you see anyone, why not give a low groan, like this? (*Groans deeply*)

CAROL: That sounds like a lonesome coyote.

MIMI: Thank you.

CAROL (*Promptly*): You're welcome.

JACKY: I could neigh like a horse.

MIMI: Now we're getting childish again.

MELANIE: What do you expect, Miss New Yorker? We aren't exactly grown-up, you know. Anyway, this is fun.

CAROL: Let's get going. Everybody will be up having breakfast before we get started haunting.

JANE: Come along, Emily. To your stations, guards.

NARRATOR: Jane leads Emily to the door and starts her on her way to the hall below. The girls giggle softly in excitement. Jacky speaks.

JACKY: If Emily sees herself in a mirror in that outfit, she'll faint.

MIMI (*In a loud whisper*): Well, I wouldn't mind taking her place. I think I would look rather nice in a sheet.

GINNY: The gorgeous ghost, eh?

MIMI: Emily looks like someone who got mixed up in a washing machine.

JULIA: Gee, this is dull. My foot's gone to sleep.

MIMI: How sensible of it. There's nothing else to do.

NARRATOR: Suddenly they hear a muffled scream and a noise from downstairs.

CAROL: What was that?

MIMI: They've seen the ghost at last. I thought maybe Emily had gone home.

JANE: That sounded like her voice. If she spoils this thing . . .

JULIA: Here she comes now, running up the steps. Oh, she's ruined everything.

EMILY: Jane, Jane!

JANE: Here I am, you . . . you Benedict Arnold!

MELANIE: What happened?

MIMI: She spoiled it, of course.

EMILY (*Gasping for breath*): Wait . . . wait a minute.

JACKY: That's what I like about horses. They aren't afraid of anything.

EMILY: If you will only keep quiet a minute. You'd think I hadn't risked life and limb and . . . and . . . everything to save Mrs. Allen, when she had her own ghost all the time.

CAROL: Was it really the lady in green, Emily?

EMILY: Of course it was. Why do you suppose I yelled?

MIMI: This is so thrilling.

EMILY: Quiet, Mimi. This is my story.

JANE: Gee, Emily, you've changed!

EMILY: Sure I have. I'll never be the same again . . . never! Well, this is what happened. I crept downstairs as you said to, Jane, and every step creaked with me, and it was awfully dark. Then, when I got to the bottom of the stairs I tried to walk up and down in the hall waving my arms like a ghost, only my legs were shaking so I could hardly stand. I heard a noise and saw someone . . .

MELANIE: The lady in green!

CAROL: Are you sure it was a real ghost?

EMILY: Well, how many people do you know who are ten feet tall? Anyway, I've never seen anyone like that before . . . with her face all sort of greeny-white and gleaming.

JULIA: Let's get out of here!

MIMI: Yes, come on. Hurry up!

MELANIE: What for?

JULIA: Are you crazy? If there is a ghost loose in this house, I'm getting out right now.

MELANIE: Without seeing it? Why, I think this is real thrilling . . . finding a sure-enough haunt. I didn't think you Northerners had anything half so romantic. I just have to see it!

NARRATOR: Melanie goes to the door and peers down the stairs into the hallway.

CAROL: Are you nuts, Melanie?

MELANIE: But you said yourself the ghost appears only about every ten years. I'm not waiting until I'm old to get my thrills!

JANE: I can wait very nicely to see a ghost.

JACKY: Hurry, Emily!

EMILY: I won't leave Melanie all by herself . . . I'll stay with you, Melanie. I'll take you down there if you really want to go, but I wish you wouldn't.

NARRATOR: Footsteps are heard coming up the stairs. Suddenly a green light glows in the hall.

JULIA: It's the lady in green! Run!

MIMI (*Wailing*): It's too late! We can't get out!

EMILY: Hide!

NARRATOR: The girls scramble to hide. A ghostly figure appears in the doorway. Its head is swathed in cloth and it carries a flashlight which reveals a white face gleaming above a flowing gown. The ghost speaks.

GHOST (*In an urgent whisper*): Where are you? You must come out of there now! Where are you hiding? Come out, I say, or I'll have to come get you.

NARRATOR: The small table Mimi is hiding behind topples over with a loud crash.

GHOST: Shhh! Do you want to wake the dead?

MIMI (*Backing away*): Oh no, Green Lady, no! Honestly, I didn't want to wake you.

NARRATOR: Emily, in her sheet, steps forward to protect Mimi.

GHOST: Good heavens! What's that?

EMILY: I'm just a little girl, really . . . we all are! And we didn't want to bother you at all. We just came here to scare humans.

GHOST: What?

EMILY: So please won't you let us go home now . . . if we promise not to interfere with your haunting anymore?

GHOST: What are you talking about? Wait until I turn a light on in here.

NARRATOR: The light reveals a young woman in a pale blue bathrobe. Her head is done up in a towel and her face is covered with cold cream.

MIMI: Oh!

MISS BLAKE: Why, my goodness!

EMILY: You're not green at all! You're blue!

MISS BLAKE: What are you talking about?

EMILY: You aren't a ghost after all, are you?

MELANIE: Oh, shucks!

MISS BLAKE: Of course I'm not a ghost. I'm Mrs. Allen's house guest, Miss Blake. I heard you children outside in the tree when you went by my window, but I didn't call out for fear of disturbing Mrs. Allen, whose room is on the other side of the house. When I heard you up here in the attic though, I decided it was time someone sent you home; so I slipped on my robe and came up here before you awakened anyone. Do you think it is a nice thing for big girls like you to break into an old lady's house at this time of night to try to frighten her?

JANE: Oh, we didn't want to do that at all! Mrs. Allen is a friend of ours.

EMILY: Yes, I was supposed to be protecting her!

MISS BLAKE: Protecting her? From what?

EMILY: From you.

JANE (*Quickly*): You see, Emily means that . . . well . . . we happen to know that Mrs. Allen doesn't really want to sell this place, and if you bought it she'd have to leave here.

MELANIE: And that would break her heart. Wouldn't it, girls?

JULIA (*Desperately*): You see, we thought it would be fun to help Mrs. Allen by scaring you so that you would go away without buying this house. Mrs. Allen's daughter-in-law would have to let her live here if people thought there were real ghosts in the house and wouldn't buy it . . . don't you see?

MISS BLAKE: I'm afraid I don't. Who said Mrs. Allen doesn't want to sell her house?

JANE: My mother did. She knows Mrs. Allen very well, and she says Mrs. Allen cried when she talked about having to leave here.

MISS BLAKE: That's strange. I thought she was anxious to sell. She wrote and told me about the place being for sale, or I wouldn't have come here.

JANE: That's just because you are a friend of her daughter-in-law's. She knows you love old things, and wouldn't try to change the house. But she hates to leave, all the same.

MISS BLAKE: I see! Well, I wouldn't be surprised if you were right, little girl.

NARRATOR: Suddenly, Mrs. Allen calls from the foot of the stairs.

MRS. ALLEN: Miss Blake? Are you all right?

MISS BLAKE: Everything's all right, Mrs. Allen. I'm up in the attic.

MRS. ALLEN: I heard a crash. What happened?

MISS BLAKE: Straighten things up quickly, girls. She's coming up the stairs.

NARRATOR: As Miss Blake hurries to help the girls with the table she suddenly stops and runs her hand over the wood.

MISS BLAKE: How perfectly beautiful this table is!

MRS. ALLEN: My gracious, what's this? A masquerade party? Children, what in the world are you doing up in this dirty attic? This is no place to play. You come right down to the parlor.

MISS BLAKE: Just a minute, Mrs. Allen . . . please! This table and that old chest over there are simply beautiful. And that chair . . . an original Duncan Phyfe! Look at those legs!

THE RELUCTANT GHOST 55

Why this is a crime! All these priceless things hidden away up here.

MRS. ALLEN: Oh, those? I've never used them. They belonged to my great-grandmother, I guess, and I never was one to throw things away, no matter how old they were. This house is so full of furniture, it just seemed there wasn't room for these old things. And I wouldn't want to insult my children or friends by giving them my old cast-offs.

MISS BLAKE: Cast-offs! Why, Mrs. Allen! This attic is a gold mine. Excuse me, I just can't keep from exploring . . . this old porcelain is lovely, and this furniture! It's simply marvelous!

MRS. ALLEN: Well, if there's anything you'd like, Miss Blake, you're welcome to it. I'll be selling the place anyway.

MISS BLAKE: No, you won't be selling your house . . . not unless you really want to. And you won't give away these things, either. I'd like to have first chance at that chair over there, and this table . . . but I couldn't ever afford the rest. However, I know people who can and will jump at the opportunity to pay a good price for them.

EMILY: You mean that Mrs. Allen can stay here if she wants to?

MISS BLAKE: If I know anything at all about antiques, I'm sure of it.

MRS. ALLEN: I guess I just can't tell you how much it will mean to me to keep this old place.

MISS BLAKE (Gently): You don't have to, Mrs. Allen. I think we know.

EMILY: Congratulations, Mimi. Am I glad you knocked over that table!

JANE: And I think you are the grandest ghost I ever saw, Emily. I hereby present you with our order of valor . . . it's only tinfoil, but it shines brightly.

EMILY: Thank you, Jane.

CAROL: We'd better make tracks for home. If my mother finds

out I climbed down that tree again . . . well, I'll have to stand up for our next meeting!

JANE: Here we go! And Emily can lead the way. She isn't afraid of anything!

MRS. ALLEN: Then maybe she'll lead the way down those awful attic stairs. I declare, I come up here about once in every ten years. I always say I'm going to take out that old green bulb and put in one that gives more light, but I never do! Just wander around here practically in the dark.

NARRATOR: As Mrs. Allen continues to talk the girls stop and stare at each other. Suddenly they understand!

GIRLS: The Green Lady!

MRS. ALLEN: Oh, that! Rubbish! Never did believe in ghosts. Come to the kitchen, all of you, and have some hot chocolate and cookies.

EMILY: Wheeeeee! Hot chocolate and cookies! Give me the flashlight, Jane. I'll go first.

JULIA: My, how that girl has changed. You didn't exactly have to push her down the stairs this time, did you, Jane?

JANE (*Laughing*): No, but this is different. Did you ever see Emily when she wasn't ready to haunt the kitchen?

THE END

The Pilgrim Painting

This is an imaginative story about a boy and girl in a painting who come to life. They help two children to understand the meaning of Thanksgiving.

The story that this play tells is not difficult to understand.

Read it to yourself to be sure you are familiar with the plot. List the things the children learned to appreciate through the help of the Pilgrim children.

Choose the best person for each part.

Read your part to yourself. If you need help with words, ask someone in the group.

Read the play aloud together. Talk over:

1. Did you pause to make the meaning clear?
2. Did you stress some words to make them important?
3. Did you pronounce every word clearly and distinctly?
4. Did you come in on time with your part?

Go back over the parts that were poor. Help each other to make them clear to the listener.

When you are ready, arrange with your teacher to read the play to the class.

THE PILGRIM PAINTING

by James Rawls

Characters

(4 boys, 3 girls, and the narrator)

NARRATOR

BONNIE BROWN, *a modern girl*

EDDIE, *her brother*

MRS. BROWN, *mother of the children*

MR. BROWN, *father of the children*

MR. MARKS, *chairman of the school board*

PILGRIM GIRL, *the girl in the painting, who is just about as old as Bonnie*

PILGRIM BOY, *the boy in the painting, who is just about Eddie's age*

NARRATOR: It is Thanksgiving Day. As the play begins, Bonnie is sitting in an armchair in the living room, bouncing a ball. Eddie is standing nearby holding an old doll upside down. Mrs. Brown is placing a bowl of fruit on the table.

EDDIE: Bonnie, I'm telling you, you won't have any doll at all unless you fix this one. Look at it. Its leg is half off, its face is all dirty, and its dress is in rags.

BONNIE: I don't care, Eddie. I'm sick of that old doll. I've had it forever. Why can't I have a new one?

EDDIE: Why can't I have a baseball bat? All I have to play with is that old rubber ball.

MRS. BROWN: Now, Bonnie, Eddie, that's no way to talk. Remember what day this is: this is Thanksgiving and you have a great deal to be thankful for. You're young and healthy, you go to a nice school, and you're going to have a good Thanksgiving dinner in just a little while.

EDDIE: A good dinner! I know what we'll have—boiled cabbage and a ham bone! I can smell it cooking.

BONNIE: Most people have turkey. Why, everyone has a turkey on Thanksgiving. That's what Thanksgiving is for!

MRS. BROWN: We can't afford a turkey, and you know it.

EDDIE: We can't afford a lot of things. Look at this old sweater I'm wearing. I can hardly get it on any more, I've worn it so long.

BONNIE: My dress is worse! It's the newest one I have, and it's already over a year old. Oh, Mother, why do we have to be so poor?

NARRATOR: Bonnie starts to cry. Mother crosses to her and strokes her hair. Then she puts an arm about Eddie and begins to talk softly to the children.

MRS. BROWN: There, there, children. No crying on Thanksgiving. Why, my darlings, I know how you feel. Bonnie, you do need some pretty new clothes and a new doll and a carriage, too—and, Eddie, you could use a real baseball with a bat and a glove to go with it.

BONNIE: Isn't Daddy ever going to sell a picture?

EDDIE: All he does is paint, paint, paint, but no one ever buys a picture. Why doesn't he stop painting pictures and paint houses or something? People pay for that.

MRS. BROWN: Now stop this, this instant! I will not have you children criticizing your father. He's an artist and he works hard. Someday he will be famous, and we must all help him. Now stop grumbling and be thankful for what you do have.

NARRATOR: As Mrs. Brown goes into the kitchen, Mr. Brown enters the living room carrying his brush and palette.

MR. BROWN: Well, my pets, have you seen my latest painting? I finished it this morning.

BONNIE: Did you, Daddy?

EDDIE: That's nice.

MR. BROWN: It's the best picture I've ever painted.

BONNIE: Is it pretty, Daddy?

MR. BROWN: I don't know if it's "pretty," but it's very life-like.

It's right behind that screen there. Why don't you look at it?

BONNIE: It's just awful that the school board no longer wants to buy it.

EDDIE: It would look wonderful hanging in our lunchroom at school. That picture's big enough to cover the whole side of the lunchroom.

MR. BROWN: Yes, it's life-size, all right, and it's taken hard work to finish it by Thanksgiving. But, as you say, Mr. Marks of the school board says they no longer want to buy it.

NARRATOR: Mr. Brown feels as discouraged as the children. He shakes his head as he enters the kitchen.

BONNIE: So what good is it? All that work for nothing.

EDDIE: Do you want to see it, now that it's finished?

BONNIE: What for?

EDDIE: Oh, come on, let's take a look. Dinner isn't ready yet.

BONNIE: All right, but what's the use? It's not going to bring us a Thanksgiving turkey.

NARRATOR: The children move the screen in the living room and sit down to look at the Pilgrim painting. It shows a Pilgrim family sitting at a wooden table, their heads bowed. On the table is a cooked turkey.

BONNIE: Eddie, those Pilgrims look almost real.

EDDIE: Yes, they do. You know something, Bonnie?

BONNIE: What?

EDDIE: Something else looks real, too.

BONNIE: What?

EDDIE: That turkey!

BONNIE: Mm-m-m, I wish it were. If only we could have one like that.

EDDIE: You know, the longer you look at them the more real they seem. Boy, I wouldn't be a bit surprised if they just raised their heads and said hello to us.

NARRATOR: Just as Eddie finishes talking, the Pilgrims slowly raise their heads and smile at the children. The Pilgrim mother and father go out. The Pilgrim girl speaks.

PILGRIM GIRL: Would you share our meal?

PILGRIM BOY: Pray join us.

NARRATOR: When they hear the Pilgrims speak, Bonnie and Eddie scream and cling to each other.

BONNIE: Eddie! I thought I heard them speak!

EDDIE: So did I! But I don't believe it!

PILGRIM BOY: I pray you, do not run from us. We are as real as you.

PILGRIM GIRL: Aye, in faith. As surely as this day is Thanksgiving Day, 1628.

BONNIE: But it isn't! I mean, it's Thanksgiving Day, but it's 1965.

EDDIE: You're a painting. You're not real. My father painted you.

PILGRIM GIRL: He painted us well, too. Do but feel the texture of my cape.

PILGRIM BOY: And my jacket. Prithee, feel the warmth of it.

PILGRIM GIRL: Do not be afraid.

BONNIE: Your cape feels rough and coarse. It's nice, but isn't it rather plain?

PILGRIM GIRL: It is the only one I have. May I touch your garment?

BONNIE: Oh, this old dress. I hate it.

PILGRIM GIRL: Why, it feels like a feather on my finger. It has the colors of the rainbow. Truly, it is the most beautiful dress I have ever seen.

NARRATOR: The Pilgrim boy holds Eddie's sweater in his hand and turns to his sister in surprise.

PILGRIM BOY: Sister, look upon this overshirt. It is heavy of loom and has the color of fire.

PILGRIM GIRL: Aye, brother, it is a wondrous thing. Oh! See there!

NARRATOR: The Pilgrim girl points to the armchair and runs over to get a close look at it.

PILGRIM GIRL: That object! Let me guess. It is for sleeping!

BONNIE (*Laughing*): No, it is a chair—for sitting!

NARRATOR: The Pilgrim children touch the chair and walk all around it. Finally Bonnie and Eddie help the boy into the chair.

PILGRIM GIRL: All chairs I know are made of wood, hewn with an axe.

PILGRIM BOY: Truly, it must be for sleeping. It is soft like a bed and would be easy to warm.

EDDIE: No, it's a chair. Our beds are in the bedroom.

PILGRIM GIRL: A separate room for beds?

EDDIE: Why, of course. Next to the bedroom is the bathroom. The kitchen is over there.

BONNIE: And this is the living room and there is the dining room.

PILGRIM GIRL: So many rooms! It is like a palace!

BONNIE: How many rooms do you have?

PILGRIM GIRL: Only one. All families have but one except the Squire, who is rich, and he has three.

PILGRIM BOY: But our cabin is warm, for I sealed the cracks between the logs with grass and clay to keep the cold wind out. Did I not, sister?

PILGRIM GIRL: Aye, brother. No grown man could have done the task better.

PILGRIM BOY: Oh, look upon this rare little creature. Is it alive?

BONNIE: Alive? Of course not. That's my old doll. She's ugly and disgusting.

PILGRIM GIRL: No! Oh, no. Why, she is like a real, true child. Real arms. Real legs. Oh! She has real hair, golden as the ripened wheat.

PILGRIM BOY: Her eyes are the blue of a summer sky.

PILGRIM GIRL: She is truly an angel.

EDDIE: Do you have a doll, Pilgrim Girl?

PILGRIM GIRL: Aye, my doll is a length of wood with a corn husk for a dress, but I love her, for she is mine.

EDDIE: Have you seen one of these?

NARRATOR: Eddie bounces his ball and the Pilgrim children are so delighted they laugh and clap their hands.

PILGRIM BOY: It jumps! It jumps!

PILGRIM GIRL: It jumps like magic! Oh, let me make it jump.

PILGRIM BOY: Nay, me. Prithee, friend, take all I possess—
these smooth round pebbles—but let me hold the ball.

EDDIE: Sure. Here.

PILGRIM BOY: See, sister, see! I am making it jump!

PILGRIM GIRL: It is magic. It must all be magic.

NARRATOR: The Pilgrim girl walks to the dining table and
stands before the bowl of fruit.

PILGRIM GIRL: I cannot look for wonder. Brother, look upon
this table. It is prepared for a feast.

PILGRIM BOY: It is prepared for a king.

EDDIE: Here, have a banana.

PILGRIM BOY: What is this?

EDDIE: A banana. Eat it. There are more.

PILGRIM BOY *and* GIRL: A bah-nah-nah?

BONNIE (*Laughing*): You sound so funny.

PILGRIM GIRL: It is an odd name.

PILGRIM BOY: A bah-nah-nah. Is that not right?

EDDIE: That's pretty close. Taste it. You'll like it.

PILGRIM BOY: This bah-nah-nah—its hide is thick.

EDDIE: Wait! You have to peel it first. I'll peel it for you.
(*Pause*) There. Now taste it.

PILGRIM GIRL: Stop, brother! Art thou not frightened of this
bah-nah-nah? It may be more magic like the jumping ball.

PILGRIM BOY: Nay, sister. Its meat is soft and strangely sweet.

BONNIE: It's a fruit.

PILGRIM GIRL: A fruit? Nay. Apples and pears and peaches
I have seen, but never this.

BONNIE: What about oranges? Do you have these?

PILGRIM GIRL: It is the magic ball again! Now it will jump
for me! Watch closely. (*Pause*) Oh! I have broken it.

BONNIE: No, an orange won't bounce like a rubber ball. Here,
squeeze the juice into your mouth.

PILGRIM GIRL: Ah, it is good. Sharp, but sweet.

PILGRIM BOY: You must be very rich to own such treasures: your shirt of fire, the magic ball, the sleeping chair.

PILGRIM GIRL: The angel doll, the rainbow dress and this strange fruit.

PILGRIM BOY: You must be richer than the Squire.

EDDIE: No, we're not rich at all. We're poor.

BONNIE: We don't even have a turkey for Thanksgiving.

NARRATOR: Suddenly there is a knock on the door. This frightens the Pilgrim children who quickly run toward the painting. The Pilgrim mother and father enter, and go to the painting, too.

PILGRIM BOY *and* GIRL: Heaven protect us! We must fly! Home! Home!

BONNIE *and* EDDIE: Don't go! Don't go!

NARRATOR: Just as the Pilgrims settle into place, Mr. Brown comes into the living room. Mrs. Brown calls from the kitchen.

MRS. BROWN: Bonnie! Eddie! See who is at the door.

MR. BROWN: I'll answer it, children.

NARRATOR: Mr. Brown opens the door. Mr. Marks enters carrying a large package.

MR. MARKS: Well, well! Caught you at home. Happy Thanksgiving!

MR. BROWN: And a happy one to you, sir.

MRS. BROWN: Oh, it's Mr. Marks, chairman of the school board. Come in, Mr. Marks. Let me take your coat.

MR. MARKS: No, no. I can't stay. Just stopped by for a moment. Hello, Eddie, my boy. What a pretty dress, Bonnie.

MRS. BROWN: I'm afraid she doesn't think so.

BONNIE: Oh, but I do, Mother. It's my favorite dress. See, Mr. Marks, it has the colors of the rainbow.

MR. MARKS: Careful there. You'll make that doll dizzy spinning around like that.

BONNIE: I wouldn't do that. I take good care of my doll.

MRS. BROWN: Now, Bonnie.

THE PILGRIM PAINTING 65

BONNIE: Yes, Mother, I do. I mean, I'm going to. I'm going to make her a new dress and wash her face and comb her hair.

EDDIE: I'll fix her leg.

MRS. BROWN: Well, I declare! What's come over you all of a sudden? Bonnie, you said you hated that old doll.

BONNIE: No, I love her. She's like an angel to me.

MR. MARKS: What a pretty thing to say!

MRS. BROWN: I don't understand it at all. Why, next, Eddie will be telling us he likes his old red sweater.

EDDIE: Yes, Mother, I do.

MRS. BROWN: What!

EDDIE: It's still warm. It hasn't faded a bit—see, it's the color of fire.

MR. MARKS: Well, Mrs. Brown, I would say that you are very lucky. Two children who appreciate their clothing and who take care of their toys—a real blessing.

MRS. BROWN: Yes, this time I believe they really mean it.

MR. MARKS: Mr. Brown, I've come here because I bring you good news. I am happy to tell you that the school board has voted to buy your Pilgrim painting.

MR. BROWN: Mr. Marks!

MRS. BROWN: How wonderful!

MR. MARKS: Yes, they finally made up their minds. We will hang it in the lunchroom as planned. What is more, we want you to do a painting for each holiday in the year. That should keep you busy for some time.

MR. BROWN: Mr. Marks, it's wonderful.

MR. MARKS: Here is the check to pay for the Pilgrim painting. I'll have someone come tomorrow and take it away.

EDDIE: Oh, no!

BONNIE: You can't!

MR. MARKS: What? What's this?

MR. BROWN: What do you mean?

BONNIE: Oh, Daddy, don't sell it! Don't sell the Pilgrims.

MR. BROWN: Why not?

BONNIE: We want them to stay. Don't we, Eddie?

EDDIE: Yes, Dad. Please don't sell it.

MRS. BROWN: I don't understand. You've done nothing all day but complain about this very thing.

BONNIE: We like the painting now.

EDDIE: We want to keep it.

BONNIE: We like the Pilgrim boy and girl.

EDDIE: They started our country!

BONNIE: They taught us many things!

EDDIE: Bonnie's right. They did teach us many things.

MR. MARKS: That is true, of course. The Pilgrims did lay the foundation for our nation when they landed at Plymouth Rock. And they did give us our heritage of freedom, for they came to this new land seeking freedom of worship.

BONNIE: That is why we celebrate Thanksgiving.

MR. MARKS: Yes, but if the painting has taught you all this, don't you think the other boys and girls at school would want to see it?

BONNIE: Yes, that's true.

EDDIE: Bonnie, we would be able to see it every day if it's hanging in the lunchroom.

BONNIE: I know it, but what would happen to—you know who?

EDDIE: Sh-h-h.

MRS. BROWN: Whom do you mean?

BONNIE: Well, I mean—I mean—

EDDIE: She doesn't know what she means, Mother. She's just talking. Forget it.

MRS. BROWN: I wonder. Excuse us, Mr. Marks. Sometimes they do imagine things.

MR. MARKS: The privilege of youth. Well, I must be going.

MR. BROWN: Mr. Marks, I don't know how to thank you and the school board for buying my paintings. It makes today the happiest Thanksgiving we have ever had.

MR. MARKS: My pleasure. Oh, I almost forgot. That package there. The Pilgrims have sent you something else besides freedom. At least, they looked like Pilgrims.

EDDIE: Who?

BONNIE: What do you mean, Mr. Marks?

MR. MARKS: It was very strange. As I was coming here, a man and woman stopped me just in front of your house and asked me to deliver this package to you. They were all dressed up like Pilgrims. On their way to a costume party, I suppose.

MRS. BROWN: Thank you for bringing it, Mr. Marks. I hope it is something for the children.

MR. BROWN: Yes, thank you. Thank you for everything, sir.

MR. MARKS: Goodbye, Bonnie. Goodbye, Eddie. Happy Thanksgiving!

MR. BROWN: Oh, my dear, we've sold it! We've sold it! Look at this check!

MRS. BROWN: It is wonderful! Really wonderful!

EDDIE: Stop, Mother! Father! Have you forgotten the package? Let's open it.

BONNIE: Yes, the package! May we open it now?

MRS. BROWN: Yes, dear. You may open it.

NARRATOR: Bonnie and Eddie quickly open the package and find a large turkey.

MRS. BROWN: A turkey!

MR. BROWN: A real Thanksgiving turkey!

MRS. BROWN: Wherever did it come from?

MR. BROWN: Who would have sent a turkey to us?

MRS. BROWN: Mr. Marks said a man and woman in Pilgrim clothes gave it to him.

MR. BROWN: That's right, he did. Do you two know anything about this?

BONNIE: Well, we—we—

MRS. BROWN: Come, Bonnie, out with it!

BONNIE: You see—oh, Eddie! Help me!

MR. BROWN: What about it, Eddie?

EDDIE: Dad, we might be able to make a guess, but even if we told you, you wouldn't believe it.

BONNIE: We don't even know whether to believe it ourselves!

EDDIE: So can't we just say that it's a secret? A secret handed down by the Pilgrims?

MR. BROWN: That's good enough for me. You keep the secret and I'll keep the turkey. Bring it along to the table, children, and let us sit down to eat.

NARRATOR: Bonnie and Eddie follow their parents to the table. As they pass the picture they hold the turkey high. The Pilgrim family waves and smiles.

MR. BROWN: Bow your heads. We have more to be thankful for this Thanksgiving Day than we could ever have imagined.

NARRATOR: As we leave the Browns, they have their heads bowed in prayer.

THE END

The Royal Cloth of China

This is a legend of how silk came to be made. Read the play to yourself and think about these questions.

1. Why was the Emperor unhappy?
2. What made the Empress so homesick?
3. How did she discover the silk thread?
4. Step by step, describe how silk cloth is made.
5. For what purpose was the first silk used?

Discuss the answers to these questions with your group. Be sure you understand the answers. Check on any difficult words.

Practice the following lines and emphasize the italicized word each time.

> *You* would *weave* with your own hands!
> *You* would *weave* with your own *hands!*
> You would *weave with your own hands!*
> (pitch rising)

Now try this line:

> I shall have your *heads* if you *breathe* a *word* of this to *anyone!*

And this one:

> That will take hundreds of *cocoons!*
> That will take *hundreds* of cocoons!
> *That* will take *hundreds of cocoons!*

Practice this line. Pause slightly at each dash and emphasize italicized words:

> It is *right* that she should be called the *Goddess* of the *Silk-*

worms—because *she*—like *them*—gave her life to *usefulness*.

Now, with your chairman, choose your part.
Read your part to yourself.
Practice the entire play aloud.

1. Are you enunciating each word distinctly?
2. Are you changing the pitch of your voice to bring out the meaning?
3. Are you coming in on time with your part?

Help each other to improve. Go back and practice again and again until you feel it goes smoothly.

Speak to your teacher when you have finished your practice and are ready to read.

THE ROYAL CLOTH OF CHINA

by Irma Fitz-Adcock

Characters

(8 boys, 8 girls, and the narrator)

NARRATOR
MOTHER
DAUGHTER
THE EMPEROR, *a great ruler of ancient China*
THE EMPRESS, *a homesick bride*
TWO MINISTERS, *advisors to the Emperor*
TWO DANCING GIRLS ⎫
TWO MUSICIANS ⎭ *people who entertain the Empress*
SERVANT, *a court servant*
TWO CARPENTERS, *workers in the court*
THREE WEAVERS

NARRATOR: In China, a mother and daughter are discussing silkworms. Let us listen to what they say.

MOTHER: Have you fed the silkworms?

DAUGHTER: Dozens of times, Mother! They eat the mulberry leaves as fast as I can pick them. Why must they eat so much? I am tired of feeding them.

MOTHER: Why, you know they must eat, my child. How can they spin the precious silk if they do not fill their fat little bodies with good food?

DAUGHTER: But I've stripped the leaves from our mulberry tree so many times, it is nearly bare. I have to hunt and hunt for leaves!

MOTHER (*Sharply*): Our tree bare! Come, we must go to the Shrine of the Goddess of the Silkworms, and ask her to give leaves to our mulberry trees and health to our silkworms. If our silkworms go hungry, there will be no lovely fiber to sell to the silk merchants. Without the money our silkworms earn for us, you will go hungry yourself, my lazy child.

DAUGHTER (*Stubbornly*): Well, there are still times when I wish that an Empress of China had not discovered silk.

MOTHER: Such a thing to say! And on the very day set aside in her honor, too! Such talk will bring us bad luck. If the Empress of all China could take care of silkworms with her own hands, is it a job you should despise?

DAUGHTER: Please tell me again the legend of the Empress and her silkworms.

MOTHER: Very well, if you promise there will be no more lazy talk! Now, you must know that this Empress lived long ago in the Golden Days of our people, when a great Emperor ruled the land. Everyone under heaven knows the fame of this Emperor! He was a just and wise ruler, and he brought wealth and happiness to his people. When he chose a young girl to be his new bride, she should have been the happiest girl in the land. But alas, she was not.

NARRATOR: This is the story the Mother tells. It is a summer day. The Emperor is talking to his ministers. He is very troubled. If you listen you will discover why.

EMPEROR: There is peace and prosperity in all the land. I have ruled the country well, but the happiness in the land is nothing but ashes to me when the Empress weeps day after day. As the sages say, before the land can be ordered, first there must be harmony in the home.

1ST MINISTER: O Son of Heaven, may you live ten thousand years! All the people know of your goodness.

EMPEROR: But if it is known that the Empress grieves for her own home, how can I bear the shame? Is there nothing that can make her happy?

2ND MINISTER: Your Majesty, rest your heart. It is common knowledge that a homesick bride will grieve. Perhaps some new amusement would please her.

EMPEROR: Well, suggest something.

1ST MINISTER: Dancing girls?

EMPEROR: A dozen danced for her and she only cried harder.

2ND MINISTER: A singing bird in a bamboo cage?

EMPEROR: She has three already, but she will not listen to them.

1ST MINISTER: New jade ornaments for her hair?

EMPEROR: She has more now than she can ever wear.

2ND MINISTER: A beautiful new robe?

EMPEROR: A new robe—hmmmmm. Last night I had a strange dream in which I saw the Empress dressed in a shimmering mist. The cloth in my dream glittered brightly like the finest gold, yet was softer than the caress of a flower petal. Ah, this fairy cloth graced the regal beauty of the Empress as nothing else could! Perhaps a robe of such cloth would give her pleasure.

1ST MINISTER: But there is no such cloth, O Son of Heaven.

EMPEROR: There shall be! I hereby order the whole nation to search for a way to weave such cloth as I dreamed of. And whoever finds the secret of this cloth finer than any known under heaven will be given a scroll that makes him ruler of my richest province.

2ND MINISTER: A worthy reward!

EMPEROR: See that my proclamation is sent throughout the land, from the northern desert to the villages which cling to the rocks by the sea.

1ST MINISTER: It shall be sent, O Son of Heaven.

MOTHER (*Resuming her story*): Imagine an Emperor who would give anything to please his Empress! But his new bride was young, and she longed for the home of her childhood. She had been the darling of devoted parents, and her homesickness could not be healed by gifts. The magnificent Imperial Palace awed her, but did not please her. Birds sang, but she did not hear them. Sunbeams danced in the garden of the Palace, but there were clouds on the face of the Empress, and tears in her eyes.

NARRATOR: And now it is another summer day. The Empress is sitting in her garden under a mulberry tree. She looks very sad. Nearby the Musicians and Dancing Girls are talking quietly together. Listen!

1ST DANCING GIRL: See how our Empress weeps day after day!

1ST MUSICIAN: And if she chooses to weep, is that your affair? She is sad, so she weeps.

2ND MUSICIAN: She is young, hardly more than a child. She is not used to this great court.

2ND DANCING GIRL: The Emperor has ordered us to cheer her up. We will feel his anger if we do not.

1ST DANCING GIRL: Let us dance for you, my lady, and banish those clouds which darken your heart.

1ST MUSICIAN: Would it please you, my lady, to hear the new song we have composed in your honor?

EMPRESS: Play. I know it is wrong of me to be homesick like this.

2ND DANCING GIRL: Wait! The Emperor is coming!

EMPEROR: Come here, Heart's Flower. Again I find you with tears on your cheeks! What is wrong this time? Musicians and dancing girls, I ordered you to amuse the Empress. Why have you not entertained her?

EMPRESS: No, no, my lord. The fault is not theirs. They always play and dance for me with great skill.

EMPEROR: Then why are your almond eyes so often dimmed with tears, so seldom sparkling with joy?

EMPRESS: I am a foolish child, my lord. But the truth is, my heart is heavy because I have nothing to do.

EMPEROR: Why should the Empress of all China do things with her hands like a common peasant? Are there not servants to attend to your every need or whim?

EMPRESS: Their service is perfect, my lord. But in my father's house I was always busy, and I cannot so quickly lose the habit. The days drag like lazy snails as I sit idle.

EMPEROR: Ah well, you will soon forget such childish fancies. Come, musicians and dancing girls, see that you amuse your Empress well!

1ST DANCING GIRL: Shall we dance for you now, my lady?

EMPRESS: No, really I have no heart for amusements. But do not worry. I shall not let anyone see my tears again.

SERVANT: I have brought your tea, my lady.

EMPRESS: I love to smell the fragrance of the hot tea while it is cooling. It gives more delight than the drink itself.

NARRATOR: As the Empress sniffs her tea, something falls from the tree overhead and lands in her cup. She jumps up and cries out.

EMPRESS: Oh! Something has fallen into my tea.

SERVANT: Let me pour you a fresh cup of tea, my lady. That one is spoiled.

EMPRESS: No, no. I wish to see what is in the cup.

SERVANT: It is only a cocoon which dropped from the mulberry tree overhead.

EMPRESS: Yes, but something is happening to it. It is becoming a tangle of fairy fibers. Give me the porcelain spoon so I can lift it out.

NARRATOR: The Empress lifts the tangle from her cup, and, pulling one end of the fiber free, she begins to unwind it from the cocoon.

2ND DANCING GIRL: Use my hair ornament to wind the thread on, my lady.

1ST DANCING GIRL: There seem to be miles of thread wrapped in that one cocoon!

EMPRESS: Have you ever seen such fiber? If only someone could spin thread like this, it would be a cloth such as is made by the Weaving Girl of Heaven.

2ND DANCING GIRL: Have you heard that the Emperor seeks for a royal cloth? Cloth woven from such fiber as this would be what the Emperor dreams of.

EMPRESS (*Excitedly*): The royal cloth that my lord seeks! Yes, I have heard of his proclamation. In our hands we hold the secret of such cloth. What thread could be more exquisite than this spun by the little silkworm? Thank you for your gift, little gray fellows in the mulberry tree. I shall use it to weave the royal cloth.

1ST DANCING GIRL: But the strands are too slender. You could never weave them.

EMPRESS: They are delicate, but I shall twist several strands together. Then the thread will be strong enough for weaving.

2ND DANCING GIRL: That will take hundreds of cocoons!

1ST DANCING GIRL: Look! The mulberry tree is full of them.

EMPRESS: They must all be plucked, soaked in hot tea, and unwound.

2ND DANCING GIRL: We will help you, Honorable Lady.

NARRATOR: The servant hurries out and returns with a large bowl of hot tea. As the cocoons are picked, they are soaked in hot tea, and the thread is wound on the silver and jade hair ornaments of the dancing girls.

EMPRESS: Now we have the thread for the royal cloth. But where is there a loom which will take such delicate thread?

1ST DANCING GIRL: There is none, my lady. But the court carpenters are clever. Surely they can build a special loom for you.

EMPRESS: Go, call the court carpenters.

NARRATOR: The servant bows and scurries off. She returns with the carpenters, who bow to the Empress.

EMPRESS: I need a special loom for weaving a very fine thread.

1ST CARPENTER: Command us, most Honorable Lady, and we obey. What sort of loom do you need?

EMPRESS: Do you see this thread? It was spun by the little silkworm, and I shall weave it into cloth.

2ND CARPENTER: You would weave with your own hands?

EMPRESS: The whole country is weaving to find the cloth my lord seeks. Why should I sit idle? In my father's house I was thought very clever with my hands. But the question is, can you build a loom which will take this thread?

1ST CARPENTER: It will not be easy, but it can be done.

EMPRESS: Good. Bring it to me as quickly as possible. But remember! I shall have your heads if you breathe a word of this to anyone! I wish to surprise my lord with the cloth. It is my secret.

1ST CARPENTER: Our mouths are sealed.

2ND CARPENTER: You will have the loom tomorrow.

NARRATOR: Mother resumes her story.

MOTHER: The little Empress forgot her homesickness as she planned her surprise for the Emperor. When the special loom arrived, she threaded it with the precious gift of the silkworm. Then under her skillful fingers a lovely cloth began to grow. She had no time now to sit idle in the garden. The days skipped by on joyous feet, as all days will when one is busy fashioning a gift of love. The Empress kept her secret well, and the Emperor knew nothing of what she was doing.

NARRATOR: Now we have come to another scene. The Emperor is sitting in his courtyard waiting to see samples of cloth. The Empress is in her room busily weaving. The Emperor is speaking.

EMPEROR: Was my proclamation sent through all of China?

1ST MINISTER: Indeed, O Son of Heaven, your proclamation was sent to every village and town.

EMPEROR: Were the people told of the reward I shall give to the weaver of the royal cloth?

2ND MINISTER: Everyone speaks of your generosity, O Son of Heaven.

EMPEROR: Well, well, but are they weaving? Are they searching for the royal cloth?

1ST MINISTER: The looms in the land are never silent.

EMPEROR: But the royal cloth? Has anyone discovered it?

2ND MINISTER: We have looked at many pieces of fine cloth, and have chosen the three finest. The weavers are here to present the cloth to you, O Son of Heaven.

EMPEROR: Let them enter.

NARRATOR: The minister leads in three weavers. Each carries a length of cloth. They kneel before the Emperor, bending so low that their foreheads touch the floor of the courtyard.

EMPEROR: Well, good woman, show me what you have brought.

1ST WEAVER: I am a contemptible insect, and dare not look upon the face of the gracious Son of Heaven. How can I show him this miserable rag which I have made?

EMPEROR: Give me the cloth. Hmmmm. The workmanship is good. The threads are fine, the weaving skilled. What did you use for your material?

1ST WEAVER: The white fluff of some cotton plants which grew by my door, O Son of Heaven.

EMPEROR: You have done honor to the cotton plant, old mother. You shall become one of the court weavers. Have you found the secret of a royal cloth, old father?

2ND WEAVER: I dare not presume such a thing, O Son of Heaven! I am but a lowly shepherd. But the hair on my sheep is fine and long, and I wove it into this cloth, which can give warmth when the great cold is upon the land.

EMPEROR: It is good. I shall use it for my winter clothes, and you will be suitably rewarded. And what have you brought?

3RD WEAVER: Your unworthy servant has brought a piece of linen, O Son of Heaven.

EMPEROR: Yes, this will be cool in the days of the great heat. My minister will give you a bag of gold.

NARRATOR: The weavers all bow and step back. The Emperor turns and talks to his ministers.

EMPEROR: The weavers have all done their work well, but I am not satisfied. These pieces are not the cloth like the shimmer of moonbeams which I saw in my dream!

1ST MINISTER: But these are the best the land can offer—the finest cotton, the finest wool, and the finest linen. What else is there?

EMPEROR: Well, show these pieces to the Empress. We shall see if they please her. Where is the Empress? Why is she not in the garden?

1ST DANCING GIRL: We have not seen the Empress for days, O Son of Heaven. She hides in her room.

EMPEROR: Hides in her room! Why have I not been told of this? I must find out what is wrong.

NARRATOR: The Emperor walks quickly into the palace. As he enters her room, the Empress tries to hide her loom.

EMPEROR: Why do you shut yourself away in here alone, my Heart's Flower? Will you weep forever?

EMPRESS: I am not weeping, my lord. I have never been happier. I have been making a surprise for you. I hope it will please you. Here is some cloth I have woven.

EMPEROR: My Heart's Flower! What have you done? How is it you have succeeded when the best weavers of the land have failed? You have woven the royal cloth, the cloth that I saw in my dreams. Will a gown of such cloth give you pleasure?

EMPRESS: But I wove it to make a robe for you, my lord! A robe fit for an Emperor!

EMPEROR: Ah well, no matter. We shall both have robes of

this royal cloth. But tell me, how did you spin such thread?

EMPRESS: I did not spin it at all. It is the gift of the little silkworm. A cocoon fell into my tea, and the hot liquid softened the fiber, and melted the sap that binds the threads together. Once soaked in the hot tea, the cocoons were easy to unwind.

EMPEROR: Come, my Heart's Flower. Since you have woven the royal cloth, you shall have the reward planned for the weaver.

NARRATOR: The Emperor takes the Empress by the hand and leads her to the garden. He turns and speaks to his ministers.

EMPEROR: Ministers! Bring the scroll that was to be awarded the weaver of the royal cloth. The Empress has woven it out of the fiber spun by the silkworm.

NARRATOR: The ministers hand the Emperor a scroll which he gives to the Empress.

EMPEROR: This scroll makes you the ruler of my richest province.

EMPRESS: Oh, my lord. I have no need for reward. I have more than I could ever wish for here in your courts. Please rule the province for me. There is but one small gift I desire.

EMPEROR: Name it! It shall be yours.

EMPRESS: I wish a grove of mulberry trees, where thousands of silkworms may eat and grow fat, and spin their lovely silk for me.

EMPEROR: Ministers! See that the grove is planted immediately. And you, my Heart's Flower, shall be known as the First Weaver of the land, as the Goddess of the Silkworms.

NARRATOR: The story has ended. We return now to the mother and daughter. Let us discover how the girl feels about silkworms now.

MOTHER: Now, my child, let this story teach you to prize work, not idleness. The Empress knew that joy comes not from amusements, but from work well done. It is right that she should be called the Goddess of the Silkworms, because she, like them, gave her life to usefulness. See that you do the same.

DAUGHTER: Yes, Mother, I will go right now and give the silk-worms such a supper as they have never had before.

THE END

A Matter of Conscience

This is a short play. It is about a boy who manages to get rid of his conscience for a day. Before you finish reading the play, you will probably be able to guess what happens to make the boy realize that he needs a conscience.

Read this play silently. Remember the place where you think you know the ending. This is the climax of the play. From this point on, everything is leading to the end. Read on to see whether you were right.

Practice these lines.

No you *don't!* Stay where you *are.*
No-you-don't! Stay where you *are.*
A *surprise* party. They are giving a *surprise party* for *me! So* I *will!*
You put *soap powder* in the cake, too!

Talk together and decide on parts.
Take time to read your part to yourself.
Decide which words to emphasize and where to pause.
Now you might read the play to the tape recorder.
Listen to the tape. Check to determine which parts you need to improve.

Read again to the tape recorder. If you are sure it is good, get permission to play the tape to the class. Have your group listen, too.

Do the other children recognize your voice?

Do you recognize your own?

Have the class evaluate your reading. Was it excellent—good—fair—or poor? Each rating must be based on good reasons.

A MATTER OF CONSCIENCE

by Rollin W. Coyle

Characters

(2 boys, 3 girls, and the narrator)
NARRATOR
GEORGE PAYNE
GEORGE'S CONSCIENCE
JUDITH PAYNE, *George's sister*
DORA MASON, *the girl next door*
MRS. PAYNE, *George's mother*

NARRATOR: As our play opens, George Payne is standing in front of the couch in his living room. Directly behind George is a figure who looks *exactly* like George—and who is, in fact, George's Conscience. George lifts his right arm slowly; his Conscience does precisely the same thing at the same time. George drops his arm suddenly; so does his Conscience. George lifts his left arm slowly and scratches his head; his Conscience follows exactly. George drops his arm; so does his Conscience. George looks annoyed, then determined. He suddenly faces right; so does his Conscience. Then George whirls and ends by facing left and looking at his Conscience defiantly, face to face.

GEORGE: There! I fooled you that time.

CONSCIENCE: You certainly were trying hard enough.

GEORGE: I knew I could eventually outfox you.

CONSCIENCE: Let us just say I finally decided to let you have your own way.

GEORGE: Who are you anyway?

CONSCIENCE: Don't you know, Georgie?

GEORGE: Well, I'm not sure. I've had a feeling for a long time that there were two of us. Am I one of those split personalities?

CONSCIENCE: Oh, no! I would call you entirely normal, Georgie.

GEORGE: I feel so different somehow, with my being here and your being there in front of me.

CONSCIENCE: Naturally! And now you had better let me get behind you again.

GEORGE: No you don't! Stay where you are. It wasn't easy to get rid of you and I don't want to give my freedom up so quickly. What do you do behind me, anyway?

CONSCIENCE: I keep you out of trouble.

GEORGE: Like a conscience, maybe?

CONSCIENCE: Precisely.

GEORGE: Think of that! You are my conscience!

CONSCIENCE: Yes, Georgie!

GEORGE: You know, you have been keeping me from having a lot of fun lately. I'm not so sure I want to have you a part of me.

CONSCIENCE: If I stayed away, you would want me back again very shortly, Georgie. You see, I am a rather essential part of you. Without me, you would always be in hot water. So let's not delay it any longer. Let's become one again.

GEORGE: Not so fast now! I think it would be nice not to have a conscience for awhile. Can't you take a little vacation?

CONSCIENCE: It's tempting, I must admit. You have kept me rather busy lately. How long did you have in mind?

GEORGE: Today at least. Next week I go to camp, with two months' allowance I've saved up to spend any way I please! Boy! Would I have fun at camp without you! But at least give me today.

CONSCIENCE: It is tempting, and it might teach you a lesson. I'm more important to you than you realize, Georgie.

GEORGE: You might stop calling me Georgie, too. It's not fair, since you are really a part of me.

CONSCIENCE: That's a reasonable request and I shall endeavor to call you George, although Georgie is a habit with me after almost thirteen years. So you want to be rid of me for today. Let's give it a whirl. After all, the results probably won't be fatal. I'll still be around if you want me, George.

GEORGE: I don't want to have to listen to you. You'll have to promise to be quiet.

CONSCIENCE: It will be difficult. I am so in the habit of speaking out.

GEORGE: What a day this is going to be!

NARRATOR: Judith, George's sister, begins calling him from her room.

GEORGE: That's my sister calling me. Now you go away. I want to try my new self on her.

CONSCIENCE: I suppose we have to start sometime. All right. I'll stand up there in the corner where no one can see me. Now, do be careful. Here comes your sister.

JUDITH: George, why didn't you answer me? Didn't you hear me?

GEORGE: I thought it was someone calling pigs.

JUDITH: Don't be insulting. I wanted to borrow your fountain pen.

GEORGE: Here, loveliest of sisters, try this pencil.

JUDITH: I can't write in my diary with a pencil, silly. I've been so busy the last two days that I've fallen behind. I need your pen.

GEORGE: O.K., here's my pen. How much rental are you prepared to pay?

JUDITH: Rental! I'll pay you nothing. George Payne, the reason I have to borrow your pen is that *you* broke my pen. The reason I'm behind in my diary is because of you, too. Now, let me have your pen.

GEORGE: On one condition! I get to read your diary.

JUDITH: Never! That's why it has a lock. Well, never mind. I'll see if I can use Mother's pen. I have never seen you so mean.

GEORGE: It's my new personality. Like it?

JUDITH: It's positively revolting!

GEORGE: Give me time. I'll perfect it.

NARRATOR: Judith runs off. A moment later, George hears Judith's friend Dora calling to her from the front door.

GEORGE: That's Dora Mason. Now I can practice on her.

CONSCIENCE: I wonder how long the Devil had to practice.

DORA: Georgie! Where is Judith?

GEORGE: Judith went to Africa this morning, Dora.

DORA: To Africa!

GEORGE: On a safari.

DORA: Why don't you try being sensible for a change? I came over to see if Judith will like my new hairdo.

GEORGE: It looks like a haystack.

DORA: George Payne, I think you're mean.

GEORGE: Judith may like it, though. She likes nature, birds' nests, and things like that.

DORA: Shame on you, George.

GEORGE: That's why Judith went to Africa.

DORA: It's just your age, I suppose. Boys your age are so often nasty.

GEORGE: All isn't lost yet. I'll have a birthday while I'm at camp next week. By then I'll be older and nicer.

DORA: I'll ask your mother where Judith is. By the way, Georgie, what is your favorite color?

GEORGE: Purple!

DORA: Purple! Do you like purple neckties?

GEORGE: I love purple neckties.

DORA: Ugh! I didn't know that anyone liked purple neckties. Well, goodbye, Georgie.

GEORGE: Boy! Was that fun!

CONSCIENCE: You know you don't like purple.

GEORGE: I know it, but Dora doesn't. I told her one lie after another, and it was fun. It's great not having you interrupt my fun for me all the time. Why, I don't even have to worry about being a gentleman at all.

CONSCIENCE: I'm sure you didn't make Dora a better friend of yours.

GEORGE: Who wants her for a friend? This is really living. I can say what I want to say, do what I want to do, and life will be full of laughs. Say, how would you like to go away permanently, old man?

CONSCIENCE: The idea has its merits. Seeing you in action without me has made me realize what a burden I have been bearing all these years.

NARRATOR: George flings himself down on the couch and throws his feet over the back of it. His mother comes into the living room and looks at him, amazed.

MRS. PAYNE: George! What are you doing with your feet on that couch?

GEORGE: I'm relaxing, Mother.

MRS. PAYNE: I haven't seen you put your feet on the couch that way for months.

GEORGE: I'm living a new life today.

MRS. PAYNE: Well, stop it. George, I'm making a cake, but I ran out of flour. Dora says her mother can lend me some. Will you go into the kitchen and watch the batter for me while I'm gone? I had to leave the electric mixer going.

GEORGE: Let Judith do it.

MRS. PAYNE: Judith is leaving right away to go shopping with Dora. If I'm gone too long, you will have to turn the mixer off.

GEORGE (*Reluctantly*): All right.

MRS. PAYNE: And will you call the dairy, George, and ask them to deliver two quarts of ice cream this afternoon?

GEORGE: Ice cream!

MRS. PAYNE: Vanilla ice cream, please. Now do it right away, before you forget it. I'm going.

GEORGE: Goodbye. Wow! Do I have an idea!

CONSCIENCE: It can't be good.

GEORGE: You'll see. Hello! Rosedale Dairy? This is the Howard

Payne residence on Lake Avenue. Can you deliver two quarts of cottage cheese this afternoon?

CONSCIENCE: George, your mother said ice cream.

GEORGE: Stop bothering me. Remember your promise. Rosedale Dairy? Did you get my order? Yes, that's right. Cottage cheese! I wonder if you could pack it in ice-cream cartons? You can! That would be fine. Thank you. Goodbye.

CONSCIENCE: I smell mischief brewing.

GEORGE: Can you imagine Mother's face when she serves cottage cheese for dessert? This is going to be a wonderful day.

CONSCIENCE: You'll be sorry!

GEORGE: How can I be if you aren't around to bother me? By the way, I wonder how a cake would taste if you put a cup of salt into it?

CONSCIENCE: I suppose you will have to find out.

GEORGE: Dad will love Mother's cake tonight. Now if I can just find the salt! 'Bye, Conscience. I'm off to the kitchen.

NARRATOR: Judith and Dora enter. Judith carries her diary. George's Conscience watches the girls.

JUDITH: I'll just be a moment, Dora. I want to leave my diary. I'll hide it under this magazine where George can't find it.

DORA: There always seem to be so many things to do when you are planning something like this. Do you think George really meant that, about wanting a purple necktie?

JUDITH: There's no accounting for taste. Maybe it's the latest fad.

DORA: Well, it's his surprise party. I'd feel better if you'd come with me to help choose it, though. A purple necktie!

JUDITH: You were careful not to give us away when you asked him, weren't you?

DORA: He didn't even get suspicious.

JUDITH: Good! After all this work trying to plan a surprise party for George, it would be a shame for him to guess it at the last minute.

NARRATOR: Mrs. Payne enters, carrying a cup of flour.

MRS. PAYNE: Honestly, there is so much to do! If I have everything ready by two o'clock when the guests arrive, I'll be the one surprised. You won't be gone long, Judith, will you? I need everyone's help. I even had George order the ice cream, but I don't think he caught on.

JUDITH: No, we won't be gone long. Mother, I left my diary on the table there. I hope it will be safe from George.

MRS. PAYNE: George wouldn't read your diary. Even George has a conscience.

DORA: I won't keep her long, Mrs. Payne. Shall we go, Judith?

MRS. PAYNE: Goodbye, girls.

GEORGE: I turned the mixer off, Mother. Everything is well mixed.

MRS. PAYNE: I hope this cake is good, considering all the trouble I have had. I'll go take a look.

GEORGE: Conscience, that cake certainly will be different. You should have seen it foam when I put the soap powder in it.

CONSCIENCE: You put soap powder in the cake, too?

GEORGE: I was inspired.

CONSCIENCE: Your sister left her diary under the magazine here on this table. You aren't supposed to look at it.

GEORGE: Judith's diary? Why, here it is. Say! Thanks! You are putting ideas into my head. I'll bet this letter opener would pry off the lock. See! It was easy.

CONSCIENCE: You shouldn't read the diary.

GEORGE: So I will!

CONSCIENCE: I thought you would.

GEORGE: If you were a little more human like this all the time, I wouldn't mind having you around. Now, let's see. "Dearest Diary, I don't know whether I am in love or not." Oh, boy, is this going to be mushy!

CONSCIENCE: Couldn't you find something a little more current?

GEORGE: Here's today's date, and something's written in, too. Judith must have found Mother's pen. Is this current enough for you?

CONSCIENCE: That should do nicely, thank you.

GEORGE: "Dear Diary. I don't have much time to write today because we are so busy." (*Scornfully*) Women are always busy, to hear them tell it.

CONSCIENCE: Read on.

GEORGE: "The invitations have all been accepted. There will be Henry, Richard, Mary, Dora, Parker, Helen, Louise, Gerald, and Ted." Invitations! Say! That's odd.

CONSCIENCE (*Mockingly*): Invitations!

GEORGE: "The games are planned. Refreshments are almost ready."

CONSCIENCE: Refreshments!

GEORGE: "Now all that remains is wrapping our presents for George."

CONSCIENCE: Now the dawn is beginning to break.

GEORGE: A surprise party! They are giving a surprise party for me!

CONSCIENCE: Such a beautiful surprise!

GEORGE: But why? It isn't my birthday.

CONSCIENCE: Could it be because when your birthday arrives next week, you will be at camp?

GEORGE: "Henry, Richard, Mary, Dora—" My friends! And I put salt in the cake!

CONSCIENCE: Not to mention a little soap.

GEORGE: Instead of ice cream, they will get cottage cheese.

CONSCIENCE: It sounds delicious.

GEORGE: What will my friends think of me?

CONSCIENCE: They will, no doubt, like your purple necktie.

GEORGE: Purple necktie? Oh, Dora knew I was only kidding.

CONSCIENCE: Twenty minutes ago you thought you had her fairly well convinced.

GEORGE: A purple tie! Ugh! That settles it. Get behind me again before I do something else that is foolish.

CONSCIENCE: Your day of liberty isn't over yet.

GEORGE: I wish it were. Hurry!

CONSCIENCE: I'll probably make this afternoon more painful for you.

GEORGE: How could you?

CONSCIENCE: Ah! It's so nice to be appreciated.

GEORGE: They will all bring presents. And what will I do for them? Cottage cheese! (*Pause*) Maybe it's not too late. I'll phone the Dairy and change the order to ice cream! (*Pause*) I suppose I'll have to explain to them what I did. (*Sighs*) Oh well, guess I asked for it. (*Pause*) The cake! Oh, the soapy cake! (*Groans*) Whatever made me do it! It wouldn't take me ten minutes to go down to the bakery and get another cake—but what would I use for money? I know! Upstairs! In my strongbox! The allowance I've been saving for camp! (*Sadly*) Guess it's the only way. All right, Conscience, let's go! What are we waiting for?

THE END

The Legend of the Christmas Rose

Many stories have been told of the miracles that happened when Jesus was born and of the many people who took gifts to the new-born child.

This is the story of what happened on that night to a little girl who helped all of her friends and did not think of herself first.

Read the story to yourself.

1. What miracle did the Angel perform?
2. Why did the Angel help Madelon?
3. Who told the children what gifts they could bring?

Talk over the answers to these questions. Now choose parts. Read your part to yourself.

Practice reading the play aloud. Be very careful to make the meaning of every sentence clear to the listener.

After reading evaluate yourself.

1. Did you use your voice to show wonder, fear, sadness, etc.?
2. Did you stop after every period?
3. Did you read smoothly and easily without awkward pauses?
4. Did you come in on time with your part?
5. Did you speak clearly and distinctly?

Practice once more to see if you can improve your reading.

Arrange with your teacher to read to the class, or perhaps you would like to tape your reading and play it to the class later.

THE LEGEND OF THE CHRISTMAS ROSE

by Eleanore Leuser

Characters

(7 boys, 3 girls, and the narrator)

NARRATOR
MADELON, *a shepherd girl*
ESTEBAN, *her oldest brother*
ALDERAN, *another brother*
JOSEF, *her youngest brother*
ANDRES, *a neighbor boy*
MICHELA, *a neighbor girl*
THE THREE WISE MEN
AN ANGEL

NARRATOR: This story takes place on the night when Jesus was born. We are on a snow-covered road near a field, where the shepherd girl, Madelon, tends her sheep. Esteban runs in breathlessly. He is looking for someone.

ESTEBAN (*Calling*): Madelon—Madelon—where are you?

NARRATOR: Madelon comes over to Esteban. She is carrying a shepherd's crook.

MADELON: I am here, Esteban, looking after my sheep. What is it?

ESTEBAN: Three most noble strangers have just now alighted at our door and are coming down the road for a drink of water at the well.

MADELON: But why so excited, my brother? We have surely seen strangers before.

ESTEBAN: Not like these! They are richly dressed and bearing gifts. They say they are going to a place of great importance not far from here.

MADELON: Bearing gifts—to a place not far from here. That is indeed strange. But why and for whom? Surely you found out more.

ESTEBAN: They were so thirsty and weary I had not the heart. See, here they come. Perhaps you can ask them, sister, after you have given them water.

NARRATOR: The Three Wise Men come along the road carrying large ornate boxes. They move over to the well.

1ST WISE MAN: May we have a drink of water from your well? We have traveled far and would quench our thirst.

NARRATOR: Madelon stoops and fills a cup from the well. Each time she refills it, she gives it to one of the men. As she works, she talks.

MADELON: Gladly! All travelers like our water. Do you still have far to go?

2ND WISE MAN: We think not, for we have been following the Star and now it moves slowly—very slowly. Soon it must stop.

MADELON: But what seek you? Whom would you find?

NARRATOR: One of the Wise Men has been sitting quietly on a rock. He now speaks to Madelon.

3RD WISE MAN: We seek the holy babe—he that was born in a manger. We bring him royal gifts, for we have heard that he is to be king and saviour of all mankind. We would worship him.

MADELON: What a wondrous tale! I, too, would see this babe.

1ST WISE MAN: You? A little girl? Had you not better stay close to home this frosty night?

2ND WISE MAN: My brother is right. (*Kindly*) Besides, one must have a gift to bring the holy babe.

NARRATOR: Madelon looks very sad and disappointed when she hears about the gift.

2ND WISE MAN: Would you like to see the treasures we are carrying to him?

MADELON (*Eagerly*): Oh, yes, if I only might!

NARRATOR: The second Wise Man opens his box and Madelon and Esteban peek inside. They are almost overcome with the beauty of its contents and cannot help crying out.

MADELON: Ooooh—it's gold, rich yellow gold!

ESTEBAN: And see all the jewels!

1ST WISE MAN: But we must be on our way, my brothers, lest the babe be moved and we do not find him. Come.

NARRATOR: The Wise Men close their boxes and begin to journey again down the road. One of the men notices that Madelon and Esteban look discouraged. He stays behind a moment and speaks kindly to the children.

3RD WISE MAN: Do not look so sad. All gifts need not be rich and magnificent.

MADELON: You mean that even humble shepherds like us might bring gifts?

3RD WISE MAN: Yes. No matter how humble the gift or the giver, the babe will rejoice. If the giver has wrought the gift himself or put something of himself into it, I think it will be as welcomed and as blessed as all the gold and jewels of kings and princes.

ESTEBAN: How wonderful of him to tell us that! I wish I could go to see this babe.

MADELON: Why not, Esteban? If this Wise Man has spoken truly, why not go? Take our little red cockerel that we raised together. Then go at once, eldest son of our father, and find the babe.

ESTEBAN: A thousand thanks, my sister. I shall go.

MADELON: How wonderful! A holy babe born in a manger and a star to lead people to him.

NARRATOR: Madelon's brother, Alderan, comes running in.

ALDERAN: Our brother has told me of the babe in the manger. He is going to find him. I wish I could go, too.

MADELON: Go then, Alderan. And take the gray goose with you. It belongs to all of us, after all. Did we not save it from dying of cold and of hunger? Is it not a pet of our house?

ALDERAN: I'll take it gladly and be on my way.

MADELON: I hope there will be many people going to worship this babe.

NARRATOR: Madelon hears sobbing and sees little Josef running up to her. He tells his sad story.

JOSEF: Sister, sister, both my brothers are going to see this new-born babe. But I cannot go with them, for I have no gift.

MADELON: Do not fret, little Josef. I will think of something.

JOSEF: They are taking the red cockerel and the gray goose. There is nothing left for me.

MADELON: Look, I will give you my little pet lamb.

JOSEF: But he is all yours. He follows you everywhere with his wobbling legs. You love him dearly.

MADELON: We all love him, little Josef. Take him. He will be a fitting gift for the new babe.

JOSEF: Oh, thank you, Madelon, thank you!

NARRATOR: As Josef runs off with the lamb, two neighbor children come into view. They, too, stop to talk to Madelon.

MADELON: Greetings, Andres! Greetings, Michela! Are you two going on a journey?

ANDRES: Indeed we are! We have been hearing about the babe who lies near here in a manger. We are off to worship him and rejoice.

MICHELA: We have heard that we do not have to offer him rich gifts but something that we ourselves treasure.

ANDRES: So I am taking him this shepherd's flute. You know how many hours I spent fashioning it from a reed. It is the best flute I ever made.

MICHELA: And I have put some honey in this basket I wove myself. Do you remember how you helped me with it— how slow I was at learning? Yet you said it was good when I was finished.

MADELON: Indeed you have woven it beautifully, Michela.

MICHELA: We stopped to see if you would not come with us, Madelon. Truly nothing so wonderful has ever happened before.

MADELON: I would love to see this babe better than anything on earth, but I cannot leave my sheep. You two go on, but be sure to stop and tell me everything about him when you return.

ANDRES: That we will, Madelon. Come, Michela, we must hurry.

NARRATOR: Andres takes Michela's hand and hurries her away. As Madelon sits sadly on the rock all alone, an angel appears holding a wand tipped with a lily. Gently, she touches Madelon with the wand.

ANGEL: What is the matter, Madelon?

MADELON (*Gasps*): An angel in my father's fields! Indeed, strange things are happening.

ANGEL: Why are you sad, Madelon?

MADELON: Indeed, I should not be. Everyone is going to see the new-born babe . . . he that is to be a king and saviour of mankind. I should be filled with happiness that he is born, but—but I should like to see him, myself.

ANGEL: And why do you not go, Madelon?

MADELON: I could not leave my sheep.

ANGEL: I will guard them for you, Madelon, for you have sent your brothers, thinking not of yourself. This is a holy night. Now will you go?

MADELON: An angel guarding my sheep! That would indeed be wonderful. But still I cannot go. I have no gift to take.

ANGEL: Are you certain, Madelon?

MADELON: Most certain! The red cockerel and the gray goose that we owned together I sent with my older brothers. To little Josef I gave my pet lamb. I cannot carve a flute like Andres, and Michela is taking honey in the basket I taught her how to weave. Gladly I saw these things go, but I have nothing I could offer.

ANGEL: Think, Madelon, think! Is there nothing else that you have worked over and put your whole heart into?

MADELON: I can think of nothing.

ANGEL: Think again! What did you do here in the spring?

Your back ached. You worked from dawn till dusk. You carried water to them and the whole neighborhood shared in their loveliness.

MADELON: Why, I had forgotten. I made a little garden here by the well and tended it. It grew fair for all to see and I gathered many flowers and sent them round about to people who had none. But it is winter now and the blossoms all have died and the snow has covered them.

ANGEL: The blossoms have not died, Madelon. They wait for you to gather them to take to the holy babe! See!

NARRATOR: The angel reaches down and touches the ground near the well with her wand. A white rose is blossoming there in the snow.

MADELON: It cannot be possible! A rose in winter!

NARRATOR: Madelon stoops and picks the precious rose.

ANGEL: And from now on there will always bloom a white rose in the middle of winter to show that one shepherd girl thought of others besides herself. Go—it is a fitting gift for this child who was born in a manger.

MADELON: I shall go, kind angel. I go and rejoice and worship the holy babe.

NARRATOR: The angel smiles as she watches Madelon trudge down the road after the other children, carrying the precious gift.

THE END

Shades of Ransom

This is a completely imaginary story of ghosts and kidnappers. Read the entire play silently and be prepared to answer these questions:

1. Why could Billy see the ghosts?
2. Why did the police arrive so quickly?
3. How does Dipper the pickpocket introduce an element of humor into the story?
4. What were the two major differences between the pixie and the ghosts?

In this play there are many instances of using words for a double meaning—"a play on words."

For example: "If you want butter—try ours. It ought to be Rancid."

Can you find others? What are they?

In reading this play you will have to use your voice to show:

disagreement
surprise or shock
astonishment
nervousness with a hint of fear

Let us try some lines from the play to see whether you use your voice well.

Disagreement

Millie Hamlet! I've been a ghost—a *good* ghost—for as long as I can remember and (*Slowly and distinctly*) *I just don't believe in people!*

Surprise

Oh! You startled me! Why, you're a little ghost-boy! For a moment I was afraid you were a *person!* How on earth did you ever get here?

Astonishment

Gang? *Whatever* are you *talking* about? I'm just a plain ordinary ghost, the same as my sister Liz, or *you*, or *anybody!*

Nervousness

Green guys! Boy, am I getting nervous. At least Dipper hasn't started stealing watches yet.

Choose two or three people to read each of these parts. Help each other after each reading by discussing how to improve.

Now each take a part.

Practice your part by reading silently. Be sure you know every word.

Read the play together. Use your voice to show how you feel.

Watch the punctuation!

Talk it over together. Are there places you need to improve? Practice again.

When you are sure you read the play well, ask your teacher to assign a time when you can read to the class.

SHADES OF RANSOM

by James R. Chisholm

Characters

(6 boys, 3 girls, and the narrator)

NARRATOR
LIZ HAMLET, *a tall, thin spinster* } *two sisters who are*
MILLIE HAMLET, *a short, stout spinster* } *ghosts*
BILLY RANCID, *a ten-year-old boy*
GUS CHICKEN, *a flashily-dressed, moustached gangster*
KIRK DIRK, *a slim, dark, young gangster*
DIPPER, *a very large gangster*
INSPECTOR DICK } *detectives*
SERGEANT WEBB } *detectives*
MRS. RANCID, *Billy's mother*

NARRATOR: This play takes place in a parlor of a house haunted by the Hamlet sisters. Liz Hamlet sits knitting in a rocking chair. She stops, puts her knitting on the table, looks about and shouts a question to her sister. Millie Hamlet enters holding a duster.

LIZ: Millie! (*Louder*) Millie, dear! Have you seen my book?

MILLIE: Which book is that, dear?

LIZ: My "Ghost Manual," of course. What else do I ever read these days? Seems the only other books there are in this house are all those silly superstitious books about people. As if there really were such things as people.

MILLIE: I don't know about that, Liz. According to one of those books, you and I once were people, long ago, before we became ghosts. It could be true.

LIZ: Now don't be ridiculous, Millie. How long have we been haunting this house?

MILLIE: Almost forty years.

LIZ: Thirty-nine this winter. And in all this time have you ever seen a person?

MILLIE: No, but that doesn't mean anything. They may be all around us. Sometimes I'm so frightened.

LIZ: Millie Hamlet! I've been a ghost—a good ghost—for as long as I can remember, and I just don't believe in people!

MILLIE: Well, I suppose you're right, dear. (*Sighing*) I guess I just have too much imagination. (*Pause*) Was that book entitled "How to Spook: A Handbook for Ghosts"?

LIZ: Why, yes, that's the one.

NARRATOR: Millie crosses the room to the couch and brings the handbook to Liz.

MILLIE: It was on the couch. Here it is, dear. And now, I have to go into the kitchen and get some food ready for supper.

LIZ: Supper? What are you talking about, Millie? We don't need food. Ghosts don't eat.

MILLIE: Liz Hamlet, you're getting so forgetful. Of course we ghosts don't eat, but pixies do! Have you forgotten all about our boarder, Mr. Caliban? Remember, he's only a pixie.

LIZ: Millie, you're right, I did forget. It's just that Mr. Caliban seems such an unsociable little man, always staying out there in the kitchen. I hardly ever see him.

MILLIE: He's not unsociable, dear. It's just that he's a water pixie and likes to stay near the sink. Don't be impatient, Mr. Caliban, I'll have your celery ready in a jiffy!

NARRATOR: Millie hurries to the kitchen and Liz begins to read her book. There is a knock at the door, but Liz does not seem to hear it. Kirk Dirk enters the room. He keeps one hand in the pocket of his coat. He cautiously circles the room, looking nervously about. He stares at the table and rocking chairs without seeing Liz and then shouts for Gus and Dipper.

KIRK: Gus! Dipper! Come on in! The place is empty.

GUS: You're right, Kirk. Not a living soul here. Boy, what a hideout! The police will never find us.

KIRK: Am I tired! Where's Big Dipper and the kid, Gus?

GUS: Dipper's putting the car away. The boy's with him. Those two get along as if they were the same age.

KIRK: Dipper may be grown-up but the kid seems smarter.

GUS: Yeah! Sometimes I worry about Dipper. He can't seem to do anything worthwhile except pick pockets.

MILLIE: Liz! Would you come out to the kitchen, dear, and help me find the peanut butter?

LIZ: Oh, all right! I don't know why that Mr. Caliban can't eat anything but peanut butter sandwiches and celery. You know, Millie, it's so quiet in this house. It makes me nervous!

KIRK: Gus?

GUS: Yes, Kirk?

KIRK: This place is too quiet. It makes me nervous. I miss all the traffic noises. What if it is *haunted* or something?

GUS: Are you fooling? Ghosts aren't real. Have you ever been near a ghost?

KIRK: No. Never. I guess you're right, Gus.

GUS: You bet I am! Gus Chicken is always right. Anyway, we won't be here long. Old Rancid will deliver the money tonight, we'll give his boy back to him, and we'll head back to the bright lights by tomorrow morning.

KIRK: Sounds good, Gus, but are you sure the kid's father can get the money?

GUS: What? W. W. Rancid, the butter king? You've heard their slogan: "If you want butter—try ours. It ought to be Rancid."

NARRATOR: There is a loud knock at the door. Kirk reaches nervously in his pocket. He walks to the door, one hand in his pocket. The door opens and Dipper enters pushing Billy Rancid ahead of him.

DIPPER: Here you are, Billy. Here's where you meet your dad.

NARRATOR: Dipper sits on the couch. Billy follows and sits on the floor at his feet. Kirk looks angrily at Dipper.

KIRK: Hey, I was using that couch. Me, Kirk Dirk!

DIPPER: Now I am.

GUS: Watch out, Dipper, he carries a knife.

DIPPER: That's all right. He doesn't fool me. It may be a weapon, but he uses it only to cut the bad spots out of apples.

BILLY: Apples! I'm hungry.

GUS: That's an idea! Come on, Kirk, let's see what there is to eat in the kitchen.

NARRATOR: Gus and Kirk go out. Dipper yawns sleepily.

DIPPER: Don't run away, Billy.

BILLY: I wish I could. Did gangsters ever take *you* away when you were a little boy?

DIPPER: Me? No! They wouldn't do that to *me*. My father was in the business. That's how I got into the Gus Chicken gang, even though I am only a pickpocket.

BILLY: I'm hungry.

NARRATOR: Dipper falls asleep. Millie enters and dusts all around the room while talking to herself. She dusts Dipper's head, the table, and moves toward the hat rack. Billy can see her and hear her talking, but she does not know it.

MILLIE: That Mr. Caliban! I swear he's just the shiest pixie we've had to board. One minute he's eating his celery, the next he stares at the empty doorway just as if somebody were there, and quick as a flash he hides in the drainpipe. I'll just never understand him.

BILLY: Are you in the gang, too?

MILLIE (*Shocked*): Oh! You startled me! Why, you're a little ghost-boy! For a moment I was afraid you were a person! How on earth did you ever get here? This must be your hat. I knew it couldn't be Mr. Caliban's, because it's not pointed.

BILLY: You mean you're not one of the gang?

MILLIE: Gang? Whatever are you talking about? I'm just a

plain ordinary ghost, the same as my sister Liz, or you, or anybody.

BILLY: You're a ghost?

MILLIE: Is there anything unusual about that?

BILLY: Why, I suppose not. I believe in ghosts. I also believe in pixies, brownies, elves, leprechauns, werewolves and vampires. I read a lot.

MILLIE: Of course you believe in them. They're all real, aren't they? But I'm glad to see you're sensible, and don't say that you believe in people.

BILLY: I am a person. I'm Billy Rancid.

MILLIE: A person! Well, Billy, I must say you're a very imaginative little ghost-boy and, though I don't know how you came to be here, your old Aunt Millie and Auntie Liz will take care of you.

BILLY: Can you get me away from the gangsters who brought me here—the Gus Chicken gang?

MILLIE: Now, Billy, there you go being imaginative again. You know perfectly well that there's no gang here. Besides, if you were really a person, how could we talk to each other?

BILLY: That's easy. In books only the innocent children like me can see the pixies and things.

DIPPER (Sleepily): Who you talking to, Billy? Yourself? What's the matter? Is this thing too much for you? I'd better tell Gus.

BILLY: I'm hungry.

MILLIE: Now don't be silly. You know ghosts don't eat. I'll go tell Liz about you, Billy. You wait right there.

BILLY: Boy! Could I use a peanut butter sandwich.

DIPPER: You'd better stop talking to yourself, Billy. It sounds crazy, and that's the one thing that makes Gus very nervous. He read in the papers one time that gangsters weren't normal, and he's been very touchy about things like that ever since, and when he gets nervous you can't tell what he'll do!

NARRATOR: Kirk and Gus come back. Kirk is nervous.

KIRK: But I tell you, Gus, I saw him when we first went in. A little green guy with pointed ears and a pointed head. He ducked right into the drainpipe when you weren't looking.

GUS (*Icily*): Kirk!

KIRK: Yes, Gus?

GUS: You're crazy. (*Pause, then threateningly*) I'm getting nervous.

KIRK: O.K., Gus.

GUS: I'm going outside to look around. Billy's father should be here soon, with the money.

KIRK: Take care of yourself, Gus. Be careful.

GUS: Don't worry. I have my little old —

NARRATOR: Gus pats his coat pocket, then gasps. Dipper walks over to Gus and hands him something.

DIPPER: I forgot I took it, Gus.

GUS: Dipper! How many times do I have to tell you not to take something that doesn't belong to you?

DIPPER: Oh, Gus! What kind of pickpocket would I be if I didn't practice?

GUS: Dipper, you aren't honest.

DIPPER: That makes me feel bad. Here, Kirk. Here's your wallet. I'm going to reform.

GUS: I'll be outside if you need me.

BILLY: I'm hungry.

KIRK: You'll have to stay hungry. There wasn't anything to eat in the kitchen except peanut butter sandwiches and celery.

BILLY: Why, they're my favorites!

KIRK: There's not enough for you. Besides, you'll be going home tonight when your father shows up with the cash. You can eat there. (*Pause*) He did hide in the sink!

MILLIE: He's right in here, Liz. He's the nicest little ghost-boy. Liz, this is Billy Rancid. Billy, this is your Auntie Liz. We're going to take care of you, Billy.

BILLY: How do you do, ma'am—I mean Auntie Liz.

LIZ: Hello, Billy. (*Sighs*) It will be so nice to have a little ghost-child around the house.

MILLIE: We have to go into the kitchen for a moment to clean up the dishes after Mr. Caliban.

LIZ: Is there anything we can do for you, Billy?

BILLY: Yes, ma'am—Auntie Liz. May I have a peanut butter sandwich and some celery? I'm awfully hungry.

KIRK: Who's he talking to, Dipper? Who's he talking to? I don't see anybody.

LIZ: Peanut butter? Celery? Millie, you don't think he could be a pixie?

MILLIE: A pixie, Liz? No, of course not. He's just pretending. He's not really hungry.

BILLY: Oh, no!

KIRK: I asked you, Dipper. Who's he talking to?

DIPPER: Don't tell Gus. He's already getting nervous. This whole business is too much for Billy. He's talking to himself now. You know what Gus is like when he gets nervous. Don't tell him.

BILLY: I wasn't talking to myself. I was talking to Aunt Millie and Auntie Liz. They're ghosts. Didn't you see them? Oh, that's right, you're not innocent.

KIRK: What do you mean? I always plead innocent! Ghosts?

DIPPER: See what I mean, Kirk?

KIRK: Don't talk like that, kid, or I'll—

NARRATOR: Kirk reaches for his knife. It is not in his pocket. He starts to search for it frantically.

DIPPER: Here, Kirk, I forgot.

KIRK: Crook!

DIPPER: Kirk, what if Billy's father doesn't bring the money? What'll we do with Billy?

KIRK: The windows are boarded up. Nobody comes near here. We'll lock him in here, leave, and let his ghost friends take care of him.

BILLY: Oh, no! I'd starve to death. They won't feed me. They think I don't eat.

DIPPER: Another thing bothers me, Kirk. Do you think Gus

should have told Mr. Rancid to bring the money here to our hideout? Somehow, it doesn't seem right.

KIRK: Stop that talk, Dipper. Gus is the brains of this gang. You let him do the thinking.

DIPPER: O.K., Kirk. I guess you're right.

KIRK (*Yawns*): Think I'll read for awhile. What's this book? "How to Spook: A Handbook for Ghosts."

NARRATOR: Kirk starts to read. Suddenly he throws the book on the table.

DIPPER: I think I'll get something to eat. Want anything, Kirk?

KIRK: Who can eat?

BILLY: Me. I'm hungry.

NARRATOR: The door bangs and Gus comes back into the house.

GUS: It's too quiet out there. Almost makes me nervous.

KIRK: You're not afraid, Gus?

GUS: What! The great Gus Chicken afraid? I'm never afraid —I'm Chicken. Where's Dipper?

KIRK: He's out there.

NARRATOR: A scream is heard and Dipper runs in excitedly, pointing back to the kitchen.

DIPPER: Little green guy! Little green guy! Hello, Gus. (*Weakly*) I—I didn't see a little green guy. He didn't throw any celery at me. He didn't dive into the sink. Honest, Gus. No green guy. No.

GUS: Kirk sees green guys, you see green guys.

KIRK: Only one, Gus.

GUS: I'm getting more and more nervous. Kirk!

KIRK: Yes, Gus?

GUS: Go out and check the car. Make sure it's ready for a getaway. Where are the keys?

DIPPER: I have them, Gus. I'm sorry.

GUS: Take Dipper with you! I'll watch the kid. Are there any papers or books around here to read?

NARRATOR: Kirk is half way to the front door but when he

hears the word *read*, he dashes back to the table, grabs the book, and hides it behind his back.

KIRK: You wouldn't like this, Gus. I'm reading it. Terrible book—no pictures.

GUS: Green guys! Boy, am I getting nervous. At least Dipper hasn't started stealing watches yet! Almost ten o'clock. Nearly time for your father, Billy. Well, at least you're still all right. What do you have to say for yourself, kid?

BILLY: I'm hungry. Oh, hello, Auntie Liz!

LIZ: Hello, dear. Did you see my "Ghost Manual"? It's almost time for the ten o'clock haunting and I just wanted to check up on the routine.

BILLY: The what?

LIZ: The ten o'clock haunting. We have to haunt at ten p.m., midnight, and two a.m. It does seem silly wandering around the house with a candle, with Millie in her chains, but we are ghosts, and duty's duty. Well, I don't see it, and it is getting near time. I'd better tell Millie to get ready. She doesn't take it nearly seriously enough. She thinks it's a lark!

BILLY: Goodbye!

GUS: Who are you talking to? You seeing green guys?

BILLY: Oh, no! Nothing like that. Just ghosts!

GUS: Him, too! Green guys. Ghosts. Some place there must be a place where nobody's crazy. *Some place!*

NARRATOR: A loud banging is heard at the door.

BILLY: Your friends are back.

GUS: Friends? Kirk and Dipper? I wonder if *they're* real.

KIRK: The car's all set, Gus. Dipper left your wallet and your gun in the glove compartment. He was just practicing, Gus.

DIPPER: Yes, that's right. I left your things there, too, Kirk. Hey, when's Billy's father coming, Gus?

GUS: Ten o'clock. It's ten now. He should be here any minute. At least that's one thing you've never stolen, Dipper— a wrist watch.

DIPPER: I never thought of it. (*Scared*) Look, Kirk! Look out there. Floating in mid-air—a candle, and chains!

KIRK: I know it, but don't let Gus know you see it! There's no telling what he might do.

NARRATOR: They huddle together very frightened. Liz enters carrying a candle. Millie follows with chains draped over her shoulders. She waves to Billy and walks around the tables and chairs.

GUS: Do you see anything strange? Kirk? Dipper?

KIRK: Green guys, you mean? No, Gus.

DIPPER: No green guys.

GUS: Like a candle, floating in mid-air?

KIRK: Candle, Gus? Do you see a candle, Dipper?

DIPPER: No candle.

GUS: And chains, waving around?

KIRK: Chains, Gus? Did you say chains? Dipper, do you see chains?

DIPPER: No chains. No, no chains, Gus.

KIRK: Do you see chains, Gus?

DIPPER: And a candle?

GUS: Who, me? No, I don't see anything. I just wondered if you did.

KIRK: No, we don't see anything, Gus.

NARRATOR: The ghosts leave the room. The ten o'clock haunting is over.

DIPPER: That's right, Gus. (*Pause*) Those chains and that candle we don't see are gone now.

KIRK: Yes, Gus, they went out there.

BILLY: I'm hungry!

GUS: That's enough! I'm very nervous! Green guys! Ghosts! Candles! Chains! There must be some place in this world where nobody's crazy.

KIRK: The only place I can think of is jail.

DIPPER: Nobody's crazy in jail.

GUS: That's it! That's it! I'll call the police! Jail will be wonderful!

NARRATOR: Gus dashes to the phone and starts to dial.

KIRK: Oh, Gus!

DIPPER: Quiet, Kirk, Gus is nervous. Besides, he's the brains.

KIRK: Yeah.

GUS: Hello, police? This is Gus Chicken, *the* Gus Chicken
. . . Yes, I want to go to jail. . . . Never mind why. . . .
I deserve it, don't I? . . . . Yes, jail. . . . You promise?
. . . . I'm at the old Hamlet house. . . . The boys are here,
too. . . . Oh, sure, Billy's all right. . . . It's me, I want to
go to jail. . . . You'll come right away to arrest me? Oh,
thank you.

NARRATOR: As Gus completes his call, he hears a loud knock
on the door.

INSPECTOR DICK: Open up, Chicken. It's the police!

GUS: That was fast! Let them in. Oh, boy! Jail! No crazy stuff.
Oh, boy!

NARRATOR: Dipper strides to the door and bows as he opens it
to Sergeant Webb and Inspector Dick.

DIPPER: Welcome, officers.

INSPECTOR DICK: So there you are, Chicken. You never thought
we'd catch you, did you?

GUS: What do you mean? I sent for you!

SERGEANT WEBB (*Ignoring him*): Do you want to know how
we found you, Gus?

KIRK: He told you to come, over the telephone.

INSPECTOR DICK: You made your mistake when you told Mr.
Rancid where to meet you. He called up and we figured out
how to find you, just like that.

DIPPER: I thought there was something wrong with this setup.

KIRK: Gus, these aren't the cops you called. These are other
cops.

GUS: What difference does it make? I want to go to jail.

SERGEANT WEBB: Want to go to jail? Are you crazy?

GUS: Don't say that!

INSPECTOR DICK: Say, there's the boy. Are you all right, Billy?
How did they treat you?

BILLY: I'm all right, but they treated me terribly.

SERGEANT WEBB: What did they do, Billy?

BILLY: They wouldn't give me any peanut butter sandwiches.

INSPECTOR DICK: What? Wait until the judge hears about this, Chicken.

GUS: What'll happen?

SERGEANT WEBB: You'll fry, Chicken!

INSPECTOR DICK: All right, let's start to the jail!

GUS: Good idea!

SERGEANT WEBB: Wait, Inspector Dick! We haven't shown them our badges yet. How do they know we're really police?

GUS: That's all right.

KIRK: We believe you.

INSPECTOR DICK: Never mind. We have to be proper. Mine is right here, pinned to my wallet.

SERGEANT WEBB: So's mine.

NARRATOR: The policemen search their pockets but cannot find their wallets.

DIPPER: Oh, here they are. I'm sorry. I just have to practice.

INSPECTOR DICK: That does it! Come on, off to jail, all of you.

GUS: Oh, good! Just think, no chains and candles!

KIRK: No ghosts!

DIPPER: No green guys!

BILLY: Hey! What about me?

INSPECTOR DICK: Don't worry, Billy. We brought someone to take you home. Here she comes!

NARRATOR: Mrs. Rancid comes rushing into the room and hugs Billy.

MRS. RANCID: Billy! My baby!

BILLY: Ma!

MRS. RANCID: They told me that you were all right, Billy. Look what I brought you, dear. A peanut butter sandwich!

BILLY: Where's the celery, Ma?

MRS. RANCID: Oh, I forgot it, dear.

BILLY: That's all right, Ma. Nothing else matters, now that I have my peanut butter sandwich! And you, Ma. You, too!

NARRATOR: Liz has been standing in the doorway and she sees Billy leave. She calls to her sister, Millie.

LIZ: Millie! Come here, dear, quickly!

MILLIE: What is it, Liz? I was just putting my chains away.

LIZ: That Billy Rancid just walked out of here all by himself without even saying goodbye, and he was eating a peanut butter sandwich.

MILLIE: You mean he took it without asking? Eating! He was eating?

LIZ: I saw him, Millie.

MILLIE: Then he must have been a pixie all the time, even though he didn't have a pointed head.

LIZ: Of course he was a pixie. You don't think he was a person, do you?

MILLIE: If only Mr. Caliban could have seen him! He always seems so lonely. He's hardly been out of the drainpipe all evening.

LIZ: Well, back to business. Let's see, how much time until the twelve o'clock haunting?

NARRATOR: Liz looks at her wrist and gasps.

MILLIE: What's wrong, dear?

LIZ: My watch is missing!

THE END

The Magic Nutmeg-Grater

Read this play to yourself. This is a kind of fairy story though you have probably never read it before.

As you read, notice certain things about the play:

1. The narrator's part tells you about any action in the play. For instance, the narrator mentions anyone coming in, going away, skipping, running, etc.
2. Notice that the dialogue tells you everything else you need to know to keep you interested. As the people talk, you learn many things that have happened and other things that are going to happen.
3. Each step in the play brings you closer to the climax or turning point in the story.
4. Decide where this play reaches a climax.

When you have finished reading the play, discuss with the group where the climax of the play lies. Try to agree. (Remember the climax is that place where the play must turn or move toward an ending. It is not the end.) You may wish to ask your teacher to check your decision.

Choose parts. Read your part carefully. Be sure you know every word.

Practice the play together. Be very careful to come in quickly with your part.

Talk over together:

1. Did you use your voice to show surprise, anger, fear?
2. Did you emphasize certain words to make the meaning clear?
3. Did you try to talk so that the character you portrayed seemed real?

When you are ready, it might be helpful to read the play to the tape recorder. Then you could play the tape to the class. Ask them to evaluate you on the three points listed above.

THE MAGIC NUTMEG-GRATER

by Adele Thane

Characters

(6 boys, 6 girls, and the narrator)
NARRATOR
KARL, *a young German boy*
ELSA, *his sister*
FRAU STROPKEN, *their mother*
TINKER HANS, *a mender of pots and pans*
FRAU WELZEL, *the mayor's wife*
LENA, *the mayor's daughter*
HEINRICH, *an artist*
HEIDI, *a milkmaid*
BEGGAR, *the king in disguise*
PLAYMATES, *two boys and a girl*

NARRATOR: It is a warm spring morning. The children are playing together in the town square. Suddenly Karl stands still and holds up his hand to quiet the group.
ELSA: What is it, Karl?
KARL: It's Tinker Hans. Don't you hear him?
ELSA: No, I don't hear anything.
FIRST PLAYMATE: Neither do I.
KARL: He's way down the street and around the corner. You'll see him soon.
TINKER HANS (*Calling faintly*): Tinker Hans, Tinker Hans, Here he comes to mend your pans.
KARL: There! Hear him now?

FIRST PLAYMATE (*Whimpering*): Oh, Karl, I'm afraid!

SECOND PLAYMATE: So am I.

THIRD PLAYMATE: Me, too.

KARL: Afraid? Of what?

PLAYMATES (*In a chorus*): Tinker Hans!

ELSA: For mercy's sake, why?

SECOND PLAYMATE: I don't like him. He looks crazy, with all those pans and things dangling around him and banging together.

FIRST PLAYMATE: They say he's a wicked sorcerer.

THIRD PLAYMATE: And a mind reader.

SECOND PLAYMATE: You mean, Tinker Hans can tell what you're thinking about without your saying a word?

THIRD PLAYMATE: That's right. All he has to do is look at you and he knows what's passing through your mind.

FIRST PLAYMATE: Mother says he bewitches the things he mends, so that the cakes all fall and the porridge burns.

THIRD PLAYMATE: That's because he uses magic metals to mend them with. He says so himself—listen!

TINKER HANS (*Calling faintly*): Tinker Hans will mend old kettles
With all sorts of magic metals.

THIRD PLAYMATE: See? What did I tell you? Magic metals.

SECOND PLAYMATE (*Squealing*): He's coming! I'm going to run!

FIRST PLAYMATE: Come on! Let's go!

NARRATOR: All the children run away as fast as they can and leave Karl and Elsa alone in the square.

ELSA: What ninnies they are—to be afraid of a poor old man!

KARL: That's because they don't understand him, Elsa. People are always afraid of what they don't understand.

ELSA (*Thoughtfully*): But if he really can read our thoughts—

KARL: Humph! I'd like to see him do it.

ELSA: Then you don't believe he can?

KARL: No-sir-ee!

TINKER HANS (*Calling*): Here I come, Tinker Hans!

Will you let me mend your pans?
Many a pleasant tale they will surely
    tell
When they come back whole and
    well.

KARL: There's a big hole in Mother's tea kettle. I wonder how much he'd charge to mend it.

TINKER HANS: I will mend it for a penny.
    If you're poor and haven't any,
    I will mend it if you say:
    "Please," and "Thank you," and "Good day."

NARRATOR: Tinker Hans walks into the town square and comes up to Karl and Elsa. Pots and pans and kettles are slung over his arms. Saucepans, frying pans and cakepans hang from his neck and waist. He wears a wide-brimmed hat and carries a brazier for heating metals.

ELSA (*Whispering, amazed*): Oh, my goodness, Karl! He answered you. And he couldn't possibly have heard what you said. He wasn't even here!

KARL: Nonsense, Elsa! He just happened to say that. It's one of his regular trade rhymes, I'll bet.

TINKER HANS: Good morning, children.

KARL *and* ELSA: Good morning.

TINKER HANS: Now, laddie, you run and fetch your mother's tea kettle, and by the time you're back with it, I'll be back, too, and I'll mend it for you.

NARRATOR: Tinker Hans takes his tools and pans and goes down the street.

ELSA: Well, that certainly wasn't one of his trade rhymes! He said it right out—your mother's tea kettle. If that isn't reading people's minds, I'd like to know what is.

KARL: You go get the kettle, Elsa, and I'll wait here.

NARRATOR: Elsa starts to run off—but just then she sees her mother coming into the town square.

ELSA: Oh, Mother, Tinker Hans wants to mend your tea kettle.

FRAU STROPKEN: No, dear. We can't afford it.

ELSA: But, Mother, he isn't charging us much—only a penny.

KARL: Or maybe nothing at all—if we say "thank you."

FRAU STROPKEN: Very well. Go fetch the kettle, Elsa.

NARRATOR: Elsa runs home as fast as she can. Frau Stropken takes a penny from her purse and gives it to Karl.

FRAU STROPKEN: Here, Karl. Give this penny to Tinker Hans, and tell him I wish it were more.

KARL: All right. (*Pause*) Mother—what's the matter? Why are we so poor all of a sudden?

FRAU STROPKEN: It's not sudden, Karl. It's been coming ever since your father died. He was ill such a long time, and his entire savings were spent on medical care. We still owe Dr. Moritz a lot of money, and now he's asking me to settle up.

KARL: The whole amount?

FRAU STROPKEN: Yes. He's been quite disagreeable about it, too. He says he must have the money by next Thursday, and not a day later.

KARL: The old skinflint! What will you do?

FRAU STROPKEN: I'm going now to plead with him again for more time (*Sighing*), though I doubt if he will give it to me.

KARL: What will happen if he doesn't?

FRAU STROPKEN (*Faltering*): Then—then I'm afraid we shall have to sell our home to raise the money.

KARL (*In dismay*): Sell our home! But, Mother, we can't do that! We'll have no place to live.

FRAU STROPKEN: I know, dear. Perhaps Dr. Moritz will have a change of heart. I'll be back as soon as I can.

NARRATOR: Mother hurries off to keep her appointment with Dr. Moritz. Karl stands still, in deep thought. Soon Elsa comes running back, carrying the broken tea kettle.

ELSA: Where's Mother?

KARL: She has gone to see Dr. Moritz about some money she owes him.

ELSA: Is it very much?

KARL: More than she can pay now—or maybe ever. Oh, Elsa! We may have to sell our home!

ELSA: Oh, no, Karl! Isn't there anyone who can help us?

TINKER HANS (*Calling*): When you're in a peck of trouble,
And expect that it will double,
Tinker Hans, if he's about,
Will be glad to help you out.

ELSA (*Excitedly*): Karl, did you hear that? Do you suppose he could do something?

KARL: Tinker Hans? How could he help?

ELSA: I don't know, but he just said he could, and it will do no harm to ask him.

NARRATOR: Tinker Hans returns and walks over to Elsa, who still holds the tea kettle.

TINKER HANS: Hand over the tea kettle, my dear, and I'll have it mended in next to no time.
I will teach it how to sing,
And to boil like anything.

NARRATOR: The tinker takes the kettle, places his brazier on the ground, opens his bag of tools and sets to work.

KARL: Tinker Hans, we—we thought perhaps—

TINKER HANS (*Humorously*): Is that so? Well, well!

ELSA (*Fidgeting*): You see, Tinker Hans—you—

TINKER HANS: Is it something about your mother?

ELSA: How did you know?

TINKER HANS: Wherever Hans the Tinker goes,
Every secret he soon knows. (*Pauses*)
Well? Is it your mother?

KARL: Yes, it is. She's in trouble.

TINKER HANS: Money matters, laddie?

KARL: Yes. We always had enough until Father was sick. Now it's all gone, and Mother is deep in debt.

ELSA (*Crying*): We may lose our home!

TINKER HANS: Dear, dear! We can't let that happen.

KARL: It's so important that something be done for Mother.

ELSA: And you're the only one we could think of who might be able to help.

TINKER HANS: You know what folks call me, don't you?

KARL: Yes.

TINKER HANS: A wicked sorcerer—that's what they call me.

ELSA (*Hotly*): *We* don't!

KARL: They're a pack of fools!

TINKER HANS: You're not afraid of me?

ELSA: I should say not!

KARL: We like you a lot. Oh, I do hope you'll be able to help us.

TINKER HANS: Hmmm. We shall see. Here is your kettle, my dear girl. As good as new. And singing already. Listen!

Since Tinker Hans has mended me,
I feel as gay as gay can be.

ELSA *and* KARL (*Laughing*): Oh, thank you, Tinker Hans.

KARL: Here's your penny. I wish it were a gold piece.

TINKER HANS: But you've already paid me—when you said "Thank you."

KARL: No, no, please take it. Mother insists.

TINKER HANS: Very well. Now I am in debt to your mother, and that means only one thing—I must help her.

NARRATOR: Hans reaches into his pocket and pulls out a nutmeg-grater which he holds out for the children to see.

TINKER HANS: Do you know what this is?

ELSA: It's a nutmeg-grater, isn't it?

KARL: But what are these strings for, stretched across the back here?

TINKER HANS: Ah, this is no ordinary nutmeg-grater, children. These four strings are tuned to the four winds. Each string has its wind, and each wind its song. And whatever the song, you will hear it when the wind blows. Hold it to your ear now, and listen.

NARRATOR: Karl and Elsa hold the nutmeg-grater between them. Each places an ear to it. They stand very still and listen.

TINKER HANS: Do you hear anything?

KARL: Oh my, yes! I hear music like a great wind wailing through the trees and the rigging of ships.

ELSA: Now I hear moaning. Oh, my gracious!

NARRATOR: Suddenly Karl and Elsa jump and drop the nutmeg-grater.

TINKER HANS: Don't be afraid of it. Pick it up. It will never vibrate enough to hurt you. Just hang on to it, no matter what.

NARRATOR: The tinker gathers his tools and brazier and starts to leave. Karl jumps up and holds his arm.

KARL: But Tinker Hans! You've forgotten about Mother.

TINKER HANS: Oh, no, I haven't. I never forget anything. Now listen to me carefully, and remember every word I say. (*Slowly, with great emphasis.*) Whoever gives the nutmeg-grater to the one who needs it most shall have good fortune. That is all. Goodbye, children.

NARRATOR: Tinker Hans leaves the children standing in the square and goes on his way, singing softly to himself.

KARL: "Whoever gives the nutmeg-grater to the one who needs it most shall have good fortune." What do you make of it, Elsa?

ELSA: I've no idea. It's such a worthless-looking thing. Not pretty at all. Smells spicy, though. Let me listen to it again.

KARL: Do you hear the wind?

ELSA: It's a different song this time—sweet and swaying.

KARL: That must be the West Wind.

ELSA: Oh! It's beginning to vibrate!

KARL: Hang on to it! Don't drop it! Remember Tinker Hans said it wouldn't hurt you.

NARRATOR: Elsa holds the nutmeg-grater to her ear and listens carefully.

ELSA (*Breathlessly*): I hear people talking. They're talking about me.

KARL: What do you mean?

ELSA: Someone is saying that I do the worst embroidery in town. That's not true!

KARL: Do you hear voices in that thing?

ELSA: Shhhhh!

KARL: You're dreaming. Give it to me.

NARRATOR: Karl takes the grater from Elsa and holds it to his ear. He listens for a moment.

KARL: I hear nothing. Nothing but the wind.

ELSA: But wait! Wait till it vibrates again. That's when I heard the voices.

KARL (*Scoffing*): Look here, Elsa. You don't think this nutmeg-grater can talk, do you?

ELSA: No, but I think it lets you hear what other people say.

KARL: Balderdash! Ow! It's beginning to vibrate.

ELSA: Quick! Listen before it stops shaking. (*Pauses*) Well? Is anyone speaking?

KARL: Yes—Dr. Moritz.

ELSA: What's he saying?

KARL: He says, "It's time that good-for-nothing boy of yours went to work, instead of loafing around like a rich man's son."

ELSA: He must be talking to Mother. Anything else?

KARL: Nothing. It's all quiet. (*Thoughtfully*) You know, Elsa, I believe I've guessed the secret of this thing.

ELSA: Oh, tell me!

KARL: Have you noticed that when you hold it, the voices say things only about you? And when I hold it, they say things only about me?

ELSA: That's right.

KARL: Then what we have to work out is whom to give it to— who is the one who needs it most?

ELSA: How shall we find the right person?

KARL: We'll have to try it out on different people and see what happens.

ELSA: You mean, just anyone?

KARL: No—people of importance, who can pay us well for it.

ELSA: Well, here comes the mayor's wife with her daughter. They're pretty important people. Shall we begin with them?

KARL: A good idea.

NARRATOR: The mayor's wife and daughter enter the square. They hold their heads high, barely noticing Karl and Elsa. Karl, however, steps forward and bows.

KARL: Good morning, Frau Welzel.

ELSA: Good morning, Lena.

KARL: Frau Welzel, I have something here that's very unusual. I think it might interest you.

FRAU WELZEL (*Haughtily*): What is it?

KARL: A nutmeg-grater, ma'am.

LENA (*Tittering affectedly*): Oh, Mama, how droll!

FRAU WELZEL: And why, pray, would I be interested in that rusty old thing?

KARL: There's not another one like it in the whole world. It is a magic nutmeg-grater.

FRAU WELZEL: What's magic about it?

LENA (*Sarcastically*): Perhaps, Mama, it will grate nutmeg all by itself.

ELSA: It will do better than that.

LENA: Indeed?

ELSA: It will tell you what people are saying about you.

FRAU WELZEL: Do you take me for a numbskull, girl?

KARL: Elsa is right, ma'am. Please try it. Hold it to your ear, and when it begins to vibrate, that means someone has mentioned your name.

FRAU WELZEL: Well, I suppose it won't do any harm to try it.

NARRATOR: Frau Welzel takes the nutmeg-grater and holds it to her ear.

LENA: I want to hear, too, Mama.

FRAU WELZEL: After me, dear.

KARL: Don't let go of it, ma'am, or the voices will not speak.

NARRATOR: The mayor's wife grips the nutmeg-grater firmly. As she listens, her face lights up with pleasure.

LENA: Who is it, Mama?

FRAU WELZEL: It's my dressmaker, dear. She's telling your Papa about my new gowns. She calls me "that most gracious, bountiful, beautiful and noble lady." Now she's asking your Papa to pay her for the dresses.

LENA: How much?

FRAU WELZEL: Two thousand guilders.

NARRATOR: Suddenly Frau Welzel's face changes. She becomes enraged.

FRAU WELZEL: Why, the wretch! The heartless wretch!

LENA: Who, Mama?

FRAU WELZEL: Your Papa! He says I'm not gracious or bountiful or beautiful or noble! I'm bad-tempered, and greedy, and ugly, and vain, and—and—oh! We're going home, Lena! Wait till I see your Papa!

LENA: But, Mama, I didn't have my turn! I want to listen!

FRAU WELZEL: And hear your Papa say disgraceful things about you? I wouldn't put it past him, the viper! Come along, now.

NARRATOR: Frau Welzel grabs Lena's arm and they hurry away to town.

KARL: Whew! I wouldn't want to be the mayor when she gets hold of him!

ELSA: Serves her right, the pompous old High-and-Mighty! And that stuck-up Lena, too! Well, what shall we do now? Wait for the next person?

KARL: It's the only way we'll find the right one. Say, there's Heinrich, the artist! Let's try him. Heinrich! Heinrich! Come here!

NARRATOR: Heinrich carries an easel, a canvas and his paintbox. He comes over to Karl and Elsa.

HEINRICH: Hello, there! I'm on my way to the river to paint the fishermen. Would you two like to come along and watch?

KARL: Not today, thank you. Uh—Heinrich?

HEINRICH: Yes?

KARL: Do you believe in magic?

HEINRICH: Well, I've seen a few strange things in my travels.

KARL: Would you be surprised if I showed you something magic?

HEINRICH (*Smiling*): What is it?

KARL: This nutmeg-grater.

HEINRICH: Let's see it. Hmmm. It looks about as magical as— well, as a nutmeg-grater.

KARL (*Laughing*): That's just it! But these strings are tuned to the four winds. And if anyone is speaking about you, no matter where—north, east, south or west—the strings will vibrate, and then you can hear what is being said by holding the grater to your ear.

HEINRICH: Amazing!

KARL: Try it.

NARRATOR: Heinrich takes the nutmeg-grater and sits down on a bench. He holds it to his ear and listens quietly. Soon he begins to smile.

HEINRICH: What lovely music!

KARL: That's the song of the wind. You can hear that any time. But it's only when the nutmeg-grater vibrates all over that voices can be heard. There! It's beginning to shake now.

HEINRICH: There's quite a babble of voices. It sounds like a gathering of some kind. Yes—it's a group of artists. They're talking about my paintings. (*Pauses*) What's that? My paintings are bad! Bah! I'm a fool to listen. Here! Take the wretched thing back.

KARL (*Anxiously*): I hope it hasn't upset you.

HEINRICH (*Bitterly*): Upset me! It has ruined my peace of mind, that's all! It has shaken my belief in myself.

KARL: I'm sorry, Heinrich, truly I am.

HEINRICH: There, there! You're not to blame. It's my own fault.

ELSA: How is it your fault?

HEINRICH: I should have more sense than to let a pack of tuppenny artists provoke me like this. Forgive me, children. Now I'm off to regain my self-confidence by painting the finest picture of my life. You wait and see! Goodbye, Karl. Goodbye, Elsa.

KARL: Well, we haven't done much to help Mother. This thing isn't so wonderful, after all. Nobody wants it.

ELSA: I wish we could see Tinker Hans again. Perhaps he would tell us more about it.

KARL: I doubt it. Folks who deal in magic never tell you much. They just say, "Take this magic ring, or hat, or stick, or whatever it is, and see what you shall see."

NARRATOR: While the children are talking together, a milkmaid comes into the square. She listens for a moment and then speaks.

HEIDI: Hello.

ELSA: Oh, hello, Heidi.

HEIDI: That's a curious thing you have, Karl. What is it?

KARL: This? It's a magic nutmeg-grater.

HEIDI: Magic, did you say?

ELSA: You sound as if you didn't believe in magic.

HEIDI: That depends. What can your nutmeg-grater do?

KARL: It can make music when the wind blows. And it lets you hear what people say about you, too.

HEIDI: You mean, gossip and such?

KARL: I suppose you'd call it that. Would you like to try it?

HEIDI: What for—just to hear myself talked about? No, thank you. Folks have to talk, I know, and if they want to talk about me, I don't mind. But listen to them? I'd rather spend my time lying in the meadow, watching the clouds sail by. I don't have time to listen to gossip. That's not my idea of magic.

ELSA (*Earnestly*): Tell me, Heidi—what is?

HEIDI: It would be magic if I could hear the footsteps of a lady-bug, walking on a blade of grass—or the splash a star makes when it shines in the river. I'd say that was true magic. Goodbye. I must be on my way.

ELSA (*Wistfully*): Karl, wouldn't it be wonderful if we could hear things like that in the nutmeg-grater?

KARL: Yes. Then, perhaps, we'd have some luck with it. As it is now, nobody will have anything to do with it.

ELSA: There must be someone who needs it, or Tinker Hans wouldn't have said so.

KARL (*Grumpily*): Oh, bother Tinker Hans!

ELSA (*Suddenly*): Karl! I know! I know someone who needs it!

KARL (*With indifference*): You do?

ELSA: Someone who really would be helped by hearing himself talked about.

KARL: Who?

ELSA: The King!

KARL (*Startled*): The King?

ELSA: Yes. Aren't people always talking about him, day and night? And isn't it important for him to know what they say, so that he can rule his kingdom well?

KARL (*Awe-struck*): Yes, but—take this to the King? I wouldn't dare.

ELSA: Not even for Mother's sake?

KARL: But how could I reach him?—I mean, get into the palace to see him?

ELSA: You'd stand a better chance than a grown person, because the King's not much more than a boy himself, and very friendly, I've heard. Why, I'll bet he'd be glad to try the nutmeg-grater.

KARL: At least he'd be rich enough to pay us for it.

ELSA: Rich enough! Why, he could pay Mother's debts ten times over and never know he had opened his purse.

KARL (*Enthusiastically*): We could walk to the palace in two hours and be back by nightfall. Mother needn't know.

ELSA: Let's start now!

NARRATOR: With Karl holding the nutmeg-grater, the children start off in the direction of the palace. They are in such a hurry that they bump into a beggar.

KARL: Oh, we're sorry!

ELSA: Are you all right?

BEGGAR: I think so. Where are you off to in such a hurry?

KARL: To see the King.

BEGGAR: Oho, that's glibly said. But will the King see you? The King is closely guarded, and few people get to see him.

ELSA: How do you know about the King?

BEGGAR (*Evasively*): I often walk near the palace. Tell me, why do you want to see the King?

KARL: We want to sell him this nutmeg-grater.

BEGGAR (*With an amused laugh*): What would the King do with a nutmeg-grater? He probably has a pantry full of them already.

KARL: Well, you know the King has many enemies—I mean, traitors who want to take his crown away—and so we figured this would help him find them out.

BEGGAR: How would it?

KARL: It's magic, and when anyone speaks about you—anyone, anywhere in the world—you can hear what's being said right inside this nutmeg-grater.

NARRATOR: The beggar stares at Karl for a moment, then he holds out his hand.

BEGGAR: Give it to me.

KARL: No, it's for the King.

ELSA: Oh, let the poor man see it, Karl.

NARRATOR: Reluctantly Karl hands the grater to the beggar, who examines it curiously.

BEGGAR: So you want to sell this thing. Why?

KARL: To help Mother. You see, our father was sick a long time before he died, and now Mother has nothing. She's about to sell our home to pay her debts.

BEGGAR: What is your name, boy?

KARL: Karl Stropken. And this is my sister, Elsa. Don't be afraid if the grater trembles. It means that someone is talking about you.

BEGGAR: Oh! There are so many voices—like a crowd chattering. It's so confused and mixed-up, I can hardly make out anything.

KARL: It will clear up soon, and then you'll be able to understand.

BEGGAR: It's still quite noisy. Everybody is talking at once— "The King this and the King that."

KARL: But why is the King's name mentioned? You must be mistaken. You should hear only your own name, and what is being said about you.

BEGGAR (*Horrified by what he hears*): It is being said about me!

ELSA (*In a whisper*): Karl, you don't think—? Can he be—?

KARL: Are you the King?

BEGGAR (*Nodding solemnly*): Yes, I am the King. And sometimes I wish I'd never heard the word. I wish I'd been born poor, like this beggar I pretend to be.

ELSA: Why do you pretend to be a beggar, Your Majesty?

BEGGAR: So that I can go among my people, unrecognized, and get to know them better. It's not the people who betray me. It's my own flesh and blood. Just now I heard my cousin plotting to overthrow me and take my throne. Luckily, I have found out in time, thanks to this magic nutmeg-grater.

KARL: At last, Elsa—here is "the one who needs it most."

BEGGAR: What did you say, Karl?

KARL: When Tinker Hans gave us the nutmeg-grater, he told us that if we found the one who needs it most, we should have good fortune.

BEGGAR: And so you shall, children. I'll settle your mother's debts, and give her five hundred gold pieces besides. As for you, Karl—how would you like to live in the palace and be my page?

KARL: Oh, Your Majesty! I'd like nothing better.

ELSA: It's just the way things happen in a fairy tale, Karl— good fortune comes from the last place you expect to find it!

THE END

Midnight Burial

Read this play as rapidly as you can. It is very short and does not contain any difficult words.

Notice the ending of the play.

How do you think the girls will react to the special treat?

Do you know the meaning of the word *suspense?*

(If you are not sure of the meaning, look for the word in the dictionary.)

This play builds suspense by having different girls prepare to eat a piece of poisoned cake.

Find the places where this happens and tell how the author prevents each girl from really eating the cake.

Can you explain why this holds you in suspense?

Does this contribute to the climax? How?

Choose your part. Practice reading to yourself. Decide just how you are going to read your lines; what kind of voice you will use; which words you will make important.

Practice reading the entire play.

Talk together and help each other to improve. Remember each part must be read well if the play is to be good.

Read the entire play again.

Tell your teacher if you feel you are ready to read to the class.

MIDNIGHT BURIAL

by Kay Hill

Characters

(8 girls, and the narrator)
NARRATOR

SUZIE   ⎫ *Three friends who*
BETTY   ⎬ *are trying to bury*
CHUBBY ⎭ *a chocolate cake*

NONA ⎫ *Three friends who are*
SALLY ⎬ *trying to discover what*
ROSIE ⎭ *the other girls are doing*

FIRST LEADER ⎫ *Camp leaders who are*
SECOND LEADER ⎭ *in charge of the girls*

NARRATOR: Suzie and Chubby are carrying a large square parcel wrapped in brown paper. They are in the woods and
it is very dark. Betty, who is following the other girls,
bumps into them and makes them drop the parcel.

SUZIE: There now! See what you've done! Can't you look
where you're going, Betty?

BETTY: Sh-h! Do you want the whole camp down on us to
see what we're doing out in the woods after lights-out? I'm
almost sure I heard something a minute ago.

SUZIE: Nonsense! You're imagining it. Well, Chubby, this is
as good a spot as any to hide the body.

CHUBBY: Don't talk about bodies! Just think, if we'd eaten
that cake, we'd have been the dead bodies!

SUZIE: Do you think they'd have buried us out here in the
woods? I'd like that—the pine trees whispering at night,
and sprinkling us with needles on a hot day.

BETTY: Will you stop, Suzie! You're giving me the creeps. How on earth, Chubby, did your mother happen to get poison in the cake, anyway?

CHUBBY: It was a terrible mistake. My mother made the cake yesterday and sent it to the post office right away. This morning, she discovered the vanilla bottle she'd used was an old one my little brother Freddy had filled up with rat poison. She got me on the telephone this afternoon just after the box arrived. She was nearly out of her mind until she found I hadn't opened the box yet.

BETTY: And it looks so good. Just think—one bite of that luscious-looking cake and (*Dramatically*) we'd be writhing in death agony!

SUZIE: Let's get it over with. We can't light a fire out here in the woods. We'll have to bury it.

BETTY: What'll we dig a hole with?

SUZIE: What a bunch of dopes we are! We need a shovel!

BETTY: I know where there's a hoe.

CHUBBY: Where?

BETTY: Over in Farmer Green's field. I saw it lying there this afternoon.

SUZIE: Come on, then, let's get it. Leave the box here.

NARRATOR: Suzie, Betty and Chubby run off to the field to find the hoe. No sooner are they out of sight than three more girls come tiptoeing into the woods.

NONA: I'm sure they went this way. Come on, we must be right on their tracks. Look at this box. I wonder what it is.

ROSIE: They were carrying something when they sneaked out of Chubby's tent. This must be it.

SALLY: What do you suppose is in it?

NONA: Only one way to find out.

NARRATOR: Nona quickly tears off the wrapping and lifts the lid from the box. She holds the box so the girls can look inside.

SALLY: A beautiful cake. Chocolate with pink peppermint icing—I can smell the peppermint.

NONA: So that's why they came out here, the greedy things. They didn't want to share the cake.

ROSIE: Why did they leave it here?

SALLY: Probably heard us coming and got scared. I don't know about you two, but I think finders are keepers.

NARRATOR: Sally breaks off a piece and raises it to her mouth. Nona quickly slaps the cake out of Sally's hand.

NONA: Greedy pig! Wait till I divide it—share and share alike. I'll have to break it. Here's your piece, Sally. One for you, Rosie.

NARRATOR: Rosie lifts her piece of cake and is just about to take a big bite when she changes her mind.

ROSIE: I'm thirsty. I wish we had something to drink with it.

SALLY: There's a brook down the hill back there. Let's fill the box—it's tin.

NARRATOR: The girls jump up and run off toward the brook. Sally trails behind and sneaks back quietly to get her piece of cake. Just as she is about to put her teeth into the cake, Nona calls to her. Sally drops the cake and follows the girls. No sooner have they disappeared from view than the other girls return with the hoe.

SUZIE: It doesn't feel very sharp. But we can try. Here's a soft spot. There, the hole is big enough! Where's the box?

CHUBBY: Look! The cake is out of the box and all broken up.

BETTY: I knew we were being followed.

SUZIE: Don't be silly! Chipmunks, of course!

BETTY: Chipmunks?

SUZIE: Or squirrels. They're inquisitive little beggars, just love to get into things. Wonder where their dead bodies are, poor things.

CHUBBY: The box is gone, too! Don't you try to tell me, Suzie Blake, that any old chipmunk ever walked off with the tin box!

SUZIE (*Patiently*): Of course, Chubby—that's just what squirrels and chipmunks love, anything bright and odd. The little imps have hidden it somewhere.

BETTY: I don't like it! I'm sure I heard the bushes crackle when we came down the path.

SUZIE: Betty, if nothing else will satisfy you, we'll take a look around. I'll go back the way we came. You and Chubby go that way. Meet here in five minutes.

NARRATOR: The girls go off. Nona, Rosie, and Sally return carrying the water. They sit down prepared to eat the cake. Sally sits on the edge of the hoe, which makes the handle fly up in the air. This startles the girls and they all jump up in dismay and stare at the hoe.

NONA: Where did it come from?

ROSIE: And look at that hole. That wasn't there before!

SALLY: I'm s-scared. Let's go back.

NONA: We might as well. We can take the cake with us.

SUZIE (*Calling faintly*): Come on, Chubby.

NONA: Quiet! It's Suzie! Hide the cake.

NARRATOR: Suzie, Betty and Chubby come back to the cake. They stop short.

SUZIE: What are you doing here?

CHUBBY (*Suddenly and loudly*): The cake! Where's the cake?

NONA: Ha! You thought you'd eat it all yourselves. Well, you're too late! We've eaten it all up!

SUZIE, CHUBBY and BETTY (*In chorus*): Wha—a-t!

SUZIE: You ate it? You ate it all!

SALLY: Certainly. It's a lesson to you not to be so stingy here-after!

CHUBBY (*Starting to sob*): Murderers, that's what we are—murderers.

SUZIE: How do you feel, Nona?

NONA: I'm fine—how are you?

SUZIE: Do you feel any pain, Sally?

SALLY: Not a twinge. Cake agrees with me, especially in the woods at midnight.

SUZIE: What about you, Rosie?

ROSIE: I'm all right.

134 *MIDNIGHT BURIAL*

CHUBBY: This is a nightmare—a horrible dream! We'll go to jail.

SUZIE: Now, Chubby, keep cool. All may not be lost. If we can get them to a doctor in time . . . maybe he has an antidote, or a stomach pump. Now you two take Rosie and Sally. I'll take care of Nona. Here, Nona, put your arm across my shoulder.

NONA: What nonsense is this?

ROSIE: I won't get up.

NARRATOR: Rosie resists Chubby's efforts to move her, but Chubby pulls desperately, and at last Rosie gets up.

ROSIE: All right, there's your old cake. But I'm going to have one piece anyway!

SUZIE: Stop! Don't eat that! It's full of rat poison.

NARRATOR: For a moment, everyone is absolutely still. Then Rosie hurls the cake as far away as possible. Chubby is the first girl to get into action.

CHUBBY: We'll bury it right now before anything else happens. Come on, everybody help!

NARRATOR: In a moment, every girl is frantically picking up pieces of cake and burying them. All of a sudden Betty jumps up and listens.

BETTY: Sh-h! I hear something. Voices. It must be the leaders.

SUZIE: Let's get out of here—but fast!

NARRATOR: The girls scurry off into the woods and disappear in the nick of time. Two older girls stroll into the woods talking together.

1ST LEADER: It's late. They'll all be asleep by now.

2ND LEADER: Oh, yes. The fresh air, you know. They can hardly keep their eyes open after nine o'clock. I have a treat for them tomorrow—a special dessert.

1ST LEADER: Oh? What is it?

2ND LEADER: A beautiful big chocolate cake with pink peppermint icing.

THE END

The Ghost Walks Tonight

There are many comical situations in this play. It is a series of strange happenings that took place when three boys decided they were brave enough to spend Halloween night in a haunted house.

There is nothing difficult in this story. Read it to yourself and see if you find it amusing.

Bud acts *brave* and *fearless* and this must show in his voice.

Henry tries to be as brave as Bud but he slips up every once in a while and *fear* and *nervousness* show in his voice.

Peewee is a younger brother and every once in a while he *cries* and *sniffles*. At other times he just enjoys himself.

Joe is very *tough* in his speech and his actions.

Al is an unfortunate man who is not too bright. He *stutters* a great deal and is very nervous.

Talk the play over together and decide who should read each part. Take time to read your part to yourself. Ask each other for help if it is needed.

Now read the entire play aloud together. This time try to read smoothly and come in on time.

Read the play aloud again. Remember not only to come in on time but to use your voice so that you sound just like the person you are supposed to be.

Decide whether there are parts you should practice again.

Arrange for a time to read to your class.

THE GHOST WALKS TONIGHT

by Jessie Nicholson

Characters

(9 boys, 3 girls, and the narrator)
NARRATOR
BUD
HENRY, *his friend*
PEEWEE, *Henry's small brother*
JOE, *a burglar*
AL, *his dull-witted partner*
POLICE OFFICER

DICK
SAM
BILLY   *school friends of*
GINNY   *Henry and Bud*
SUSAN
NANCY

NARRATOR: As the play opens, we find three boys standing outside the window of the living room of an abandoned house. Bud and Henry are holding lanterns and examining the room. Peewee wears a sheet and carries a jack-o'-lantern. All of the boys are trying to get enough courage to enter the room.

HENRY: Gosh, it looks awfully spooky in there.

BUD: So what? That's the way a haunted house is supposed to look. Come on—I'll go first.

NARRATOR: The boys climb into the room through the window.

HENRY: L-look at the pile of—of bones!

BUD: They aren't bones, silly. They're just chunks of fallen plaster from that hole in the ceiling. (*Enthusiastically*) What a perfectly swell place for a ghost!

PEEWEE (*Loudly*): I want to go home.

BUD: Aw, there's nothing to be scared of, Peewee. Just an old, empty house, isn't it, Henry?

HENRY: Yeah, I guess so. I wish we weren't going to stay here all night, though. After all, it is Halloween.

PEEWEE (*Howling*): I want to go home.

HENRY (*In disgust*): Why didn't you think of that sooner? I would have been glad to leave you there. But no, you bawled until Mom said we had to take you along.

PEEWEE (*Dejectedly*): I thought we were going to everybody's houses and collect candy.

BUD: Shucks—that's only for little kids.

PEEWEE: But I am a little kid.

BUD: What are we going to do with him?

NARRATOR: Reluctantly, Henry takes a bag of candy from his pocket and dumps it into Peewee's bag.

HENRY: I was saving these for later but I guess we have to shut him up. Now, Peewee, you can take your jack-o'-lantern and walk up and down in front of the house. Then you can warn us if you see anybody coming.

PEEWEE: Who are you expecting?

BUD: Oh, just some old ghosts, goblins and witches.

NARRATOR: At this point Peewee begins to howl louder than ever.

HENRY (*In disgust*): Now, see what you did.

BUD: They're just kids dressed up in costumes, Peewee. And they're going to try to scare us out of here. Hen and I bet them we'd stay all night in this fine old haunted house. If we win we each get a double scoop ice cream cone. And we'll share with you if you'll be good and do what you're told.

PEEWEE (*Wailing*): No!

HENRY (*In exasperation*): What's the matter now?

PEEWEE: I want a whole ice cream cone for myself!

HENRY: All right—all right—so you get a whole ice cream cone. Come on, out the window you go.

NARRATOR: The boys lift Peewee over the window sill and station him outside to keep watch.

BUD: Now, since it's nice and quiet around here, we can really enjoy this fine old haunted house.

HENRY: It's too quiet if you ask me. W-what was that?

BUD: Aw, just the wind blowing a shutter. There are a lot of loose ones on the front of the house. I noticed them when we came in.

HENRY: Oh-h—say, where did you tell your mother you were going to stay tonight?

BUD: At your house—what'd you tell your mother?

HENRY: That I was going to stay at yours. I kind of wish I was.

BUD: You getting cold feet or something?

HENRY: I guess not. Only it is kind of lonesome here all by ourselves.

BUD (*Enthusiastically*): What do you say we explore?

HENRY (*Falteringly*): Ex-explore?

BUD: Sure—why not? We might find some hidden treasure in this good old haunted house.

HENRY: Or a ghost.

BUD: I don't believe in ghosts.

HENRY: Me either.

NARRATOR: Just then the rattle of a heavy chain is heard. Henry grabs Bud for protection. Even Bud looks a little startled.

BUD: Creepers—what do you suppose that was?

NARRATOR: Henry and Bud turn their backs to the window and look around the room. Peewee leans in the window and drops an old automobile chain on the floor. The sound scares the older boys who howl and jump a foot. When he sees how startled they are, Peewee giggles and calls to them.

PEEWEE (*Still giggling*): It sure doesn't take much to scare you fellows. Just a little bitty old chain I found under the window.

HENRY (*Furiously*): What's the big idea?

THE GHOST WALKS TONIGHT 139

BUD: Yeah—what are you trying to do, Peewee? Hen thought the ghost was walking for sure.

HENRY: *I* thought—what do you mean, I thought?

BUD: Aw, come on, Hen, let's explore.

HENRY: Well—you go first, then.

NARRATOR: No sooner have the boys left the living room than Peewee scrambles through the window and calls again.

PEEWEE: Hey, Henry—Bud—where are you? There's someone coming down the road. I don't want to meet up with any old goblins, witches or ghosts. I'll just hide behind the sofa so they won't see me.

NARRATOR: Peewee takes his jack-o'-lantern and squeezes behind the sofa. Two burglars with flashlights creep cautiously into the room. Al is very big and carries a small black bag which he places on the table. Joe is small and thin with a sharp voice. Both men wear black kerchiefs tied over the lower part of their faces. They remove them and start to talk.

JOE: I figger this oughta be a good place to lie low for a couple of hours.

AL (*Stutters*): If th-there are no h-haunts!

JOE: Whatcha talkin' about?

AL: You know, Joe—g-g-ghosties in their nighties!

JOE: Aw, cut it out, Al. Be your age.

AL (*Protestingly*): But J-Joe, it's Halloween, when the g-g-graves give up their d-d-dead. I know. I've seen 'em walkin'.

JOE (*Disgusted*): Seen what, stupid?

AL: Just what I s-s-said—haunts and ghosts—yeow!

NARRATOR: As Peewee's sheet-covered figure creeps out from behind the sofa, Al spies him. When Peewee hears Al's cry, he quickly ducks behind the sofa again.

JOE: What ails you anyhow?

NARRATOR: Al is far too frightened to talk but he points to the sofa. Joe looks but sees nothing.

JOE: Sometimes I think you're not quite right in the head. Nobody's there. Come on, we'll look the joint over. We might even get a little shut-eye before we have to lam outa here.

AL: But Joe, I s-s-saw a haunt—honest. I saw it with my own eyes.

JOE (*Growling*): You see too much—that's what. Come on now, get movin'.

NARRATOR: Joe and Al leave to explore the rest of the house. Peewee comes from behind the sofa and places his pumpkin on the table. Let's listen to what he says.

PEEWEE: Gosh—they must have bet somebody they could sleep in this good, old haunted house all night, too. I wonder if they're going to get double scoop ice cream cones if they win. I didn't notice this black bag before. I guess I'll just see what it has in it.

NARRATOR: Peewee takes the black bag from the table and prepares to open it when he hears more voices outside of the window. He scurries behind the sofa, taking the bag with him. Three boys and three girls in Halloween costumes enter the room.

SUSAN: Look, kids—a jack-o'-lantern. They must be here.

DICK: I guess they've run off—left their lantern in their hurry.

SAM: Say, what's this black kerchief doing here? Do you suppose Henry's started wearing bandannas?

BILLY: I know what to use it for.

NARRATOR: Billy is dressed to look like a tramp. He quickly ties the kerchief over the lower part of his face, and points his finger like a gun.

BILLY: Stick 'em up!

NANCY: Oh, Billy, you're a panic.

NARRATOR: There is a loud noise as if someone has fallen. Everyone stands still and listens. Then quietly, they begin to talk together again.

GINNY (*Falteringly*): W-what was that?

DICK (*Cheerfully*): Must be Hen and Bud tripping over the ghost.

BILLY: Come on, kids, let's hide in the other room and give them a real scare when they come in.

SAM: We'll take this old chain with us. We can make plenty of ghostly noises with that.

NARRATOR: With the chain and the lantern, the girls and boys leave the living room to prepare to frighten Henry and Bud. Joe and Al come back from the hall. Al is limping and groaning.

JOE: Pipe down, will you? Why couldn't you look where you were goin'?

AL: In the d-d-dark, Joe?

JOE (*Disgustedly*): Those big feet of yours would fall over each other in the middle of Main Street at high noon! Now, where's that bag?

AL: I'm s-s-sure I left it right here on the t-t-table, Joe.

JOE: You're sure—that's just fine and dandy. How can you be sure you're sure?

AL: Maybe I'm not s-s-sure, Joe.

JOE (*Slowly, painstakingly*): Listen Al, try to think—way back to five minutes ago. (*Then shouting*) What did you do with that bag?

AL: Maybe the g-g-ghost took it!

JOE (*Groaning*): You oughta have your brains examined—what there is of 'em.

AL (*Pleased*): My b-b-brains, Joe? Gee, thanks.

JOE: Come on, find that bag.

NARRATOR: Joe searches frantically for the bag. He throws things to the left and right. Al follows him, picking up and replacing everything Joe throws around.

AL (*Muttering*): Gee, you're making an awful m-m-mess of this place, Joe.

NARRATOR: While Al and Joe are looking the other way, Peewee creeps out and draws one of the cushions behind the sofa. For a while Al, who is tidying the room, cannot figure out why the sofa looks different. When he realizes a sofa pillow has disappeared, he runs over and tugs at Joe's sleeve.

JOE: Let go of me. What's the matter with you, anyhow?

AL: One of the cushions is m-m-missin', Joe. It just sort of d-d-disappeared.

NARRATOR: Peewee slides the cushion out into the room while Al is talking to Joe.

JOE (*Turning around*): There's your cushion, dummy—right in front of your eyes.

AL: I'm g-g-gettin' outa here—but fast.

JOE (*Shouting*): Come back here, stupid.

NARRATOR: Al leaps through the window and Joe follows close on his heels. They have been gone only a few minutes when the boys and girls return to the living room.

DICK: Come on, kids, they're gone. Whew—did we give them a scare! You should have seen Bud's legs flying through the window.

SAM: I wish we could have heard what they were saying. These old walls must be pretty thick.

NARRATOR: While Sam speaks, he knocks on the wall to test the thickness. Immediately, his knock is returned. The boys look at each other in surprise. The girls are very frightened. Finally Billy speaks.

BILLY: Try it again, Sam. See what happens.

NARRATOR: Sam knocks on the wall again, very timidly. His knock is returned as before.

GINNY: Let's go home, kids. I don't like this place.

NANCY: Me either.

DICK: Now, wait a minute. We have to view this thing scientifically. There must be some kind of echo here. It was the same number of raps each time. See, I'll show you.

NARRATOR: This time Dick knocks on the wall very distinctly, three times. The knocks are not returned. Instead, they hear a terrific clatter as if an iron bar were falling down a flight of stairs.

BILLY: Some echo!

GINNY: Someone's coming. I hear footsteps.

SAM: Must be Bud and Henry again. Nobody else ever uses

this old back road but kids. Let's hide before they get here.

NARRATOR: As before, the boys and girls run into the next room. Very soon Joe returns, pushing Al ahead of him.

JOE: Now, you do what you're told when you're told to do it, dummy—understand?

AL: Y-y-yes, Joe.

JOE: You gotta stir them cobwebs outa your brain and remember what you did with that bag—understand?

AL: C-c-cobwebs, Joe? Did you say cobwebs?

JOE (*Growling*): Stop asking questions and start answering a few.

AL: Yes, Joe. Maybe if I lie d-d-down on the sofa, the blood'll rush to my feet outa my head and I can t-t-think more clearly.

NARRATOR: Al lies on the sofa, thinking. Joe prowls about the room still searching for the bag. Suddenly Al howls with pain.

AL: I've b-b-been stabbed in the back. I told you g-g-ghosts were walkin' tonight!

JOE: Nonsense! What kind of ghost could stab you in the back? It's probably that pin in your suspenders. What am I gonna do with you? Here we pull a job that would put us on easy street and you gum up the works per usual. You bring me nothin' but bad luck.

AL: I'm s-s-sorry, Joe. Maybe I should go and d-d-drown myself or somethin'.

JOE: I pretty near knock my brains out tryin' to make somethin' worthwhile outa you and what do I get?

NARRATOR: As he talks, Al pounds on the wall in a fury. The pounding is answered from above.

JOE (*Slowly*): And—and what do I get?

AL (*Shakily*): A—a message from the d-d-dead—maybe? You can't s-s-say you didn't hear that, Joe boy.

JOE: No, I guess I can't. What's goin' on here anyhow? Are we bein' double-crossed? Come on upstairs. We'll look into this right off.

AL: If it's all the s-s-same to you, Joe, I'll stay here.

JOE: Oh, no you don't. I don't trust you outa my sight. Come on, we'll try this other door. It oughta get us upstairs.

NARRATOR: Joe goes out, and Al shuffles after him. Henry and Bud climb into the living room through the window.

HENRY: It was lucky that trellis was right by the window so we could get away before the gang got upstairs. They're going to get good and fooled when they try to find us. Boy, I bet we gave them a scare.

BUD: Hey—I just thought of something. Where's Peewee?

HENRY (*In a stage whisper*): Ps-st, Peewee—where are you?

BUD: He must have gone home.

HENRY (*Worriedly*): Mom's not going to like this very much. Maybe I'd better go home, too.

BUD: Now, Hen, you've got to stick this thing out. Remember, our honor is at stake.

HENRY: Yeah, I suppose so. Hey, look—what's that moving there beside the sofa?

BUD: It's just a little, old black bag. It couldn't have been moving.

HENRY: But I tell you I saw it come sliding out. Come on, let's go home.

BUD: Don't you see—it's just one of the kids trying to scare us. Act as though you didn't notice anything.

HENRY: I wonder what's in it?

BUD: That's what they want you to wonder. I wouldn't touch it with a ten-foot pole.

HENRY: Still, I'd kind of like to know.

NARRATOR: While Bud tries to peer under the sofa, Henry tiptoes over to the black bag and opens it. He lifts out a handful of money. Surprised and awed, he shouts to Bud.

HENRY: Jiminy crickets! Look what's in here!

BUD (*Sitting up and staring in awe*): Jeepers—those kids must have found the hidden treasure in this house before we did.

HENRY: I don't think it's hidden treasure. It's nice and new and clean looking. I think it's—stolen money! (*Fearfully*) Somebody may even be bound and—and gagged behind the sofa there.

BUD: Or shot maybe—that sounded like a groan before!

HENRY: We have to do something.

BUD: Yeah—but what?

HENRY: We have to look—and—see!

NARRATOR: Henry pulls the sofa out from the wall. There is Peewee all curled up on the floor. Henry is frightened and cries out.

HENRY: But—it's Peewee. He's unconscious.

BUD: Shucks, he's just asleep. Must have kicked that old bag out while he was dreaming. (*Shouting*) Peewee!

PEEWEE: Where—where am I?

HENRY (*In disgust*): Well, you're not home in bed. What's the big idea—sleeping under the sofa?

PEEWEE (*Indignantly*): I was not asleep. I—I was just hiding.

HENRY: Who were you hiding from?

PEEWEE: Oh, from all the ghosts, goblins and witches and—and Al and Joe, of course.

BUD *and* HENRY (*Together*): Al and Joe?

PEEWEE: Yeah. Boy, did I have a good time scaring them! (*Giggling*) I like Halloween.

HENRY: Yes, but who are Al and Joe?

PEEWEE: Why, they're staying here all night.

HENRY: S-staying all night?

PEEWEE (*Yawning*): Yeah—I bet they've gone to bed already. Joe was pretty angry when they couldn't find that old bag. I guess maybe it has their pajamas in it.

BUD: Some pajamas!

HENRY (*Excitedly*): Al and Joe must be burglars, all right. And they're hiding out somewhere here this very minute!

NARRATOR: A door opens and closes with a noisy squeak. Bud jumps outside through the window with a wild yell.

BUD: Ye-ow!

PEEWEE: Who's afraid of ghosts now?

HENRY: Me. Come on.

PEEWEE: But Henry, that's only—

NARRATOR: Peewee gets no further for Henry pushes him through the window and follows hastily. The other boys and girls come into the living room. They are all laughing and talking.

DICK: That sure was showing them. Do they scare easily.

GINNY: I'm getting tired of this silly game. I'd rather be out ringing doorbells.

NANCY: Me, too.

BILLY: Say, look—they left a little bag on the table.

SAM: Probably on purpose. I wouldn't touch that little old bag with a ten-foot pole.

DICK: Me either. They needn't think they can catch us that easily. I wonder what's in it?

NANCY: Maybe a midnight snack.

SAM: Do you really think so? I'm awfully hungry.

BILLY: It's kind of heavy, but not too heavy. Say kids, did you ever taste Mrs. Baxter's banana cream pie? It's one of Henry's favorite dishes.

GINNY: Yum, yum!

DICK: And Bud's mother makes swell fudge cake with frosting two inches thick!

BILLY: Could be, fellows.

CHILDREN (*In chorus*): Let's open it.

NARRATOR: Everyone crowds around Billy as he opens the bag.

BILLY (*Disgustedly*): Aw, look at this. Only some old money!

SAM: Must be play money. Bud and Henry are trying to make an impression. Did they think they were going to fool us with this stuff?

SUSAN: Yeah, what a joke! Play money. Let's throw it around. Whee!

BILLY: Give me some to throw, too. Wow! This is fun.

GINNY (*Suddenly*): Shush, kids. I think I heard something.

BILLY: Maybe Bud and Henry have come back and are sneaking around the place. Let's hide before they come in here.

NARRATOR: The children go out. A moment later, Al and Joe

return to the living room. They stare at the money thrown all over the room.

AL (*In dismay*): G-g-gee, Joe, there must have b-b-been a strong wind blowin' in here or—or somethin'.

JOE: Well—how do you like that?

AL: I t-t-told you there was a g-g-ghost at work. See the sofa's even been pushed out. That's where it was hiding. I told you, J-J-Joe.

JOE: Let's pick up the dough quick and scram outa here. I don't like the looks of things.

AL: Me either, Joe. They say you c-c-can't take it with you but some g-g-ghost was tryin' to, I guess.

NARRATOR: While the burglars are crawling about trying to gather their money, Billy steps into the room. The kerchief is over the lower part of his face. He holds his hand in his pocket as if he has a gun.

BILLY: Stick 'em up, you lugs, or I'll fill you with slugs!

NARRATOR: Al and Joe slowly raise their hands. When Billy sees that they are burglars, his knees buckle and he begins to groan. Joe makes a dive for him. Fortunately at this moment, Bud, Henry and Peewee enter with a police officer.

OFFICER (*Sharply*): Hands up, men.

JOE: I'll take care of this little punk. Al, you take care of that one.

AL: B-b-but, Joe—this is no t-t-time for playin' cops and robbers.

NARRATOR: Joe wrestles with Billy. The other boys and girls enter. The boys pitch in to help Billy, while the girls gasp in fright. Joe is finally pinned to the floor. The officer places handcuffs on both men.

OFFICER: Boys, I have to hand it to you. You've all done a splendid job. You reported a suspected crime promptly and you helped bring down a criminal courageously.

GINNY (*Indignantly*): How about the girls? Don't we get any credit?

SUSAN: Yeah—how about us?

OFFICER: Ah—er—yes, of course you get credit. A beautiful girl always acts as an incentive to encourage a man's bravery.

SAM (*Disgustedly*): All they did was scream.

OFFICER: And what's more, there's a reward offered for these crooks, Rat-face Joe McGirk and Dopey Al Swenson. I recognized them right off. They're wanted in a good many cities, and you children will get a share of the reward money.

AL (*Happily*): D-d-did you hear that, Joe? They're going to w-w-win money on us! That's nice. I guess it s-s-sort of makes us famous—huh, Joe?

JOE (*Sullenly*): Pipe down, dummy.

NARRATOR: Suddenly Peewee, still wearing his sheet, steps forward and begins to howl.

HENRY: Now what's the matter with you?

PEEWEE: You said we were going to win ice cream cones!

AL: Ye-ow—Joe—a g-g-ghostie in his nightie!

NARRATOR: The sight of Peewee in the sheet is too much for Al, who falls to the floor in a dead faint—a fitting end to a most confusing Halloween.

THE END

The Happy Prince

"The Happy Prince" is a well-known story by Oscar Wilde.

This play was *adapted* from Wilde's story. What does the word *adapted* mean? (Use your dictionary to find the meaning.)

Read the entire play to yourself.

What is the message that this play tries to bring to people? Was the prince happy? Why?

How did the swallow help the prince to achieve happiness? How did the swallow prove her love for the prince?

What was lacking in the professor and the councillor? Do you feel this same lack in the vendor and the girls? Why?

Choose parts.

Practice your own part until you read every line smoothly. Ask the other children for help on words you do not know.

Read the entire play together.

Remember:

1. Read so well that you sound as if you were talking.
2. Stay alert—be ready to come in with your part.
3. Speak clearly and distinctly.
4. Watch all marks of punctuation.

THE HAPPY PRINCE

by Oscar Wilde
adapted by Virginia Bartholome

Characters

(7 boys, 7 girls, and the narrator)

NARRATOR

THE HAPPY PRINCE, *a prince whose happiness comes from helping others*

SWALLOW, *the prince's faithful messenger*

TOWN COUNCILLOR, *a man concerned only with the superficial*

PROFESSOR

MOTHER, *a flustered, overindulgent, young mother*

ALBERT, *a spoiled, young child*

TWO GIRLS, *young schoolgirls*

SEAMSTRESS, *a poor woman working to make a living*

LITTLE BOY, *the son of the seamstress*

MAID-OF-HONOR, *a vain young woman*

POET, *a sad man, clutching at an unfulfilled dream*

MATCH GIRL, *a poor little girl*

FRUIT VENDOR, *a kind and generous man*

NARRATOR: This play takes place on an evening early in autumn in a small park in a European town. In the center of the park is a statue of the Happy Prince standing on a pedestal. As the play begins, the Town Councillor stands looking at the statue of the Prince. The Fruit Vendor is at his cart, the Professor is seated on a bench, and the Swallow is hidden behind a bush. The Councillor speaks to the Professor.

COUNCILLOR: Yes, indeed, it was a very wise suggestion I made to the town council, Professor.

PROFESSOR: A very wise suggestion, Councillor.

COUNCILLOR: To put the statue of the Happy Prince here where the poor can enjoy the sight of something cultural, Professor.

PROFESSOR: Yes, the sight of something cultural, Councillor.

COUNCILLOR: He is as beautiful as a weathercock, only not quite so useful.

PROFESSOR: Not quite so useful.

NARRATOR: A mother and her young son come walking along and we hear little Albert scream, as only a young child can.

ALBERT: I want a sucker! I want a red sucker! Mommy!

MOTHER: But you cannot have any more sweets today, little one. Be still.

ALBERT: I want a sucker!

NARRATOR: He screams again while trying to run away. Suddenly he stops. He sees the balloons on the Vendor's cart.

ALBERT: No, I want a balloon, the biggest red balloon!

MOTHER: It's always something new that you want. Why can't you be like the Happy Prince? He never dreams of crying for anything.

ALBERT: But I want a balloon!

MOTHER: Wouldn't you rather have an orange? You'll get so much more good out of it. Here—let me pay the Vendor for an orange.

VENDOR: They are very good oranges. Wouldn't you like to buy more than just one?

MOTHER: No, I just want one for my little boy. Here, little one, is a delicious orange.

ALBERT: I want a balloon! I hate oranges. And I hate that old statue. There!

NARRATOR: Albert throws the orange at the Happy Prince, but misses.

VENDOR: Why is it that you don't want your son to have a balloon? I will gladly give him one. Here is the biggest and the reddest.

ALBERT: Hurrah!

NARRATOR: Albert grabs the balloon and runs off, with his mother frantically running after him. Two girls stroll into the park as the Councillor speaks to the Vendor.

COUNCILLOR: Why did you give away the balloon? You obviously don't make much money, and you know you could have sold the balloon to his mother in a few minutes. She would have had to buy it to keep him quiet.

VENDOR: Because it was a beautiful balloon. Let's say it was because I believe we should learn while we are young not to put a price on beauty. And now I think I shall take my wares home for the day.

GIRLS (*Speak together*): Hello, Mr. Vendor. Are you going home now?

VENDOR: Yes, girls. Would you like to take my balloons?

FIRST GIRL: Yes, yes, thank you. We just came to the park to see the statue of the Happy Prince. Isn't he beautiful?

VENDOR: He is very beautiful. Good evening.

GIRLS: Goodbye.

NARRATOR: As the Vendor leaves, pushing his cart, both girls wave and run up to the statue.

SECOND GIRL: He looks just like an angel!

PROFESSOR: How do you know? You have never seen an angel.

FIRST GIRL: We have in our dreams.

PROFESSOR: I do not approve of little children dreaming. It would be far better if you forgot all such nonsense as angels.

SECOND GIRL (*Laughing*): No, no, he looks just like an angel.

NARRATOR: The two girls run out, laughing. The Councillor shakes his head, puzzled.

COUNCILLOR: Professor, you're a funny fellow. First you sit here in the park as if you enjoyed being here, then you agree with me that it was a wise suggestion to erect the statue, then you scold the little girls who have come to look at the Happy Prince.

PROFESSOR: You are in error in the first instance, Councillor. I do not enjoy being here. I do not enjoy anything. Just as the fruit vendor regards it as his duty to foster a love of the beautiful in young children, I regard it my duty to teach them to beware of love. Love will betray them.

COUNCILLOR: That is nonsense. Why, this very evening I have an engagement with a beautiful girl whom I have grown to love. Would you teach me not to love?

PROFESSOR: You are too old. The damage has been done.

COUNCILLOR: I must say I believe you are mistaken. I'm sorry I don't have time to continue our conversation further, but I must hurry on now. Goodbye. Perhaps we shall meet here again someday.

PROFESSOR: Goodbye. I, too, must leave.

NARRATOR: As the Councillor and Professor leave, the Swallow steps out from behind the bush and speaks to the statue.

SWALLOW: The little girls were right, you know. You look just like an angel, tall and majestic and beautiful. Oh, I should have gone away to Egypt six weeks ago with my friends, but I so love you. Do you know that I find you fascinating, my Prince?

PRINCE: It seems I have heard you say those words before, Swallow.

NARRATOR: While the Swallow and Prince talk, the light of day fades away and darkness falls.

SWALLOW: I remember the first day I saw you, my Happy Prince. It was early in the spring as I was flying over the treetops after a big yellow moth when I saw your golden shoulders and your beautiful eyes glinting and sparkling and dancing in the sunlight. I can see myself in your eyes. Do you know that, my Prince?

PRINCE: Yes, my Swallow, I know why it is you look into my eyes.

SWALLOW: And that day, I flew down to look at you and I flew round and round you and I said, "Shall I love you, most beautiful Prince in the world?"

PRINCE: Yes, I remember that day.

NARRATOR: Suddenly the Swallow becomes annoyed and speaks sharply to the Prince.

SWALLOW: Oh, but I am beginning to tire of you. You have no conversation. You have no pretty phrases. You never tell me what a slender waist I have or how graceful my flight is. I do not believe you love me.

PRINCE: I do love you, little Swallow. But in a different way than you love. We are so different, little Swallow. My feet are fastened to this pedestal. My roots go deep down, through the hard stone and into the ground. But you, little Swallow, you love to travel.

SWALLOW: Will you come away with me?

PRINCE: I cannot. I belong to my people in this city.

SWALLOW: You have been trifling with me. I will go to the pyramids and I will not wait any longer. Goodbye.

NARRATOR: The Swallow starts to go away but she slowly returns.

SWALLOW: But, oh, it is getting dark now and I do not have anywhere else to stay. I will stay here at your feet for this last night.

NARRATOR: She lies down and sleeps. The Prince speaks, but as he does he begins to cry.

PRINCE: Good night, little Swallow. Oh, I am much too unhappy to be called the Happy Prince.

NARRATOR: Starting suddenly, the Swallow looks up at the sky and wipes a drop off her cheek.

SWALLOW: What a curious thing! There is not a single cloud in the sky, the stars are quite clear and bright, and yet it is raining. This climate is really quite dreadful. What is the use of a statue if it cannot keep the rain off?

NARRATOR: In sudden alarm, the Swallow stands and looks up at the Prince.

SWALLOW: But you, my Prince, why are you weeping? You have quite drenched me.

PRINCE: When I was alive and had a human heart, I did not know what tears were, for I lived in the Palace of Sans-Souci, where sorrow is not allowed to enter. In the daytime I played with my companions in the garden, and in the evening I led the dance in the Great Hall. Round the garden ran a very lofty wall, but I never cared to ask what lay beyond it, for everything around me was so beautiful. My courtiers called me the Happy Prince, and happy indeed I was, if pleasure be happiness. So I lived and so I died.

SWALLOW: It all sounds perfectly lovely to me. I still do not understand why you weep. Is it because I am leaving that you weep?

PRINCE: No, no, little Swallow. You see, now that I am dead they have set me up here so high that I can see all the ugliness and misery of my city, and though my heart is made of lead, I cannot choose but weep.

SWALLOW: What do you mean, ugliness and misery? I have flown over this city many times and I never see anything ugly. I see my reflection in the sparkling clear lakes in the park and in the beautiful blue of your eyes.

PRINCE: Oh, little Swallow, let me explain. Watch with me tonight and listen to the voices of my people. Look over there on that little street.

NARRATOR: They look into the home of a poor seamstress. She is bent over her sewing. Her boy lies near her.

BOY: Mother, why must you sew late at night?

SEAMSTRESS: My child, I am embroidering passionflowers on a satin gown for the loveliest of the queen's maids-of-honor to wear at the next court ball.

BOY: My mother, I wish you would stop sewing and embroidering and come and sit by my bed and bring me something wonderful and cool to put on my forehead. There is a fire inside my head, Mother, and in my hands.

SEAMSTRESS: Little one, I have nothing but river water to give you and that would only make you worse.

BOY: I wish I had an orange, Mother. I would love to have an orange. Please stop sewing and get me an orange.

SEAMSTRESS: But you see, little one, I cannot stop sewing or I will never have enough money to pay for the orange.

PRINCE: Do you see why I weep? Oh, Swallow, Swallow,

little Swallow, will you not bring her the ruby out of my sword hilt? My feet are fastened to this pedestal and I cannot move.

SWALLOW: I thought that perhaps you were weeping because I was leaving and could no longer do your bidding. It serves you right. I cannot stay.

PRINCE: Oh, please, Swallow.

SWALLOW: I am waited for in Egypt. My friends are flying up and down the Nile and talking to the large lotus flowers. Soon they will go to sleep in the tomb of the great king.

PRINCE: Swallow, little Swallow, will you not stay with me and be my messenger? The boy is so thirsty, and the mother so sad. Oh, dearest Swallow, if you ever really loved me, do this one thing for me.

SWALLOW: Autumn nights are very cold here, but I will stay with you one night, and be your messenger.

PRINCE: Thank you, little Swallow. Here, take this ruby from my sword and bring it to the poor seamstress and her little boy.

NARRATOR: The Swallow takes the ruby and prepares to go to the home of the sick boy.

SWALLOW: And I shall bring something of my own. You are very generous, my Prince, but rubies do not quench thirst. It takes a woman to care for a little child, really. I shall bring the orange that wretched little boy threw at you this evening if I can only find it. Ah, here it is.

NARRATOR: The Swallow flies off carrying the orange and the ruby. As she leaves, the Maid-of-Honor and the Councillor come toward the statue.

COUNCILLOR: How wonderful the stars are, and how wonderful is the power of love.

MAID-OF-HONOR: I hope my dress will be ready in time for the court ball. I have ordered passionflowers to be embroidered on it, but the seamstresses are so lazy.

COUNCILLOR: I am sure you will be radiantly beautiful. But look—here is the statue I was telling you about. I suggested that it be placed here among the poor so they would have something beautiful to enjoy. That was a wise suggestion, was it not?

MAID-OF-HONOR: Really, I believe it was rather stupid of you to waste the town's money on the people who do not really know how to enjoy it. But, of course, I suppose you must make the attempt. I don't care for this neighborhood at all. Shall we walk back to my coach?

COUNCILLOR: Yes, I suppose that would be a wise suggestion.

NARRATOR: The Swallow has flown to the Seamstress' home. There she sees the tired woman's head dropped down over her work. The boy is tossing feverishly. The Swallow puts the ruby on the Seamstress' lap, then gently fans the boy and places the orange in his hand.

BOY (*Half-asleep*): How cool I feel. I must be getting better.

NARRATOR: With a deep contented sigh, the boy turns over and goes to sleep, still clutching the orange. The Swallow flies back to the Prince.

SWALLOW: It is curious, but I feel quite warm now, although it is cold.

PRINCE: That is because you have done a good deed.

SWALLOW: I must think about that. But, oh, I am so sleepy. Thinking always makes me sleepy.

PRINCE: Good night again, then, little Swallow.

SWALLOW: Tomorrow I go to Egypt. I'm much too excited to go to sleep. Perhaps I shall start my trip tonight! Have you any commissions for Egypt, my Happy Prince?

PRINCE: No, my commissions are all here. Will you not stay here a little longer?

SWALLOW: I am waited for in Egypt. Tomorrow my friends will fly up to the Second Cataract. The river-horse is there among the bulrushes. At noon the yellow lions come down to the water's edge to drink. They have eyes like green beryls and their roar is louder than the roar of the cataract.

PRINCE: Oh, Swallow, Swallow, little Swallow, I see why it is that you long so to leave, but first I beg you to look in the window of that garret over there. Look at that young man with his large and dreamy eyes.

SWALLOW: I will admit that he is rather good looking.

PRINCE: But, listen, listen to what it is he is saying.

POET: Ah, withered violets, as your scent fades when it is cut off from its source of life, so do my talent and my ambition fade when hunger smothers all my desire to write. Oh, for a crust, a moldy crust of bread and a stick of wood to give me the strength and the warmth to continue my work!

SWALLOW: Yes, I see that he is in need of your help just as much as the seamstress and her child. I will wait with you a little longer.

PRINCE: Ah, little Swallow, you truly have a good heart.

SWALLOW: Shall I take him a ruby?

PRINCE: Alas! I have no ruby now. My eyes are all that I have left. They are made of rare sapphires, which were brought out of India a thousand years ago. Pluck out one of them and take it to him. He will sell it to the jeweler, and buy food and firewood, and finish his poem.

SWALLOW: Dear Prince, I cannot do that.

PRINCE: Swallow, Swallow, little Swallow, do as I command you.

SWALLOW: I will, my Prince.

NARRATOR: Taking the eye, the Swallow flies over to the Poet who does not hear her as she places the sapphire on the violets, and leaves. The Poet suddenly looks at the flowers.

POET: Ah, this is from some great admirer. I am beginning to be appreciated. Now I can finish my poem!

SWALLOW: I am come to bid you goodbye forever now, my Prince.

PRINCE: Swallow, Swallow, little Swallow, will you not stay with me a few hours longer?

SWALLOW: It is almost winter and the chill snow will soon be here. In Egypt the sun is warm on the green palm trees, and the crocodiles lie in the mud and look lazily about them. My companions are building a nest in the Temple of Baalbec, and the pink and white doves are watching them, and cooing to each other. Dear Prince, I must leave you, but I will never forget you, and next spring I will bring you back two beautiful jewels in place of those you have given away. The ruby shall be redder than a red rose, and the sapphire shall be as blue as the great sea.

PRINCE: But look, look, down into the square; there stands a little match girl. She has no shoes or stockings, and her little head is bare. Listen to her crying.

NARRATOR: The little Match Girl drops her carton of matches into the street. She is frightened and starts to talk to herself.

MATCH GIRL: Oh, all of my matches have fallen into the gutter and they are spoiled! My father will beat me if I do not bring home some money.

PRINCE: Listen, Swallow, pluck out my other eye, and give it to her, and her father will not beat her.

SWALLOW: I will stay with you, my Prince, but I cannot pluck out your eye. You would be quite blind then.

PRINCE: Swallow, Swallow, do as I command you.

SWALLOW: I cannot. Your generosity has become unreasonable. You no longer think of yourself.

PRINCE: Swallow, Swallow, if you ever loved me, do as I command you.

SWALLOW: I will, my Prince.

NARRATOR: Reluctantly the Swallow takes the other eye. She goes to the square and slips the jewel into the little Match Girl's hand.

MATCH GIRL: What is this? A lovely bit of glass! I must run home immediately and show it to all of them. Perhaps they will forget about my spoiled matches.

SWALLOW: You are blind now, my Prince.

PRINCE: Not really. I feel that I see more clearly now.

SWALLOW: I will stay with you always.

PRINCE: No, little Swallow, you must go away to Egypt, for each night is colder than the last here.

SWALLOW: I will stay with you always. Now I will be your

eyes. And I will tell you stories of what I have seen in the strange lands where you have never travelled. I will tell you of the red ibises, who stand in long rows on the banks of the Nile, and catch goldfish in their beaks; of the Sphinx, who is as old as the world itself, and knows everything. I will tell you of the merchants, who walk slowly by the sides of their camels, and carry amber beads in their hands. I will tell you of the pygmies who sail over a big lake on large flat leaves, and are always at war with the butterflies.

PRINCE: Dear little Swallow, you tell me of marvelous things, but more of a marvel than anything is the suffering of men and women. There is no mystery so great as misery. Be my eyes now, little Swallow, and look at the people of my city. Climb up high next to me and tell me what you see.

SWALLOW: Oh, my Prince, I see the rich making merry in their beautiful houses, while the beggars sit at the gates. I see the white faces of starving children looking out listlessly at the black streets. Oh, it is so very sad, my Prince.

PRINCE: Now, my little Swallow, you must take off my cloak and give it to the poorest of the poor that you see.

SWALLOW: But, Prince, you will be cold without your cloak.

PRINCE: No, little Swallow, my splendid gold cloak is only an ornament. I am dead and do not feel the cold. Take my cloak.

SWALLOW: Yes, I will.

NARRATOR: The Swallow takes the cloak. She returns without it, rubbing her wings together to keep warm.

SWALLOW: This time I must say goodbye forever, my Prince. Will you let me kiss your hand?

PRINCE: I am glad that you are going to Egypt at last, little Swallow. You have stayed too long here; but you must kiss me on the lips, for I love you.

SWALLOW: It is not to Egypt that I am going. I am going to the House of Death, my Prince. Death is the brother of Sleep, is he not?

NARRATOR: The Swallow kisses the Prince and falls dead at his feet.

PRINCE: Ah, my little Swallow, you have learned to love me well. But now day is coming, and the townspeople come once again to marvel at my beauty that is no more for their eyes.

NARRATOR: The people of the town enter and cluster around the statue.

COUNCILLOR: Dear me! How shabby the Happy Prince looks in the broad light of day.

PROFESSOR: How shabby, indeed!

COUNCILLOR: The ruby has fallen out of his sword, his eyes are gone, as well as his golden cloak. In fact, he is little better than a beggar.

PROFESSOR: Little better than a beggar.

FIRST GIRL: And look! Here at his feet is a dead bird, poor thing, caught in the cold.

COUNCILLOR: There actually is a dead bird at his feet. We must really issue a proclamation that birds are not to be allowed to die here.

MOTHER: This statue is definitely no longer a subject of pride for our city. We can no longer hold him up as a symbol of real happiness. Let us pull the statue down.

PROFESSOR: But, of course, you are correct. As he is no longer beautiful, he is no longer useful.

COUNCILLOR: And we must see that the proper department takes charge of the removal of the dead bird.

SECOND GIRL: Let us take care of the poor dead swallow. For we have known her to fly often over our city and to have been a companion to our Happy Prince.

PROFESSOR: That is all nonsense. One bird is much the same as another. Children must get rid of such sentimental notions.

COUNCILLOR: Oh, it will be all right for this time. And besides, they will do it right now, and it would take some time for the proper department to take care of the matter.

NARRATOR: Everyone goes away leaving only the two girls with the Prince and the dead Swallow.

FIRST GIRL: Ah, poor Swallow, her heart stopped beating. It was far too cold for her in this city. Why is it that she stayed so long into the winter?

THE END

Bobby and the Lincoln Speech

This play is about boys and girls just like you. It takes place in the month of February, just before Lincoln's Birthday. Read the play to yourself and find the answers to these questions.

1. What was Mother concerned about?
2. What were two of the incidents that had made Mr. Carter unpopular?
3. In what way did Bobby behave like Lincoln?
4. How did Bobby memorize the Gettysburg Address?

All the boys should practice these lines from the Gettysburg Address. Be sure to say them rapidly, as you would if you were eager to say them and run.

"Fourscore and seven years ago our fathers brought forth on this continent a new nation, conceived in liberty. . . ."

"And that government of the people, by the people, for the people, shall not perish from the earth."

Now try these lines again. Say them slowly and distinctly and with a great deal of meaning. Let different boys try.

Have the girls practice some of Mother's part.

Make your voice sound *worried:*

"Oh, dear me! You think you'll reach them all right, don't you, Mary?"

Make your voice sound *nervous* and *hurried:*

"I should think so! You're making me nervous, too. I wish the girls would hurry and get home."

Make your voice sound *mysterious:*

"He was home—and—and there's something I haven't told

anyone because it was *so weird.* I listened through the door and *somewhere in that house* was a slow thud—thud—thud."

Decide who should be Mother and who should be Bobby. Talk it over and decide on all the other parts.

Read your part over to yourself. Be sure you know every word and understand what you have to say.

Practice reading the entire play.

Check yourself on these things:

1. Did you sound like a real person talking to other people?
2. Did you come in on time with your part?
3. Did you speak in a voice that could be heard?
4. Did you use your voice to show excitement, mystery, fear, etc.?

Go back and practice the parts that did not go smoothly.

Read the entire play again if you need to.

Arrange to read the play to your class.

BOBBY AND THE LINCOLN SPEECH

by Edrie Pendleton

Characters

(3 boys, 3 girls, and the narrator)

NARRATOR

MOTHER, *Alice Brown*

FATHER, *Fred Brown*

BOBBY BROWN, *a ten-year-old boy*

MARY BROWN, *Bobby's eleven-year-old sister*

LUCILLE BROWN, *another sister, thirteen years old*

MR. CARTER, *a neighbor*

NARRATOR: This play opens in the Browns' living room in the late afternoon, a few days before Lincoln's Birthday. Mother is sitting in an armchair, while Bobby rehearses the Gettysburg Address. Bobby is wearing a high stovepipe hat, long black frock coat and blue jeans. He recites the Address much too rapidly.

BOBBY: "And that government of the people, by the people, for the people, shall not perish from the earth." (*He stops.*) There. See, Mom, I guess I know it all right.

MOTHER: Yes, Bobby, you seem to know the words. But can't you speak with a little more feeling, the way Mr. Lincoln would do it?

BOBBY: But Mom—

MOTHER: And Mr. Lincoln was a dignified man. Try to stand a little straighter. You look as though you're going to jump.

BOBBY: Oh, Mom, it's these blue jeans. They're baggy at the knees. I'll look all right when I put on the pants to the costume.

MOTHER: Yes, I suppose that will make a difference. But now you'd better try it once more.

BOBBY: O.K. (*He sighs.*) "Fourscore and seven years ago our fathers brought forth on this continent a new nation, conceived in liberty. . . ."

MOTHER: Now, what's the matter? You haven't forgotten it, have you?

BOBBY: Of course not, but listen, Mom. The gang's playing baseball on the vacant lot.

MOTHER: Baseball? In the middle of winter?

BOBBY: It's the first good day we've had. And gee, Mom, I ought to get out and practice. The baseball season will be here soon.

MOTHER: This is February, Bobby. The baseball season is a long way off. The program is tonight.

BOBBY: Oh, Mom.

MOTHER: Now, just try it once more. And this time, with feeling.

BOBBY (*Rapidly*): "Fourscore and seven years ago our fathers brought forth. . . ."

MOTHER: No, no, Bobby. Not so fast.

BOBBY: But Mom, I'm in a hurry.

FATHER: Hello, Alice. What are you disguised as, Bobby?

MOTHER (*Surprised*): Why, Fred, you're home early. Is anything wrong?

FATHER: Not a thing. We weren't very busy so I thought I'd come home and just relax. Any objections?

MOTHER (*Laughing*): Of course not. In fact, it's wonderful. You'll be all rested up for the program tonight.

FATHER: What's that? What program?

MOTHER: You know very well. The Lincoln program at school. All the children are taking part. Mary is going to sing a folk song and Lucille is in charge of the seating. She's the head usher.

BOBBY: And gosh, Dad, why do you suppose I'm rehearsing the Gettysburg Address?

FATHER: Are you?

BOBBY: Well, I was. But Mom, now that Dad's home and wants to rest, I guess we don't want to disturb him, do we?

MOTHER: That's very thoughtful of you, Bobby, but you're not going to get out of it that easily. Now, try it just once more.

FATHER: Alice, if we hear it so many times now, we won't enjoy it tonight.

MOTHER: Now, Fred. You can listen to Bobby just once. All right, Bobby, begin again, and this time speak with some feeling, please.

BOBBY (*Making an effort. Almost shouting*): "Fourscore and seven years ago. . . ."

MOTHER: No, no, not so loud, Bobby.

FATHER: Does he have to do it now, Alice? Haven't I heard somewhere that performers can overdo their rehearsing? They're inclined to get nervous if they practice too much.

BOBBY: Gee, Mom, Dad's right. That's exactly what the teacher said. She said not to worry about the speech on the day of the program, not to think about it until tonight. She said just forget it.

MOTHER: Forget it, indeed! That's just what I'm afraid of, that you'll forget the whole thing. But as long as your father has sided with you, I give up. Go on out and play ball.

BOBBY: Boy! Thanks, Mom. Gee, I sure wish I had my new baseball glove. That reminds me, Dad. I hauled all that junk out of the basement. You owe me thirty-five cents.

FATHER: Do I? Well, here you are. Don't lose it.

BOBBY: Don't worry. I'm going to put it right in my bank before I go out.

FATHER (*Laughing*): That bank of yours ought to be getting pretty heavy.

BOBBY: It is. This makes almost three dollars I have in the bank —but my glove will cost five. Well, I'm going out. See you later.

MOTHER: Bobby, wait. Tell the boys not to make too much noise. It disturbs Mr. Carter.

BOBBY (*Disgustedly*): Gee, Mom, you tell me that every time I go out. I wish he'd never moved next door.

MOTHER: Well, he did, and we've had trouble ever since. I don't know what he does all alone in that house but apparently he doesn't like noise. So be careful.

BOBBY: O.K.

MOTHER: And maybe you can say the Lincoln speech over while you play.

BOBBY: Oh, Mom, I know that backwards and forwards. (*Quickly*) "Fourscore and seven years ago our fathers brought forth on this continent a new nation. . . ."

NARRATOR: Father shakes his head thoughtfully as Bobby quickly leaves the room.

FATHER: The boy sounds as though he's selling papers. Alice, will you please tell me why they picked Bobby to recite the Gettysburg Address?

MOTHER: Well, that's a fine thing to say. I should think you'd be proud that your son was chosen to be Abraham Lincoln.

FATHER: I suppose I am. But I still think they must choose them by picking numbers from a hat.

MOTHER: No, they wanted a fifth-grade boy for the Gettysburg Address and Bobby has a good memory. I wish you'd stop fussing about the program, Fred. You were the same way about the Christmas program.

FATHER: Now, Alice—

MOTHER: Yes, you fussed and fussed, but when it was over you were as proud as anything. You went around telling everyone that your daughter Mary was the Christmas angel.

FATHER: Alice, that was different. Besides, that's not the point. The Gettysburg Address is one of the great speeches in the history of our country. But Bobby doesn't seem to have any idea of what it means. Nor does he have any idea of the true greatness of Abraham Lincoln. He doesn't understand the qualities of the man.

MOTHER: Oh, for goodness' sake, Fred, he's young. He's only a little boy.

FATHER: Then why give him the speech? I wonder sometimes about these programs—mere children playing our great men.

MOTHER: That's the whole idea of the programs, Fred. The children learn about our great men. They grow interested.

FATHER: Bobby doesn't seem very interested. All he's interested in as far as I can see is baseball. Why don't they let him play Babe Ruth?

MOTHER: Fred, we're celebrating Lincoln's Birthday, not Babe Ruth's. And will you please stop pacing about and waving your hands? Why don't you sit down? Read your paper. I thought you wanted to relax.

FATHER (*With a sigh*): Very well, Alice. I'll try again.

MOTHER: I should think so. You're making me nervous, too. There's a lot to do before the program. I wish the girls would hurry and get home. We'll have to have an early supper.

FATHER: Why on earth?

MOTHER: The program, of course. The children have to be at school by seven. You'll have to drive them over and then come back for me.

NARRATOR: Boys' voices are heard outside, shouting: "Bobby, Bobby, slide!" "Get him at second." "Safe, safe!" "No, he's out!"

MOTHER: Oh, dear me, listen to those boys shouting. Fred, you have to do something.

FATHER: Alice, I thought you said I was to relax. And besides, what can I do? Go out and gag the boys? Or shall I tell them to tiptoe round the bases and whisper to each other as they play?

MOTHER: Fred, it's not funny. We don't want any trouble with Mr. Carter today. There's enough to worry about with the program. Oh, I'd give anything if we had our old neighbors back. I wish that man had never moved next door.

FATHER: Well, Alice, we can't very well tell him to move away.

MOTHER: Something has to be done. I worry all the time. It's impossible to keep children quiet. All the mothers in the neighborhood are upset about Mr. Carter.

FATHER: Has there been any more trouble, Alice? Maybe you've all been exaggerating this whole thing.

MOTHER: Exaggerating? When he shouted at the boys—

FATHER: I thought he told them just once to be quiet.

MOTHER: He shouted at them to stop making such noise. But that isn't all, Fred. He seems so unfriendly.

MARY: Hi, Mom and Dad. I'll bet you're talking about Mr. Carter. I just saw him.

MOTHER: You did, Mary? Where?

MARY: Glaring out his side window at the boys playing ball.

MOTHER: Oh dear, I just don't know what to do. It's because they are making noise.

MARY: Gee, what's a little noise? The only time we ever see Mr. Carter, he's staring out of that window and he's always frowning. Why does he have to look so cross all the time?

MOTHER: I don't know, dear. He's a strange man.

FATHER: Now, Alice—

MOTHER: No, Fred. I told you I went to call on him last Tuesday, and he wouldn't answer the door.

FATHER: But maybe he wasn't home.

MOTHER: He was home—and—and there's something I haven't told anyone because it was so weird. I listened through the door and somewhere in that house was a slow thud—thud—thud.

FATHER: Hmmm, a slow thud—thud—thud. I'll admit it's strange, but there's no reason for jumping to conclusions.

MOTHER: Perhaps not, but I don't like the looks of it. I tell you, there's something very mysterious about that Mr. Carter.

MARY: That's what the kids are saying, Mom. Susie Remple says maybe he's a gangster.

FATHER: Mary, you and your mother have been listening to too many soap operas.

MARY: Some soap operas are true-to-life, Dad. And suppose this is true? Perhaps we have a gangster living right next door to us! It gives me the shivers just thinking about it. And I'm nervous enough already—about my song tonight.

FATHER: What kind of song are you singing, Mary?

MARY: An old folk song, Dad, of the Lincoln period. It has lots of high notes.

MOTHER: Oh, dear me. You think you'll reach them all right, don't you, Mary?

MARY: I don't know, Mom. Sometimes I do—but then again if I'm nervous, sometimes I don't.

MOTHER: Well, dear, we just mustn't be nervous. Let's stop thinking about Mr. Carter. After all, he has no connection with the program. We'll just relax.

FATHER: Alice, you've been saying that ever since I got home.

MOTHER: Well, this time I mean it. Mary, why isn't Lucille home?

MARY: The ushers had a meeting, Mom.

MOTHER: Oh. Well, I guess she'll be here soon and she can

help me with the supper. Fred, you can read your paper. Mary, you'd better call to your brother. It's time he came in to get cleaned up and that will settle the noise business.

MARY: O.K., Mom.

NARRATOR: Lucille enters, full of excitement.

LUCILLE: Hello, everybody. Have I got news!

FATHER: Well, it's the head usher herself. I understand we're going to get the best seats in the house tonight.

LUCILLE (*Laughing*): I should say not. No favoritism. But listen, guess who is going to be the guest of honor at the program?

MARY: Guest of honor? I haven't heard anything about a guest of honor.

LUCILLE: I know you haven't. Nobody knows except our committee. Miss Davis, the librarian, told us this afternoon. I have to escort him to the platform. And oh, you'd never guess!

FATHER: Lucille, this suspense is killing me. Surely I haven't been chosen?

LUCILLE (*Laughing*): No, Dad, but you're close. It's your next-door neighbor.

MARY: Neighbor?

MOTHER: Lucille, you don't—you can't mean Mr. Carter?

LUCILLE: Yes, isn't it fantastic?

MOTHER: But why should he be guest of honor?

LUCILLE: Because he went to the library last night to use some reference books and Miss Davis found out all about him.

MOTHER: Indeed?

FATHER: Did she find out what kind of bombs he is making in his spare time?

LUCILLE: Don't be silly, Dad. Mr. Carter is a writer. And what's more, he's writing a book about Lincoln. I guess he's written others, too. So Miss Davis asked him to be guest of honor and he's going to speak after the rest of us are all through.

MARY: My goodness. I'll be scared stiff. I won't be able to sing a note with him glaring at me.

MOTHER: Now, Mary, you mustn't be nervous. Maybe we've misjudged the man.

LUCILLE: Sure. Miss Davis seemed to think he was nice. And I guess he's quite well-known. Miss Davis says he's a Lincoln scholar and he came here to live because he wanted a quiet place to do his writing.

MOTHER: A quiet place. Why, the poor man! No wonder the boys' shouting has annoyed him.

MARY: But I still don't see why he has to act so grouchy.

FATHER: Mary is right, Alice. Just because he's a writer is no reason why he can't be neighborly. And what about the thud—thud—thuds?

MOTHER: Yes, I'd forgotten that for the minute.

LUCILLE: What thud—thuds?

MOTHER: I heard strange sounds the day I went over there. Maybe he just made that up about being a writer.

LUCILLE: But why would he go to the library?

FATHER: Obviously to look up information about atom bombs.

MOTHER: Fred, I wish you wouldn't joke about it. It's not funny.

NARRATOR: Again, the shouting outside is heard. "Lean on one, Bobby." "He can't hit it." "Home run, Bobby. He can't pitch!"

MOTHER: Oh, there they are shouting again! Mary, go tell Bobby to come home right away.

MARY: With all this excitement I'd forgotten all about him. Wait till Bobby hears he's going to have to recite the Gettysburg Address in front of Mr. Carter.

MOTHER: Oh dear, we'll have to go over it again to make sure he's letter perfect.

NARRATOR: The sound of the bat is heard as it strikes the ball. Then come yells of: "Look out—the window, the window." The crash of splintering glass is heard. Then a voice yells, "Run, run, everybody!"

MOTHER (*Frantically*): Oh, oh, my goodness, they've broken a window!

MARY: Bobby must have done it. They were yelling for him to hit a home run. And it's Mr. Carter's window. I can see it from here. The top pane is smashed.

LUCILLE: Wouldn't you know it! And tonight I have to conduct Mr. Carter to his seat.

MOTHER: But where are the boys? I can't see any of them.

FATHER: My dear, do you expect them just to stand there and face the wrath of the terrible Mr. Carter? My guess is that they're at least a block away and moving fast.

MOTHER: But Fred, we'll have to do something. You'll have to go over and see Mr. Carter.

FATHER: *I'll* have to go over? Alice, I wasn't playing baseball. You know very well that I've been right here—relaxing.

NARRATOR: The slam of a door echoes throughout the house as Bobby rushes in and across the room.

FATHER: Bobby, Bobby, wait a minute.

BOBBY: I—I can't, Dad.

FATHER: Bobby, did you break that window?

BOBBY: Yeah, I—I hit a home run.

LUCILLE (*Laughing*): I'll say it was a home run. In more ways than one. Bobby, wait a minute. Come back here.

MARY: Poor Bobby.

MOTHER: But I don't like his running away and hiding like this.

FATHER: No, you're right, Alice. He'll have to face the music. And it might as well be now. I'll have to get him and take him over.

MOTHER: Yes, Fred. Oh dear, why did this have to happen on the day of the program?

NARRATOR: The doorbell rings once. Then, after a minute, it begins ringing again and again.

MARY: Gee, I bet that's Mr. Carter now, looking for Bobby.

MOTHER: Oh—oh dear. Fred, you can't leave now.

LUCILLE: No, Dad, don't leave us to face Mr. Carter.

FATHER: Very well. Answer the door, Lucille.

LUCILLE: Me? Why me?

FATHER: Well, you're going to have to escort him up the aisle tonight. You may as well get used to him.

LUCILLE: Oh, all right. But he—he sounds as though he's angry.

MARY: Oh, what'll I do? I'm getting more nervous all the time. I'll never be able to sing.

MOTHER: Please, Mary, not now.

NARRATOR: Mr. Carter enters followed by Lucille. He is a scholarly-looking man and seems very excited.

CARTER: Where is he? Where's the boy who broke my window?

FATHER: He'll be here in a moment, Mr. Carter. But there's no need to be quite so excited.

CARTER: But I can't help it. I want to see him. He ran in here.

FATHER: Yes, I know. He is our son, Bobby. And this is Mrs. Brown and our daughters, Lucille and Mary.

MOTHER, LUCILLE *and* MARY: How do you do?

CARTER: Oh, I—I should apologize for rushing in this way. I'm glad to know you all. But I was anxious to catch that boy and talk to him.

MOTHER: Mr. Carter, we realize that breaking the window was serious and Bobby shouldn't have run away, but he was frightened.

CARTER: Frightened? He didn't seem frightened. The rest of them were flying off in all directions but he came right up to the side of the house and shouted at me.

MOTHER: Oh, my goodness! Mr. Carter, he—he wasn't insulting, was he?

CARTER: Not at all. He just shouted, "It was my fault, Mr. Carter. I did it." Then off he ran.

FATHER: Well, then, so he admitted it.

CARTER: Yes, with no hesitation. That's why I was—well, rather excited. I didn't know boys were like that any more. You read so much about the younger generation being irresponsible.

MOTHER: Oh, you mustn't believe all those articles, Mr. Carter.

CARTER: I can see you're right. That Bobby has sterling qualities.

FATHER: I'm—I'm sure he has. Won't you sit down, Mr. Carter?

CARTER: Thank you. He's real, he's honest. Not unlike Abe Lincoln.

MOTHER: There, you hear that, Fred? Our Bobby is like Mr. Lincoln.

FATHER: What's that? Oh, Bobby, there you are.

BOBBY: Pop, I had to get my bank. Oh, Mr. Carter, you're here. I—I was coming right over to pay you for the window.

MOTHER: Why, Bobby, we thought you were hiding.

BOBBY: Gosh no, Mom, what do you think I am?

FATHER: Son, I'm proud of you. Mr. Carter, he's been saving that money for months to buy a baseball glove.

CARTER: See, what did I tell you? Like Lincoln again.

BOBBY: Gosh, you—you mean me?

CARTER: Certainly I mean you. When Lincoln's store went bankrupt, he didn't rest till he'd paid off every debt. But Bobby, I don't want the money you've been saving. I'd much rather see you get the baseball glove.

BOBBY: You—you would?

MOTHER: Bobby, that's no way to talk.

BOBBY: But Mom, everybody thought he was an old grouch. You said yourself that time he yelled at us to stop shouting—

FATHER: Bobby, that's enough.

CARTER: Well, now, I think I'm beginning to understand something.

MOTHER: Mr. Carter, please don't mind what he said.

CARTER: No, no, I admit to the charge of having shouted to the boys to quiet down. I'd been calling to them from the window but they were making such a racket they couldn't hear me. I wanted to tell them that I had some soft drinks on ice if they cared to come in and have some.

MOTHER: Well, of all things. Did you hear that, Bobby?

BOBBY: Gosh, and we just made more noise on purpose. But gee, Mr. Carter, how were we to know? You always seem to be frowning when you look out the window so we thought you were angry with us.

CARTER: No, I wasn't angry, Bobby. You see, I'm frowning right now and I'm not angry with anybody. Sometimes thinking hard about a problem makes a person frown. And if I get stuck for ideas while I'm writing, I often get up and pace about the room or look out the window.

MARY: Why, Mr. Carter, that's just what you were doing a little while ago when I walked past. I thought you were angry with the boys.

CARTER: No, I was just trying to get a little change from staring at my typewriter. Why, one day last week I even went down to the basement and chopped wood. I'd just written something about how Lincoln could chop through a four-inch log in eight strokes and I got to wondering if that was an interesting fact or not. So I decided to try it myself. I chopped through a piece of firewood I had in the basement. It took me over thirty strokes.

FATHER: And I take it you left the fact in.

CARTER: I certainly did.

MOTHER: Mr. Carter, was it last Tuesday that you were chopping wood?

CARTER: Why, I believe it was. But how did you know?

MOTHER: Well, Mr. Carter, I went to call on you. I knocked on the door and there was no answer. But I could hear a thudding noise. It must have been you chopping wood.

CARTER: Undoubtedly. And I'm so sorry I didn't hear you. I've wanted to get acquainted with my neighbors but somehow it doesn't seem easy for me to make the first move.

MOTHER: Why, Mr. Carter, I do believe you are shy.

CARTER (*Little laugh*): Yes, I—I imagine I am, and it seems to take something like a broken window to make me forget myself. When I think of how I came bursting in here—

FATHER: Now, don't you worry about that, Mr. Carter. We're all glad that you did.

BOBBY: Sure, Mr. Carter, if you hadn't, we'd never have found out that you were a swell guy.

CARTER: Thank you, Bobby. You see, your breaking the window was really a favor to me.

BOBBY: Well, maybe, but I've been thinking. Lincoln just didn't offer to pay his debts. He really paid them. So you better take my money. And—and if it's not enough I can pay the rest a little at a time.

CARTER: Hmmm, so you had saved up all this toward a baseball glove.

BOBBY: Sure, but that's all right. I owe it to you.

CARTER: My, you seem to have pennies of every date here.

BOBBY: Listen, Mr. Carter—I broke the window. So I ought to pay you.

CARTER: Well, now, what have we here? A Lincoln penny and the very one. Bobby, if you want to pay money for that window, I'll accept this Lincoln penny in full payment.

BOBBY: But Mr. Carter, that's only a penny.

CARTER: Yes, I know, but it's worth more than just a penny to me. You see, I've made a hobby of collecting Lincoln pennies for each year since they were first made. I'm missing a few and this happens to be one of them. I don't know what it's worth in dollars but it's as valuable as that window to me. Is it a deal?

BOBBY: Well, gee, of course, Mr. Carter, if you're sure I've honestly paid off my debt.

CARTER: As honestly as Honest Abe paid off his.

BOBBY: Whee-ee, I've paid for the window and still have money for my baseball glove.

CARTER: And don't forget, Bobby, the next time you're playing baseball, bring that gang of yours in to see me.

BOBBY: You—you mean the whole gang?

CARTER: Yes. I think getting to know more boys would help

me to make my description of Lincoln's boyhood more true-to-life.

BOBBY: But how could we help?

CARTER: Well, all boys are pretty much alike in some ways. For instance, when Lincoln was a boy he enjoyed sports. He liked to wrestle, you like to play ball. I hope I can make Lincoln seem more like one of us instead of like a statue in a park.

FATHER: I know just what you mean, Mr. Carter. I think we're often inclined to take our famous characters too seriously. I—I know I do that. We remember dates from history books and forget that in between those dates, they were pretty much like friends we know today. Not just figureheads.

BOBBY: Say, Mr. Carter, do you really write lots of books about Mr. Lincoln?

MARY: Does he write books! Why, he's an authority. He's going to be the guest of honor at the program tonight.

BOBBY: He is? Are you, Mr. Carter?

CARTER: Oh, dear me, yes. I'd almost forgotten about that. I'd better get home and try to figure out what I'm going to say. I get so nervous before one of these affairs that I sometimes can't even remember the year that Lincoln was born.

MOTHER: Well, Mr. Carter, to think of you being nervous, too. We've all been as nervous as can be.

MARY: Especially after we heard that you were going to be there, Mr. Carter. I have to sing.

LUCILLE: And I have to escort you to the seat of honor.

CARTER: Well, well, a charming escort. Perhaps we can buck each other up. I wouldn't get so nervous if it weren't for my memory. Invariably someone will ask me to recite the Gettysburg Address. Usually I start out "Fourscore and seven years ago—" and then I get stuck.

BOBBY (*Going right on*): "Our fathers brought forth on this continent a new nation. . . ." Gee, you don't have to worry about that, Mr. Carter. I'm going to say it.

CARTER: You are?

MOTHER: Yes—our Bobby was chosen.

CARTER: An excellent choice.

FATHER: I think I agree with you.

CARTER: Bobby, do you mind telling me—what's your secret? I mean, for memorizing the Gettysburg Address?

BOBBY: Well, gee, I—I don't know. My teacher said to try to think about the ideas, not just the words. To think about what it means.

CARTER: Ah, so that's it. Well! If only more of us would do that.

BOBBY: So I'm pretty sure I know it now. 'Course I still might forget.

MOTHER: Oh, Bobby—you don't think you will?

BOBBY: No, Mom, but even if I did forget some of the middle part, I could still finish up all right. I know I won't forget the end. And I guess that's the most important part of all— "And that government of the people, by the people, for the people, shall not perish from the earth."

THE END

Heidi Finds the Way

Heidi is a book that you have all read or heard about. This play is a very short version of the story. It does not cover all of the adventures you read in the book.

Read the play to yourself. As you read, try to understand the feelings of the different characters in the play. Decide how you would speak the different parts.

Look through Peter's part. See how many times he changes his voice. He must be cross, angry, belligerent, and moody.

Check the part of Alm Uncle. He must use the voice of an old man. Sometimes he is stern, sometimes cross, sometimes kind, but always *dignified* and *old*.

Look closely at the things Aunt Dete has to say. This part must be read to show that she is selfish and unkind.

Heidi is kind, cheerful, good-natured, eager for everyone to be happy. How would she speak?

Decide on the parts. Read your part to yourself. If you need help, ask for it. Remember to read smoothly and easily, as if you were talking.

Read the play together.

Check on these things:

1. Did you know every word in your part?
2. Did you read smoothly?
3. Did you come in right on time?
4. Did you use your voice well, changing pitch and tone?

If you can't all answer *yes* to these questions, practice again. Help each other until you feel the play is good enough to read for others.

HEIDI FINDS THE WAY

by Johanna Spyri
adapted by Karin Asbrand

Characters

(4 boys, 6 girls, and the narrator)

NARRATOR

HEIDI, *a happy good-natured girl who lives in the mountains
with her grandfather*

PETER, *a goatherd who lives near Heidi*

THE ALM UNCLE, *Heidi's grandfather*

BRIGIDA, *Peter's sister*

AUNT DETE, *Heidi's aunt who found it too much trouble to
keep Heidi in the city*

CLARA, *a rich little girl who is an invalid*

TWO GOATHERDS, *boys who work with Peter*

TWO CHILDREN, *friends of Heidi*

NARRATOR: It is a summer morning in a mountain pasture in
Switzerland. Several goatherds are standing around, idly talking together.

1ST GOATHERD (*Impatiently*): What are we waiting for all this
long time? Why don't we go along? The sun will soon be
high over the mountains.

2ND GOATHERD: Didn't you know? Peter has a new girl friend.

PETER (*Crossly*): Heidi is not my girl friend, any more than
she is yours. She wants to be everybody's friend.

1ST GOATHERD: Who wants a silly girl for a friend?

PETER: I do, for one. Anyway, her grandfather wants me to
wait for her, and to see that no harm comes to her.

2ND GOATHERD: Imagine having to sit around and wait for just a girl! If it were a dog or a goat or something, that would be better.

PETER (*Angrily*): Don't you call her just a girl. She's Heidi. Anyway, you don't have to wait. I'm waiting because I promised the Alm Uncle that I would take care of her. So go along, all of you.

2ND GOATHERD: That's the most sensible thing you've said yet. Let's go.

1ST GOATHERD: Let's go. I'm tired of sitting around waiting for a dumb city girl.

PETER (*Belligerently*): She isn't dumb. She can do as much as the girls around here. She can cook and sew and even milk the goats. Oh! Here comes Heidi now.

1ST GOATHERD: You'd think she was a princess, the way you kowtow to her, Peter.

PETER: I do not kowtow to her, but her father and mother are dead, and she was left here because her Aunt Dete didn't want her. Her grandfather didn't want her at first, either, but now he does. She is like a princess, and she has been very kind to poor old blind Granny.

NARRATOR: Heidi enters carrying a basket covered with a white cloth.

HEIDI (*Cheerfully*): Good morning, boys.

2ND GOATHERD: Good morning, she says. Good afternoon, you mean.

HEIDI: You didn't have to wait for me. I know my way up the mountainside now.

PETER: I had to wait. I promised the Alm Uncle. I'm glad we all waited. You are fun to be with, even though you are a girl.

1ST GOATHERD: We wouldn't want to see the Alm Uncle angry. He is so big and strong.

HEIDI: I'm glad you all waited, too. It's more fun going up the mountain when you have company. Let's go. The Alm Uncle has given me enough bread and cheese to feed a whole army, so I will share it with all of you.

NARRATOR: Just as they are about to leave, Heidi's Aunt Dete catches up to them. She is out of breath from hurrying.

AUNT DETE (*With a gasp*): So here you are, Heidi. I was afraid I would never find you without having to climb up and see the Alm Uncle.

HEIDI: Why, Aunt Dete, what brings you here after all these weeks?

AUNT DETE (*A little huffily*): You, of course. Who else? I've missed you, child. And that's a fine way to greet me when you haven't seen me for so long.

HEIDI: You said you never wanted to see me again. You didn't want me around, remember?

AUNT DETE: Now, Heidi. That was only because I couldn't afford to take care of you properly.

HEIDI: Have you come to stay with me and the Alm Uncle?

AUNT DETE (*Mimics her*): No, I have not come to stay with you and the Alm Uncle. The less I see of him, the happier I'll be. But I've found you a lovely place to stay, so I have come to take you away with me to Frankfort, to a beautiful fine house where you will have everything you want.

NARRATOR: While Aunt Dete is talking, the Alm Uncle comes up to the group, and listens quietly in the background.

HEIDI: I have everything I want now.

AUNT DETE: Nonsense. You have nothing. You will have beautiful clothes of satin and velvet, just like Clara, the little girl you will live with. She is sick and cannot walk. And you will have pretty bows for your hair.

PETER: Heidi has pretty flowers for her hair here. They are prettier than bows.

AUNT DETE: Who asked you? I'll thank you to keep your mouth shut until you're spoken to.

HEIDI: I don't want all those things.

AUNT DETE (*Angrily*): You are only a little girl, Heidi, but you are stubborn as a mule.

NARRATOR: The Alm Uncle, who has been listening to Aunt

Dete, becomes very upset. He steps forward and shakes his stick angrily.

THE ALM UNCLE (*Angrily*): Hah! I thought I smelled a rat. That is why I came to see if Heidi was all right. Take her away, did you say? You brought her here only a short while ago, and we are just getting used to each other.

AUNT DETE: You weren't very anxious to have her in the first place. You should be glad that I have come to relieve you of the burden.

THE ALM UNCLE: Who said Heidi was a burden? If I wanted to be relieved of her, I would let you know soon enough. Heidi is happy here with me. Aren't you, child?

HEIDI: Oh, yes, Grandfather.

THE ALM UNCLE: There, you see! And here she is going to stay.

AUNT DETE: Listen to the stubborn old goat. Now, you listen to me. There is a very rich family in Frankfort that is looking for a girl to be a companion to their sick daughter, Clara. Heidi is a little young, but they are willing to try her because Clara must be in a wheelchair all day.

HEIDI: Oh, Aunt Dete! The poor, poor thing!

THE ALM UNCLE: Don't let yourself be taken in by her tall tales, Heidi. Heidi is not going there, you understand?

AUNT DETE: They would make it worth her while. They are very rich.

THE ALM UNCLE: They'll make it worth your while, too, I'll warrant.

AUNT DETE: Naturally, I get paid for my services in finding them such a fine girl as Heidi.

THE ALM UNCLE: Get out of here, Dete. Heidi does not need money. She has everything she needs to keep her healthy and happy.

AUNT DETE: Heidi looks healthy enough, to be sure. You have done well by her, that I can see. But she can do better.

THE ALM UNCLE: Don't try your honey on this old bee, Dete. I don't know what you are up to, but none of it is good.

AUNT DETE: Wouldn't you like to have a lot of money?

HEIDI: No, I don't need money.

AUNT DETE: Everybody needs money, and you would just love Clara.

THE ALM UNCLE: I love Heidi, and Heidi loves me.

AUNT DETE: Much love you have for her, to deprive her of such a fine opportunity. You are out of your mind. There isn't a soul in Prattigan who wouldn't thank her lucky stars for such a chance.

THE ALM UNCLE (*Shouts*): Go find these souls then, and give them the chance. I will have none of it for Heidi. Do you hear?

AUNT DETE (*Angrily*): Of course I hear. I am not deaf. But let me tell you something. Heidi is eight years old, and they tell me you do not send her to school.

HEIDI: The Alm Uncle teaches me himself.

PETER: Heidi can read better than any of us. She reads every day to my blind old Granny.

AUNT DETE: Who asked you? And you do not send her to church, either.

THE ALM UNCLE: What need has she of church when she can meet God every day on the mountainside beneath the clear blue sky?

AUNT DETE: Such rubbish! She is the child of my only sister. I will not allow her to grow up into an ignoramus.

HEIDI: Please, Aunt Dete, leave Grandfather alone.

AUNT DETE: I will go to court. The law has a way of tracking down things one thinks are forgotten.

1ST GOATHERD: This is no place for us. Let's go.

2ND GOATHERD: You might know we'd run into trouble when we let a girl come along with us.

THE ALM UNCLE (*Shouts*): Yes, run along, all of you. Scoot!

AUNT DETE (*Persistently*): You would not wish me to go to court, would you?

THE ALM UNCLE (*Thunders at her*): Silence! Take the child! Ruin her! But never bring her back to me again.

NARRATOR: Heidi runs to her grandfather, crying. She throws her arms around him and pleads with him.

HEIDI: Please don't say that, Grandfather.

THE ALM UNCLE (*Ignoring* HEIDI): You heard me, Dete. If you take her away, I never want to set eyes on her again, or you, either. And never let her be seen with a feather in her hat such as you have, nor with such words on her tongue as you have spoken.

HEIDI (*Forlornly*): Now you have hurt his feelings, Aunt Dete.

NARRATOR: The Alm Uncle turns and stalks away from Heidi and Aunt Dete. He is too disturbed to talk.

AUNT DETE: He will get over it. Come along. We must hurry.

HEIDI: I am not going. I want to stay here with Grandfather, and with Peter and the goats. See, I have lunch here for all of us.

AUNT DETE: Fine. We can eat it on the train, you and I. Come!

HEIDI: No!

AUNT DETE (*Crossly*): You are a stupid little goat yourself. Come.

HEIDI: No!

NARRATOR: Aunt Dete raises her hand and prepares to strike Heidi but suddenly she changes her mind. She turns to the child and speaks in coaxing tones.

AUNT DETE: Don't be silly now, there's my good girl!

HEIDI: I am not a good girl, and I am not your girl, either. I'm Grandfather's girl, and he didn't even say goodbye to me.

AUNT DETE (*Coaxingly*): All right. Be a bad girl then, but come along. You can come back, if you don't like it.

HEIDI: Can I come back tonight?

AUNT DETE: Of course not, silly. We won't even get there until tomorrow.

HEIDI: But I have not gone yet. Grandfather will miss me.

AUNT DETE: Believe me, Heidi, when your Grandfather thinks things over, he will be glad you went.

HEIDI (*Sighs*): I suppose I must go. Goodbye, Peter.

PETER: Don't ask me to say goodbye, Heidi, because I won't do it.

NARRATOR: Brigida, Peter's sister, comes running into the mountain pasture.

BRIGIDA: I thought I saw you coming up the mountainside, Dete. I'll wager you are up to no good. Heidi, Granny has been calling for you. I hope you will come and see her later today.

HEIDI: See there, Aunt Dete. I can't go. Granny needs me, too.

AUNT DETE: Poor little sick Clara needs you, too. She can't even walk. And after all, Granny has Peter and Brigida, but Clara has nobody. Her father, Mr. Seseman, is away most of the time making barrels of money.

BRIGIDA: I suppose you are trying hard to get Heidi away from us all. What does the Alm Uncle say to all this?

AUNT DETE: Why don't you go ask him?

BRIGIDA: Don't worry, I will.

HEIDI: I cannot go, Aunt Dete. I must go to Granny.

AUNT DETE: Listen, Heidi, you shall bring back fine presents for Granny. Wouldn't you like that?

HEIDI (*Eagerly*): Oh, yes. Could I bring her some fine white rolls? She can't eat the hard black bread any more.

AUNT DETE: That's easy.

HEIDI: Could we bring some back tomorrow?

AUNT DETE: I told you Frankfort was a long way off, stupid. Come along or we will miss our train.

NARRATOR: Aunt Dete suddenly loses her patience. She grabs Heidi by the arm and forces her to hurry away.

PETER (*Sadly*): Poor Heidi.

BRIGIDA: She will be back, Peter. Don't worry. You will see.

PETER: I guess I'd better go tend my goats. Poor Heidi.

NARRATOR: The next scene takes place two months later. Again Peter, Brigida and their friends are together in the pasture in the mountains.

BRIGIDA: Here is a letter from Heidi. I suppose you are all eager to hear what she has to say.

PETER: Naturally. (*Sighs*) If I could only read, then I could read it myself.

BRIGIDA: Such nice writing she has for such a little girl.

1ST CHILD: What does she say?

BRIGIDA: She says that she and her teacher are having such fun together, learning things.

1ST GOATHERD: That's fun?

2ND GOATHERD: She isn't a little blockhead, like you. She wants to learn.

BRIGIDA: She has been very lonely for all of you.

2ND CHILD: Well, we've missed her, too.

1ST CHILD: I am sure I would never be lonely if I could live in a fine big house in Frankfort and have everything I wanted.

PETER: She doesn't have everything she wants. She doesn't have the mountains, or the Alm Uncle, or Granny, or me.

1ST GOATHERD: I'll bet she misses the goats, too.

BRIGIDA: She does. She says so here. Listen! "I miss the goats a lot, especially Brown Bear and Little Swan and the Snow-hopper. And the milk isn't as good here as the goat's milk was."

2ND GOATHERD: Poor Heidi.

PETER: What's poor about her? She wears fine clothes and rides around in a carriage drawn by two milk-white horses, and she has all the money she wants.

2ND CHILD (*Sighs*): Poor little rich Heidi!

1ST CHILD: Sometimes rich people become very proud. Do you think Heidi would recognize us if she passed us in the street?

PETER: Heidi would never forget her friends.

2ND CHILD: She has been away a long time.

PETER: It has been only two months, but it seems like a year.

BRIGIDA: The people are good to her, and Heidi loves them very much, especially Clara, the little sick girl. But she is homesick for the mountains, for her grandfather, for her friends, and even for you, Peter.

PETER: She just says that.

1ST GOATHERD: Why doesn't she come back home then?

BRIGIDA: She writes that she *is* coming. She would a thousand times rather be here with us in the mountains than anywhere else in the world.

2ND GOATHERD: I think she should have her head examined.

PETER: Look, there is someone coming up the mountainside.

BRIGIDA: It looks like a very rich little lady.

1ST CHILD: What fine clothes she has. She must be visiting someone in the village.

2ND CHILD: Maybe she is lost.

2ND GOATHERD: That's no lady, Peter. That's Heidi.

PETER (*Excited*): That's right! It is Heidi, come back to us again.

NARRATOR: Heidi comes into the pasture. She wears a velvet dress and plumed hat, and carries a bundle in a kerchief. She runs around speaking to all of the children and ends with a big hug for Brigida.

HEIDI: Brigida! How glad I am to see you again!

BRIGIDA: We have just been talking about you, Heidi, and reading your letter. Your ears must have been burning.

HEIDI (*Gaily*): I am so glad to see everybody. How are you, Peter, and how is Grandfather? I want to hear all about everyone.

BRIGIDA: Everybody is just fine. The Alm Uncle has missed you, Heidi. He has been getting more and more like a cross old bear every day since you left.

PETER: Nobody dares go near him, except Brigida.

HEIDI: Poor Grandfather. He will change now, for I shall never leave him again. He needs someone to take care of him, that's all, and that is why I came back. I ran away, but I left a note for Clara and Mr. Seseman.

PETER: I don't blame you. They shall never have you back again.

HEIDI: No, I will never go back again. Such fun we will have, all of us together. Now I can go up every morning with you again, and help you watch the goats. Here, Brigida, you wanted a plumed hat like this. You can have mine.

BRIGIDA: For me, Heidi? Why, I never owned anything so fine in all my life. I won't know how to wear it.

HEIDI: You'll learn easily, and it looks well on you. I must go and take off all my fine clothes before Grandfather sees me. I will change at your house, Brigida.

BRIGIDA: I will come with you.

HEIDI: I have something fine to give every one of you, silk and velvet dresses, fine shoes and handkerchiefs.

1ST CHILD: You are good, Heidi, to give all your fine clothes away.

HEIDI: Oh, no. I just like my mountain clothes better, and so does Grandfather.

PETER (*Shyly*): I like you better in your mountain clothes, too, Heidi. You look like a stranger in those fine things.

BRIGIDA: Come, Heidi. You can change your clothes. Then we will go with you to the Alm Uncle. I want to see how happy he will be.

NARRATOR: Five weeks pass quickly for Heidi, now that she is back in her mountains again. She has been patiently trying to teach Peter to read but he is not too interested.

HEIDI (*Patiently*): Now, Peter, you told me you wanted to learn to read, and here you are, just wasting your time looking at the sky. Don't you want to learn to read now?

PETER: No, I don't. I changed my mind again. It's too hard work, and there are too many smart people in the world now that can read.

HEIDI: Oh, no, Peter, there are too many people that don't know how to read, and you don't want to be one of them. Besides, you could read to Granny, you know. She would like that.

PETER: You read to her. That's enough.

HEIDI (*Severely*): Peter, you are quite hopeless. I should box your ears. Look, if you don't learn to read, I'll—I'll go back to Frankfort.

PETER (*Alarmed*): You wouldn't, Heidi!

HEIDI (*Laughs merrily*): No, I wouldn't, Peter.

PETER: I'll learn to read, Heidi, if you want me to. I guess it's no good to be dumb.

HEIDI: I'm so glad, Peter. You will see, you will have lots of fun when you can read. Here, I have marked some things for you to learn.

PETER: All right, I'll try. But I wouldn't do it for anyone but you, Heidi.

HEIDI: You aren't doing it for me, Peter. You are doing it for yourself. (*Sighs*) I hope this is the day Clara will come. I have been home five weeks already, and they haven't come yet. Clara wrote that she and Grandmamma and Mr. Seseman were all coming. They are staying in Ragatz now.

PETER: They can just stay away.

HEIDI (*Severely*): They are my friends, Peter. I want them to come.

PETER: I don't. They will take you away again.

HEIDI: No, they never will. You will like Clara, Peter.

PETER: I won't. Girls that can walk are bad enough. She will keep you away from the mountainside.

HEIDI: Peter, you must help me to help Clara walk. She took a few steps when I was there with her, but she's scared. I think if she comes to the mountains, she will soon be all well again.

PETER: I just wish she would stay in Ragatz.

HEIDI: What a selfish wish, Peter!

CLARA: Heidi! Heidi!

NARRATOR: Heidi turns and sees Brigida pushing Clara in her wheelchair. She runs over to them.

HEIDI: Clara, you look just like an angel from heaven! We were just talking about you, Peter and I, and saying how nice it would be when you came.

PETER: I wasn't.

HEIDI (*Sternly*): Peter, mind your manners! You and Clara will like each other when you get to know each other better. I'm glad you didn't stay longer in Ragatz.

PETER: I'm not! I wish you'd stayed there.

CLARA: The treatments in Ragatz didn't seem to be doing me any good. Besides, I wanted to see you so badly, Heidi. I was so lonesome after you left. Why did you run away from us?

HEIDI: I was homesick, Clara.

CLARA: I don't blame you. The mountains are beautiful. Your grandfather is a dear. Brigida wheeled me over here from his place. Papa and Grandmamma are going to leave me here with you when Grandmamma goes back to Ragatz for a while. Isn't that exciting?

HEIDI: It's the nicest news I've had for a long time. Peter, we three will have many good times together.

CLARA: Of course we will, Peter. Look, if you could have your wish, what would you like best in all the world? Grandmamma told me to give you a present because you were Heidi's very best friend.

PETER: Did she really say that?

CLARA: Indeed she did. Now, what would you like to have?

PETER: I would like ten bright shiny pennies every Sunday of my life.

NARRATOR: Clara takes out her purse and opens it. She counts out ten shiny pennies and places them in Peter's hand.

CLARA: Well, you can have them for as long as Grandmamma lives, I know. She loves to do nice things for people.

HEIDI: When you are bigger you will earn the pennies yourself.

PETER: I will try to earn them now.

CLARA: That's the spirit, Peter. (*Curiously*) What are you going to do with the pennies, Peter?

PETER: I will do nice things every day for my old blind

Granny. I can buy her fine white rolls, and maybe I can save enough to get her a nice soft bed so she will sleep better at night, and life will be more comfortable for her.

CLARA: You are a good boy, and I like you, Peter.

PETER: I like you, too, Clara. Shake!

NARRATOR: Just as Peter and Clara are shaking hands, the Alm Uncle comes up to them. He is looking very happy, for Heidi has returned to him.

THE ALM UNCLE: So here you are, my little ones. Now it is time for a surprise for Heidi, isn't it, Clara?

HEIDI: Oh, I love surprises!

CLARA: Yes, Heidi. In the short time that I have known you, you have done more for me than all the doctors in the world. See?

NARRATOR: The Alm Uncle leans over and helps Clara from the wheelchair. She walks slowly and carefully, leaning on the Alm Uncle's arm.

CLARA: After you left, I could no longer walk because you were not there to help me. But the Alm Uncle told me I could walk if I tried very hard and wasn't afraid, just the same as you did.

HEIDI: How wonderful! Can she come up the mountainside with us tomorrow morning, Grandfather?

THE ALM UNCLE: Well, maybe not tomorrow, Heidi, or even the next day, but it won't be long before she will be able to run and play with all of you, when she gets stronger and more sure of herself.

BRIGIDA: You see, Clara, you can always do things, if you believe you can, with God's help.

CLARA: I am not a bit tired. At home I was always tired.

THE ALM UNCLE (*Briskly*): It is the mountain air. But come now, tired or not tired, it is time to fill your stomach and I have supper all ready for you. We will see what goat's milk and fresh eggs will do for your appetite. Peter, how would you and Brigida like to come and have supper with us?

PETER: Oh, thank you, sir. I would like that very much, now that I am Clara's friend.

BRIGIDA: Thank you, too, but I think I will have to be getting back to Granny. She is waiting.

CLARA: I feel as though I could eat a house, chimney and all, and as though I could run and jump all day.

THE ALM UNCLE (*With mock severity*): Back in the chair you go, young lady. We must take it easy at first and not overdo it. I think I can give you better fare than a house, even with a chimney. There you go.

PETER: May I wheel the chair, sir?

THE ALM UNCLE: With the greatest of pleasure, Peter. Push it carefully. Come, Heidi, let's be on our way, for Mr. Seseman and Clara's Grandmamma are waiting.

THE END

The Wise Wife

This is an old Chinese legend retold in a new way.

Practice the Chinese names until you can say them correctly and easily without hesitation.

Cha-Ming — Chah Ming
Me-Ching — May Ching
Ah-Ling — Ah Ling

Read the story quickly to yourself. Then answer these questions:

1. How did they set about finding a wife for the Emperor's son?
2. Why did Ah-Ling send Me-Ching to the rice paddy?
3. How did Me-Ching come to be interviewed by the Marriage-Maker?
4. What questions did he ask?
5. How does this differ from the way a wife is chosen for our President or his son?

Let us practice using our voices:

Never *fear*, you'll be back before he *arrives!*
Never *fear*, you'll be *back* before he arrives!
Never fear, you'll be back *before* he arrives!
Never *fear*, you'll be *back* before *he* arrives!

Notice how placing emphasis on different words can change the meaning of a sentence just a little.

Choose your part.

Practice your own part. Each time you have a speech to read, decide which word you will emphasize so that you will make the meaning clear.

Ask for the tape-recorder. Record the reading of the play.
Play the recording and listen to it carefully.

Discuss together how you could improve the reading.

Read again and record it.

Listen to your reading. Have you improved enough to read
it to the class?

Decide with your teacher whether to read the play to the
class or to play the recording.

THE WISE WIFE

by Mary Ann Nicholson

Characters

(4 boys, 3 girls, and the narrator)

NARRATOR
CHA-MING, the oldest sister
AH-LING, the middle sister
ME-CHING, the youngest sister
FARMER CHU, the father of the girls
COURIER, a young man
MARRIAGE-MAKER, an old man
SCRIBE, a young man

NARRATOR: The play that you are about to hear took place
long, long ago. The scene is the courtyard of a Chinese farm
house. Cha-Ming is showing her new gown to her sister Me-
Ching, while another sister, Ah-Ling, stirs rice in a bowl
and watches them.

CHA-MING: How do I look, Me-Ching?

ME-CHING: You look splendid in your new embroidered silk
gown, Cha-Ming.

CHA-MING: I have been working on this design for a year.

ME-CHING: You have the finest embroidering hand in the kingdom.

CHA-MING: Thank you. You are kind to say so.

AH-LING: And what do you have to say to me, Me-Ching?

ME-CHING: You make the best rice soup in the land, Ah-Ling.

AH-LING: I'm glad you know good cooking when you eat it. Some day I may teach you my secret recipes.

ME-CHING: I shall be most grateful to you if you do.

AH-LING: Now I must have some more fresh rice from the far rice paddy for this special soup I'm making. Because you are the youngest, Me-Ching, you have the swiftest feet. Please fetch me the rice while I stir the soup.

ME-CHING: But what if the Emperor's Marriage-Maker comes while I am gone?

AH-LING: Never fear, you'll be back before he arrives, if you hurry.

ME-CHING: I don't want to miss his visit. Call me loudly when he comes so that I may run home quickly.

AH-LING: I will, Me-Ching.

NARRATOR: Me-Ching runs off down the road. She hurries so that she will be sure to be back in time to see the Marriage-Maker.

CHA-MING: Why did you send Me-Ching away, Ah-Ling? It is such a distance to the far rice paddy and you have more than enough rice for your soup.

AH-LING: The Marriage-Maker is due here very soon and I don't want him to see her. She is pretty and she is intelligent.

CHA-MING: Our father will be angry with you when he finds out.

AH-LING: It will be too late for him to do anything about it then. Me-Ching is too young to marry anyway. We should marry first.

CHA-MING: But the Marriage-Maker insists on seeing every girl in the land in his search for a suitable wife for the Emperor's son.

AH-LING: Ours is the last village he is to visit. If Me-Ching isn't home, then greater will be the chance of his choosing one of us.

CHA-MING: Of course, how clever of you, Ah-Ling. But you will have to explain Me-Ching's absence to Father. Here he comes.

FARMER: Good day, daughters. Are you ready to receive the Emperor's Marriage-Maker?

BOTH GIRLS: We are, Father.

FARMER: What talent will you offer as a bride, Cha-Ming?

CHA-MING: I will offer my skill with an embroidery needle. The silk gown that I'm wearing is an example of my handiwork.

FARMER: And you, Ah-Ling?

AH-LING: Here in this bowl is a sample of my cooking skill. It is a very special rice soup which cannot fail to please both the Marriage-Maker and the Emperor's son.

FARMER: The Marriage-Maker will have a difficult choice to make between two such talented girls. But where is your youngest sister?

CHA-MING: She has gone to the far rice paddy.

FARMER: Why?

AH-LING (*Quickly*): I think she was afraid to meet the Marriage-Maker, Father. She has so little talent for cooking and sewing.

FARMER: Still, she is pretty and quick-witted. It is a rare combination in one so young.

AH-LING: She has disobeyed your wishes, Father. What is to be done?

FARMER: So she has. I said none of you was to leave the courtyard today. For punishment she will just have to miss her chance to be considered by the Marriage-Maker. Hark, I hear voices approaching. It must be the Marriage-Maker now.

NARRATOR: The Courier enters the courtyard gate. Farmer Chu and the girls bow low.

COURIER: Farmer Chu, you are about to be honored by the presence of the Emperor's Marriage-Maker. Are these your daughters?

FARMER: Indeed they are, Courier.

COURIER: Good. His Eminence, the Emperor's Marriage-Maker.

NARRATOR: The old Marriage-Maker comes into the courtyard accompanied by his Scribe.

MARRIAGE-MAKER: You may go on to the next farm, Courier. I shall not be here long.

FARMER: Honored guest, I beg to inform you that this is the last farm outside our village.

MARRIAGE-MAKER: That is pleasant news. My ancient feet are protesting every step I walk.

FARMER: Please be seated.

NARRATOR: The Marriage-Maker finds it difficult to move about and is helped to his seat by the Courier and the Scribe.

MARRIAGE-MAKER: Ah, this is better. Courier, proceed down the road and see which way back to the Emperor's Palace is the shortest. Now to business. Which daughter is the elder, Farmer Chu?

FARMER: Cha-Ming is, Honored Marriage-Maker. Step forward, Cha-Ming.

MARRIAGE-MAKER: List her with the others, Scribe.

NARRATOR: The Scribe sits at the table, takes out his scroll and quill and gets ready to write.

MARRIAGE-MAKER: Ahem, Cha-Ming, I have some questions to ask you. First of all, I want to know what talent you have to offer as the bride of the Emperor's son.

CHA-MING: I embroider silk, Honored Marriage-Maker. This gown I am wearing I made entirely by hand.

MARRIAGE-MAKER: Hmmm, very lovely. But then, many girls I have seen embroider just as well. I'll have to test your intelligence, also. Scribe, the test questions.

NARRATOR: The Scribe hands the scroll to the Marriage-Maker. Somehow or other the scroll is upside down, and the Marriage-Maker cannot read it.

MARRIAGE-MAKER: This is the wrong scroll. It doesn't make a bit of sense.

SCRIBE: Begging your pardon, Honored Marriage-Maker, it is upside down. Would you like me to read it for you?

MARRIAGE-MAKER: By the great dragon's tooth, no. There's nothing wrong with my eyesight. You are the one with the poor eyesight, giving me an upside-down scroll.

SCRIBE: I'm very sorry.

MARRIAGE-MAKER: Cha-Ming, answer this if you can: How could you take some fire wrapped in paper to the Emperor?

CHA-MING (*Flustered*): I . . . I don't know. The fire would burn the paper. It can't be done.

MARRIAGE-MAKER: Sorry, you have failed the first question. To become the bride of the Emperor's son you must be wise as well as skilled in sewing.

FARMER: Perhaps my second daughter, Ah-Ling, will be able to pass your test, Honored Marriage-Maker.

MARRIAGE-MAKER: We shall soon see. What talent have you to offer, Ah-Ling?

AH-LING: I have many secret recipes. Here is a sample of my special rice soup.

MARRIAGE-MAKER: Scribe, be sure to put down Ah-Ling's cooking as her talent.

SCRIBE: Yes, I will. It smells delicious.

MARRIAGE-MAKER: You realize, of course, that many other girls know how to cook fancy dishes. There is more to being a suitable wife for the Emperor's son than just knowing how to cook. As his wife, you would have servants to do your cooking for you. Now to the test questions. Can you answer the one I asked your sister?

AH-LING (*Boldly*): I would carry a piece of coal wrapped in a paper.

MARRIAGE-MAKER: But if the coal were burning?

AH-LING: Well, then, I could not do it, Honored Marriage-Maker.

MARRIAGE-MAKER: A noble try, Ah-Ling, but not good enough to pass the test. I must be on my way back to the Imperial Palace, Farmer Chu.

NARRATOR: The Scribe gathers up his writing materials and stands, preparing to leave. Just at this moment the Courier enters pulling Me-Ching by the hand.

COURIER: Honored Marriage-Maker, I've found another girl.

MARRIAGE-MAKER: And you told me there were no more girls along this road, Farmer Chu.

FARMER: Well, that is. . . .

MARRIAGE-MAKER: Where did you find her, Courier?

COURIER: She was running across the rice paddies. She was afraid of missing your visit to her father's house.

MARRIAGE-MAKER: And where is her father's house?

COURIER: *This* is her father's house. She is the youngest sister.

MARRIAGE-MAKER: Farmer Chu, how do you explain this?

FARMER: It is true that she is my youngest daughter, Me-Ching. I ordered her to stay in the courtyard, but she ran off to the rice paddies and disobeyed me.

ME-CHING: I did not mean to disobey your wishes, Father, but Ah-Ling sent me to gather fresh rice for her soup. I hope I am not too late, Ah-Ling. I ran as fast as I could.

MARRIAGE-MAKER: I suspect that your sister wanted you out of the way when I came, Me-Ching. Well, no matter, she has failed my test, so all of her tricks have done her no good. Evil deeds do not bring good luck, Ah-Ling.

FARMER: As you can see, Me-Ching is unselfish and kind.

MARRIAGE-MAKER: It is to her favor, Farmer Chu. Since your older daughters have failed to pass the test, I shall ask the same questions of Me-Ching. Now, my child, what talents have you to offer?

ME-CHING: Very few, Honored Marriage-Maker.

COURIER: She runs swiftly, I can swear to that, and she's pretty, too.

MARRIAGE-MAKER: You are quite observant today, Courier, but we are not trying to find a bride for you.

COURIER: Forgive my speaking out of turn.

ME-CHING: I do many things, but none of them especially well.

MARRIAGE-MAKER: At least you are modest. Let me test your wit. This question neither of your sisters could answer. How would you carry fire wrapped in paper to the Emperor?

ME-CHING: I would carry a lighted paper lantern to the Emperor.

MARRIAGE-MAKER (*Delighted*): Very good. You show signs of real intelligence. Are you recording all this, Scribe?

SCRIBE: I'm writing down every word spoken in the report for the Emperor.

MARRIAGE-MAKER: Then here is the next question, Me-Ching. How could you carry some wind in a paper to the Emperor?

ME-CHING: A paper fan would do for that. When a fan is moved back and forth, wind comes from it.

MARRIAGE-MAKER: Indeed, you are proving to be a most clever girl, answering my test questions so easily. As a future Empress of China you would have various duties in managing the Emperor's household. One of these duties would be the instructing of the Palace servants in such domestic chores as cooking and sewing. For instance, if the Emperor were to ask you to weave a silken cloth as long as the road that goes past this house, could you do it?

ME-CHING: Before I could do it, Honored Marriage-Maker, he would first have to find both ends of the road and tell me the number of feet in its length. Then and only then could I show the servants how long to weave such a cloth.

MARRIAGE-MAKER: I thought this test was difficult. I made up these questions myself. Try this next question: If the Emperor wanted a banquet prepared and asked you to cook as many rice grains as there are drops of water in the sea, could you do that?

ME-CHING: After he counted the number of drops in the sea, I could cook the correct number of rice grains for him.

MARRIAGE-MAKER: An excellent answer, Me-Ching. Farmer Chu, your youngest daughter is the cleverest girl I have met in all my travels.

FARMER: I am honored to hear you say it.

MARRIAGE-MAKER: Now let me ask you some riddles.

ME-CHING: I grow weary of your questions, Honored Marriage-Maker. Surely you have decided by now whether or not I'm wise enough to marry the Emperor's son.

MARRIAGE-MAKER: Oh, I certainly have decided, but I won't announce my decision until I have asked you all the riddles I know.

ME-CHING: This could go on forever. Let us make a bargain. I will answer one of your riddles and then I will ask you one. If you can't answer mine, you cannot ask me any more.

MARRIAGE-MAKER: Fair enough, Me-Ching. Ahem. This riddle no one has ever answered correctly.

NARRATOR: Quickly the Marriage-Maker reaches into the air, catches a fly and holds it in his fist.

MARRIAGE-MAKER: In my hand I have a fly. Do I mean to crush it to death or let it go?

ME-CHING: If I say you mean to crush it to death, you can let it go and I will have been proven wrong. If I say you mean to let it go, you can crush it and prove me wrong. Yours is not a fair riddle.

MARRIAGE-MAKER (*Peeved*): Hrruumph.

ME-CHING: Now you must answer my riddle.

NARRATOR: Me-Ching crosses to the house and steps over the threshold with one foot inside and the other outside.

ME-CHING: I am standing with one foot in the house and one foot outside. Do I mean to go into the house or out?

MARRIAGE-MAKER: Indeed, you confuse me, Me-Ching. No one can guess your intentions; you can go in either direction.

ME-CHING: Since you did not answer my riddle, you cannot ask me any more, Honored Marriage-Maker.

MARRIAGE-MAKER: True, true. What a pity, too; I was having so much fun. Oh well, back to business.

FARMER (*Breathlessly*): Your decision?

COURIER: Is Me-Ching to marry the Emperor's son?

SCRIBE: I am ready for your announcement.

MARRIAGE-MAKER: I have come to this great decision after

having questioned all the girls in the land and found the wisest one.

COURIER: She's pretty, too.

MARRIAGE-MAKER: As the Emperor's chosen Marriage-Maker, it is my privilege to ask Farmer Chu for Me-Ching's hand in marriage to the Emperor's son. What is your answer, Farmer Chu?

FARMER: I give my consent, yes, yes.

MARRIAGE-MAKER: Me-Ching, are you ready to go to the Emperor's palace for your wedding?

ME-CHING: I am, but may I ask one favor of you, Honored Marriage-Maker?

MARRIAGE-MAKER: What is it, Me-Ching?

ME-CHING: As I have told you already, I can do many things but none of them well. I would like to have my first sister, Cha-Ming, go with me to the palace to sew my wedding dress, and my second sister, Ah-Ling, to cook the wedding feast.

MARRIAGE-MAKER: I have no objection to granting your favor, Me-Ching. It shows your very generous and loving nature. They will be welcome at the palace.

FARMER (*Sadly*): I shall miss my daughters when they leave. Will I be allowed to visit them at the palace?

MARRIAGE-MAKER: As the future Empress of China, Me-Ching can command you to visit her often, Farmer Chu, and I think she will do that.

FARMER: I am glad.

MARRIAGE-MAKER: Courier, Scribe, let us start back to the palace. There will be much rejoicing in the land tonight, because we have found a wise wife for the son of the Emperor.

THE END

Catastrophe Clarence

You will enjoy the humor in this play about a man from outer space.

Before you read the play to yourself, be sure you can say these words. If you do not know the meaning of a word, check in your dictionary.

> catastrophe
> smog
> pollutes
> analyst
> astronomer
> spiral nebulae
> self-luminous
> celestial
> atmospheric conditions

There are several words in this play that the author has made up or "coined": *litronium, hermoplated,* etc. Can you think of any words that scientists have coined which have been added to our language in recent years?

Read the story silently.

Choose parts.

Practice your part to yourself.

When you are ready, read the play aloud.

Evaluate your reading by checking yourself on the following list.

1. Did you speak clearly and distinctly?
2. Did you use your voice to show surprise, fear, excitement, amusement?
3. Did you come in on time with your part?

4. Did you know all the words or did you stumble over some of them?
5. Did you pay attention to marks of punctuation?

Read the play again to see if you can improve the weak parts. When you are ready, arrange for a convenient time to read it to the rest of the class.

CATASTROPHE CLARENCE

by Maxine Shore

Characters

(6 boys and the narrator)

NARRATOR

BOB MEADOWS, a *young boy about thirteen years old*

ANDY THOMPSON, *his pal*

PROFESSOR WADSWORTH W. CLARK, *Bob's uncle, an astronomer*

HOWARD, *the professor's chef*

GLENN MATTHEWS, *the professor's secretary and assistant*

CATASTROPHE CLARENCE, *space man of the Universal Meteor Patrol*

NARRATOR: Our play takes place on a summer evening in Professor Wadsworth Clark's observatory, located in the San Bernardino Mountains of California. Bob and Andy enter carrying luggage. Bob is also carrying a dusty quart jar. He is holding it with great care.

ANDY: Gee, what a neat place! I've never been in an observatory before.

BOB: My uncle built it himself, to carry on special research.

ANDY: But where is he?

BOB: Oh, he's around somewhere—probably in his office in the next room. I guess no one heard us come in. We'll look for him in a minute. Right now, I just want to take a breather.

ANDY: Yeah. That was a long hike through the woods, and uphill all the way. Your uncle ought to have a road built up here.

BOB: He doesn't want one. Says he gets more privacy this way.

ANDY: I'll bet.

NARRATOR: Howard enters the room. He gives the boys a curious glance.

HOWARD: Well, who are you boys? How did you get in here?

BOB: You remember me, Howard. I'm Bob Meadows, Professor Clark's nephew, and this is my friend, Andy Thompson. Andy, this is Howard. He does the cooking here.

ANDY: How do you do?

HOWARD: Hello, young man. But—the professor didn't tell me you were coming.

BOB: *You* were supposed to tell him we were coming, Howard. I called up a couple of days ago from Los Angeles, long distance. You answered the phone, don't you remember? You said the professor and Mr. Matthews were both busy in the observatory, and you'd take the message and would let us know if it wasn't O.K. for us to come. Don't you remember?

HOWARD: Well, I do remember some sort of conversation about a visit—but—

BOB: But you forgot to tell Uncle Wadsworth, didn't you? Gosh, Howard, it's professors who're supposed to be absent-minded, not cooks!

NARRATOR: The Professor enters. He greets Bob and smiles in a friendly fashion at Andy.

PROFESSOR: Why, Bob! What a pleasant surprise! Where on earth did you come from? And who's this young man with you?

HOWARD: He's Bob's brother, isn't that nice?

BOB: No, no, Howard. He's my friend, Andy Thompson.

HOWARD: They don't look much alike, do they, Professor? You'd never guess they were twins.

ANDY: No, no. You don't understand. I'm not Bob's—

PROFESSOR: Never mind. I understand. Howard gets a bit absent-minded sometimes.

HOWARD: I do not. Now, let's see, what did I come in here for? Oh, I guess I meant to go into the kitchen and—and scrub out the bathtub.

PROFESSOR: Howard's a bit confused sometimes, I'm afraid, but he means well. Now, Bob, tell me how you boys happen to be here. Who brought you?

BOB: My dad. He had to go to Barstow on a business trip and this was only a little out of his way. You said I should come up any time I could this summer and bring one of my friends—

PROFESSOR (*Heartily*): Of course, Bob, and I'm very glad to see you and your friend, Andy. Too bad your father couldn't stop, too.

BOB: He was in a hurry to keep an appointment and didn't have time. He dropped us off down below. We called long distance a couple of days ago, Uncle Wadsworth, and talked to Howard. I guess he forgot to tell you.

PROFESSOR: Well, it doesn't really matter. I like surprises. Now that you're here, I hope you'll enjoy yourselves, boys.

BOB: Oh, we will! But—we've come to see you on business, sort of, too.

PROFESSOR: Business?

ANDY: Yes, sir. You see, we have a problem.

PROFESSOR: A problem? What is it, boys?

BOB: It's in this jar here.

PROFESSOR (*Puzzled*): But—the jar looks empty!

ANDY: It isn't, though. It's full of smog—from Los Angeles.

BOB: Sure—see?

PROFESSOR: Uh—yes, I see. I mean, I smell.

ANDY: Close it up quickly, Bob, before it all leaks out.

PROFESSOR: Yes, please do, Bob, before it pollutes our nice pure mountain air. But I'm afraid I still don't see just what I can do.

BOB: We want you to analyze it for us. Andy's dad says if the smog gets any worse, he'll move to Alaska.

ANDY: And I don't want to move. I like it here in California.

BOB: I don't want Andy to move, either. He's my best friend.

PROFESSOR: But, boys, you don't understand. I'm not—I can't—

BOB: I told Andy what a famous scientist you are, Uncle Wadsworth, and about all the awards you've won. I told him you could find out what makes smog, and we could tell the mayor of L.A., and then he could get rid of it.

PROFESSOR: But, boys, I'm an astronomer, not a smog analyst.

BOB: But—I thought you knew everything.

PROFESSOR: I'm afraid not. I'd like to help you, Bob, but this is out of my line. Now, how about something to eat? You boys must be hungry after your long trip.

ANDY: We sure are!

BOB: I'm starved!

PROFESSOR: And here's Howard, ready to take your orders.

HOWARD: Professor, how do you want your eggs this morning —scrambled or poached? And would your nephews like oatmeal or corn flakes?

ANDY: Corn flakes—for dinner?

PROFESSOR: Howard, look out the window.

HOWARD: Why, it's dark out! Must be another thunderstorm coming up. And it started out to be a real nice day, too.

PROFESSOR: No, Howard. It's dark out because it's night. Dinner time.

HOWARD: Well now, is that right? How time flies. I'd better go right out and start the potatoes.

PROFESSOR: Well, it looks as if dinner will be a little late again tonight. While we're waiting, perhaps you boys would like to look through the telescope.

ANDY: Gee! That would be keen. I'd love to look through it, sir.

BOB: Go ahead, then, Andy. I've done it lots of times.

PROFESSOR: Come on, Andy, have a look at our marvelous solar system.

NARRATOR: The Professor adjusts the telescope so that Andy can see clearly.

ANDY: Gee, thanks! Wow! Millions of stars!

PROFESSOR: Correction. Trillions. And they're not all stars, either, my boy. Some of them are planets, some are comets, some spiral nebulae, and still others may be meteors.

ANDY: What's the difference—they all shine.

PROFESSOR: There's a vast difference. A star, for instance, is any self-luminous celestial body exclusive of comets, meteors and nebulae.

ANDY: Oh, I see.

PROFESSOR: Planets are much smaller than stars, and shine by reflected light.

ANDY: Planets are smaller than stars? I always thought it was the other way around.

PROFESSOR: Oh, no, Andy. The sun, for example, is a star of about average brightness and size, while the earth, Mars, Venus, Jupiter, Neptune, Saturn and so on are planets.

ANDY: How about the moon?

BOB: Oh, I know that. The moon is a satellite.

ANDY: Well, it may only be a satellite, but it sure looks big through this telescope! If the moon were a little closer, I bet I could see the people walking around on it.

PROFESSOR: It's extremely doubtful that life could exist on the moon or any other planet except, perhaps, in its very lowest forms.

ANDY: How do you know? After all, nobody's ever been there.

PROFESSOR (*Clearing throat*): No, Andy, but astronomers have made certain scientific deductions.

ANDY: How's that again?

BOB: Well, I don't know, Uncle Wadsworth. I bet there could be people just like us living up there somewhere. Why not?

CATASTROPHE CLARENCE 211

ANDY: Sure, why not? Why should we think we're the only planet in the whole universe that's inhabited? That's—conceited!

NARRATOR: Glenn Matthews, the Professor's assistant, comes into the room. He is carrying a notebook.

GLENN: Why, hello there, Bob! Glad to see you. I just met Howard and he said something about visitors. The professor's twin nephews, I believe he said, but—

BOB: Hi, Glenn. Howard got it all mixed up, as usual. He thinks my friend, Andy Thompson here, is my twin brother. Can't talk him out of it. You know Howard!

GLENN: You bet I know Howard. But I doubt if he knows me yet, even though I've been the professor's assistant for over a year. He's still confused about me.

PROFESSOR: Never mind. Howard's an excellent cook.

GLENN: True. Even if you do get cereal for dinner more often than steak.

ANDY (*Groaning*): I was afraid of that. I don't even like cereal for breakfast.

GLENN: Well, you'll like things here. For breakfast, we often have fried chicken. With ice cream for dessert.

ANDY: Wow! That's for me!

GLENN: Professor, I have a few questions about these notes you dictated yesterday regarding the rings of Saturn.

PROFESSOR: All right, Glenn. I'll go over them with you in the office right now, before dinner. Will you excuse us, boys? You can entertain yourselves here all right until we eat, can't you?

ANDY: Sure! I love looking through this telescope!

PROFESSOR: Oh. We'd better take these suitcases to your room, boys—you know which one, Bob.

BOB: Sure. Thanks, Uncle Wadsworth.

GLENN: Here, let me take them, sir. See you later, boys.

ANDY (*Whistling*): Well, what do you know! Huh! Say, Bob, look here through the telescope!

BOB: Huh—where? What do you see? People on the moon?

ANDY: Sorry, no people. But there's a real bright red star here that I'm sure I didn't see a minute ago. Gosh, it's pretty! Looks just like the tail light on my bike!

BOB: Let's see. Say, that's neat! It looks as if it's moving, too, coming right this way. Maybe—maybe it's a—a flying saucer!

ANDY: Gosh—do you suppose it could be? I've always wanted to see a flying saucer. Let me look at it again. Wait until we tell the professor!

NARRATOR: Andy continues to peer through the telescope while Bob waits impatiently for his turn. They are too absorbed to see the space man look into the window and then hop into the room. Suddenly Bob sees the visitor. The space man speaks as Bob circles him curiously.

CLARENCE: Wow! What an experience! Where am I?

BOB: Why, you're in Professor Wadsworth W. Clark's observatory, that's where. But I don't think my uncle will like your hopping in through the window that way. And what a crazy-looking costume!

CLARENCE: But—what planet is this?

BOB: What planet? Why, Earth, of course! Are you kidding? What're you all rigged out like that for? Oh, I know! I bet Uncle Wadsworth is playing a joke on us. Ha, ha! Wait'll Andy gets a load of you. He'll die laughing! Hey, Andy! Look at him!

NARRATOR: Andy turns to see what is happening. He is startled by the strange creature.

ANDY: Gosh! A real space man!

CLARENCE: Right, earth boy! You're a smart one. I am a real space man. They call me Catastrophe Clarence from Clarion. I'm attached to the Universal Meteor Patrol, a very select outfit, I'll have you know.

BOB: You mean, you're for real?

ANDY: Sure he is, Bob. Can't you tell? But what I want to know is what's he doing here on earth? Is this an invasion from outer space? Come on, Bob—let's rush him!

CLARENCE: Wait, earth boys, wait! Not so fast. Hold it! You don't understand. Stop! Stop, I say!

NARRATOR: The boys try to tackle the visitor, but they fall back, as if blocked by an invisible wall. They rub their bruises and rise slowly.

BOB: Ouch—my head! What hit me? Wh—what happened?

CLARENCE: Sorry, earth boys, you ran into my energy wall. I had to put it up to protect myself. You wouldn't wait for my explanation. I'm not leading any invasion of your earth. You earth people are always too suspicious of strangers. The rest of the universe wants to be friendly, but you're too excitable.

ANDY: I guess you're right.

BOB: But you still haven't told us why you're here.

CLARENCE (*Slowly*): Well, it's an embarrassing story. As I said, I'm on duty with the Universal Meteor Patrol. I was cruising along out in space on regular patrol duty when I got too interested in looking at a man from Earth in a comic book I'd brought along from home—the planet Clarion— and I kind of lost track of what I was doing. First thing I knew, this meteor was streaking toward earth. It's the business of the Universal Meteor Patrolmen to keep dangerous meteors away from inhabited planets, you know. Then I realized I was running out of litronium, too, and had forgotten to bring along my extra supply from the base.

ANDY: Gee! How terrible!

BOB: Then what happened?

CLARENCE: What happened? I was so close to Earth by this time that I got caught in the gravitational pull and couldn't get free because my litronium was so low and I was too weak.

ANDY: That must have been tough! You say you fell toward earth? You don't seem hurt.

CLARENCE: Oh, I'm not. Fortunately, I had just enough litronium left to float down easily. But what worries me now is that the meteor is out of control and all the Space officials will blame me for letting it crash into the earth. I may be grounded on Clarion for life!

BOB: You mean that meteor is going to—crash?

ANDY: What'll it do to Earth?

CLARENCE (*Sadly*): It may destroy your entire planet, I'm afraid. Or at least this hemisphere. And all of us have had so much fun studying your Earth, too. No planet in the universe is as full of crazy characters as this one is! It's a museum piece.

ANDY: But that's terrible!

BOB: Yes! Can't you do something—before it's too late?

CLARENCE: Not unless I can find some litronium someplace quickly.

BOB: What's litronium?

ANDY: We never heard of it before.

CLARENCE: What's litronium! Why, that's the stuff that gives Space Patrolmen the energy and courage we need to meet every obstacle—to fly, jump a mile, keep alert!

BOB: You mean it's some kind of fuel—or food?

CLARENCE: Without litronium, no one could steer the comets and meteors safely away from the planets. Litronium's nourishment.

ANDY (*Puzzled*): You mean—like hot dogs?

CLARENCE: Hot dogs?

BOB: Wieners, frankfurters. We eat 'em. How I wish I had some right now. I'm starved!

CLARENCE (*Doubtfully*): Well, it's true we take litronium internally—

ANDY: Bob, litronium might be the same thing as hot dogs!

BOB: Yeah! Say, maybe Howard has some in the refrigerator. I'll go see!

ANDY: He'll hurry right back, space man.

CLARENCE (*Wearily*): I—certainly—hope so. All this talking has further exhausted my litronium supply. I'm getting—hermoplated.

ANDY: Hermoplated? What's that?

CLARENCE: In your language it means—pooped, I believe. At least—that's what—they call it—in the Men from Earth—Comic Books.

NARRATOR: Clarence staggers to a chair and falls into it, exhausted.

ANDY: Gosh, that's too bad. We just have to get you some litronium quick! Oh, here comes Bob back with Howard, the professor's cook.

HOWARD: Well, I must say you're a strange one! I suppose you're from Hollywood.

CLARENCE: No, I'm from Clarion.

HOWARD: Clarion . . . Clarion. Let's see, isn't that near Chicago? My, you're a long way from home, aren't you, sonny?

BOB: If you only knew, Howard!

HOWARD: You look all worn out. That's a long trip.

CLARENCE: What a strange earth character! Did you bring the litronium, earth boy?

HOWARD: Young man, watch your language. The professor is very particular.

BOB: Try one of these. It's a hot dog.

CLARENCE: Is this—a hot dog? It—doesn't look—very much —like litronium. But maybe it's inside the skin. No, there's no litronium in here.

BOB: Gee, I'm sorry. Do—do you feel as bad as you look?

CLARENCE (*Groaning*): Much worse!

BOB: Maybe the professor can figure out what to do. He's a brain. Andy, go get my uncle and his secretary from the office.

ANDY: O.K.

BOB: What about the meteor heading toward earth, Catastrophe Clarence? What are we going to do?

HOWARD: Oh, is your name Clarence, young man? I had a brother named Clarence, or was it a sister named Clara? Isn't that funny, I can't quite remember, it was so long ago, but I know he had long, yellow curls. I'll go see if I can find a picture of him.

CLARENCE (*Despairingly*): The meteor will crash into the Earth and destroy it in just fifteen minutes if I can't get back up there some way to steer it out of danger. My first big assignment since I got out of training school—and I'm failing at it!

NARRATOR: The professor and his secretary, Glenn Matthews, enter the room.

PROFESSOR: Bob, what's all this about? Your friend Andy claims we're entertaining a visitor from outer space. Ridiculous! Nothing but the very lowest forms of life exist on other planets. Atmospheric conditions just won't support evolution there, you know. What kind of joke is this, anyway?

CLARENCE: Sir, I am *not* a low form of life! And I can prove I'm from space. Let me introduce myself. I'm Catastrophe Clarence from the planet, Clarion, on the other side of the moon—and a member of the Universal Meteor Patrol. I had to land here because I ran out of litronium.

PROFESSOR: I can't believe it. I have never heard of Clarion or the Universal Meteor Patrol or—or litronium, whatever that is.

BOB: Honest, Uncle Wadsworth, I'm sure he's telling the truth. Andy and I saw the meteor right in your telescope over there. I'm sure that red thing we saw must have been a meteor, Andy!

ANDY: Sure, that's it! It must have been!

NARRATOR: Andy, followed by the Professor and Glenn, runs to look into the telescope.

ANDY: Yes, there it is—and now it's as big as an orange!

PROFESSOR: Here. Let me look. It's there! The meteor! And it's growing larger every second, too. I can't believe my eyes. I've never seen one that size before. It looks as if nothing could stop it from hitting the earth! Glenn!

GLENN: Yes, Professor?

PROFESSOR: Notify the proper authorities. Make my will. Lock all the doors and windows. No, on second thought, leave them open. And tell Howard not to bother about dinner. We probably won't have time to eat it.

GLENN: Heavens, sir! Is it that bad?

PROFESSOR: Take a look for yourself.

GLENN: Jumping Jupiter! Yes! It's terrible! I'll call Washington, notify the newspapers, get in touch with Palomar, call my mother—

PROFESSOR: I can't believe it! It can't be happening!

HOWARD: Oh, there you are, Professor! I can't remember how you wanted your eggs this morning.

PROFESSOR: Never mind that now, Howard. We won't be eating.

CLARENCE (*Despairingly*): Are you sure you don't have any litronium around here?

BOB: I don't know. There might be, I suppose, if we only knew what it was. What color is it, anyhow?

CLARENCE: It's the—most beautiful—color in—the universe, a soft delicate tender shade—

ANDY: Come on, we're wasting time, and there isn't much of it left! Let's all go out into the kitchen and see what we can find there. Come on, Clarence!

CLARENCE: Can't—stand up. Too—weak. Almost—out of— litronium. Must get some—soon. Meteor will crash—in just —twelve minutes. My—responsibility. Must—save earth.

BOB: I'll stay here. The rest of you go. And hurry! Don't worry, Clarence. I'm sure they'll find some litronium for you. They just have to!

CLARENCE: I—hope—so. Earth is such—an interesting— planet. Such—crazy—people. My—duty—to save—earth.

BOB: You will. Don't worry. See, here come the others with all kinds of food. See?

NARRATOR: The Professor, Andy and Glenn bring in every type of food they can think of—milk, eggs, vegetables, meat and cornflakes.

HOWARD: But I still don't understand what this is all about.

Why are we moving everything out of the kitchen into the observatory, Professor? This is quite upsetting.

BOB: Poor Catastrophe Clarence! He feels awful. Quick, let's see if any of the stuff you brought is litronium. Gee, I hope it is!

PROFESSOR: That meteor is almost as big as the sun now.

ANDY: Only it's even redder.

GLENN: And see how light it's getting outside—and quite warm, too!

BOB: Here, space man. Is this wheat bread your litronium?

CLARENCE: No, not—litronium. Oh, dear!

ANDY: Then how about this milk?

PROFESSOR: Are these cornflakes anything like litronium?

BOB: How about this root beer? It tastes good.

CLARENCE: No. No—not that.

ANDY: Then what about this chocolate ice cream? Come on, try some!

GLENN: Try some of these nice California prunes—or some of these figs. They're full of vitamins.

CLARENCE (*Sadly*): Not—litronium.

BOB: Gee, I guess none of this stuff is litronium. What'll we do? That meteor's getting closer and closer and hotter and hotter every minute. Whew! It feels like Palm Springs on the Fourth of July!

HOWARD: Well, if everyone has finished playing this crazy parlor game, I'll just take everything back to the kitchen where it belongs. I want to get on with breakfast. Great Jumping Jupiter, but it's getting warm! Looks like it's going to be a real scorcher today, all right.

CLARENCE: Just—three minutes—left! Sorry—earth people. I've—failed!

PROFESSOR: Er—before it's too late—ah, Mr. Catastrophe—I feel I owe you an apology for referring to you, as an inhabitant of another planet, as a—a low form of life. Forgive me, sir.

CLARENCE: It's—all right. I—understand.

NARRATOR: Suddenly Howard notices the jar of smog on the table beside the milk. He picks it up and opens it.

HOWARD: Now, what's this? What's this dirty jar doing here? Yes, it's empty, just as I thought!

BOB: Oh, it's just a jar of smog Andy and I brought from L.A., Howard. Good old Los Angeles smog! I'm going to miss it.

ANDY: Me, too! Just thinking about it makes me choke up.

CLARENCE: Litronium! I smell litronium. Where is it? Oh, it's coming from that jar! Quick, let me have it! Ah, thank the planetary powers—litronium at last!

PROFESSOR: You mean to say that smog is—litronium?

CLARENCE: Yes, sir! Richest blend I've ever inhaled. Ah—dee-licious! Better than anything available on Clarion or any-where in outer space.

BOB: You mean—you're going to be all right now?

CLARENCE: Yep. This'll do it. This'll fix me up fine, earth boy. Quick, earth friends, let me out of here! There may still be time to avert disaster.

NARRATOR: Clarence heads for the window, running and jump-ing with increasing energy as he continues to inhale the smog from the jar.

CLARENCE: Goodbye, earth friends! Thanks for the litronium! I hope I'm not too late to save your planet. One minute to go!

BOB: Goodbye, Clarence—goodbye! Good luck!

ANDY: Gee, I sure hope he gets to that meteor in time! It must be awfully close to earth now.

PROFESSOR (*Astonished*): Why, he was out of sight in just one long jump! Never saw anything like it! Remarkable fellow! Highly evolved. This changes everything.

GLENN (*Shouting excitedly*): The meteor's heading west—toward the Pacific Ocean and—and it's getting smaller!

HOWARD: Great heavens, it seems to be getting darker—much

darker. Must be clouding up again. Perhaps hot cakes would be better for breakfast than cold cereal.

BOB: Hurrah! Catastrophe Clarence has steered the meteor away from earth!

ANDY: Hurrah for Clarence! Hurrah for smog!

PROFESSOR: Well, as the old saying goes, one man's meat is another man's poison—and vice versa.

ANDY: What?

BOB: Oh, I get it. You mean that what's smog for some people is litronium for others, huh?

PROFESSOR: Something like that, Bob.

ANDY: Hey! Wait until the Los Angeles Chamber of Commerce hears about this!

BOB: And L.A. isn't the only city in the world with smog. There's St. Louis and London and—and Detroit and lots of others. All big cities have some of it sometimes. And now, just think, smog has saved the whole earth from destruction —and space men need it to live on!

ANDY: Well, I'm glad *I* don't have to live on it. Say, I'm starved!

BOB: So am I. How about something to eat, Howard?

HOWARD: Just as—as soon as the professor tells me how he wants his eggs this morning.

PROFESSOR: Scrambled, Howard—scrambled!

ANDY: Well, I guess Howard is still in a smog!

THE END

Express to Valley Forge

This play takes place during a bitter cold winter when the American colonists seemed to be losing their struggle for independence.

While many of the colonists fought with Washington's army, or worked for the cause of freedom, many others sympathized with the British. Some colonists were not sure how they felt. In this play, you will learn about all of these attitudes.

Read the entire play to yourself.

1. Name the characters who are British sympathizers.
2. Name those who are undecided.
3. Name those who are for Washington.
4. What fine thing did Washington do for Granny?
5. Why was it a fine thing to do?

Do you know the meaning of these phrases? If not, use your dictionary. Ask your teacher for help on the starred phrases:

old Erin
*mild-mannered man
with a wen on his nose
learned it by rote
let's have some repose
*talk like a cloth head
*fair raises my hackles
a miniature
my stomach is so queasy
do not hamper the freedom of others

Kathleen speaks with an Irish brogue. Discuss the meaning of the word *brogue*.

Let's take turns practicing some of Kathleen's lines and see who does them best.

> By all the *saints*, '*tis* cold!
> 'Tis enough *to chill the* Divil himself.
> Sure, and *who'll be* wantin' a cool breeze?
> 'Tis only that at times I miss the green grass and *the peat bogs* of old Erin.
> Sure, *and a parrot* could answer them.
> Faith an' I thought he'd never go. 'Tis quick I must be now.

Now that you have tried a brogue, you should know the best person to be Kathleen.

Choose people for the other parts.

Practice your part to yourself. Get help on words you do not know.

Read the play out loud.

1. Did Grandmother sound impatient and angry at times?
2. Did Kathleen use her brogue?
3. Did you all read smoothly and easily?
4. Did you come in on time with your part?

Read the play over once more together. Practice the difficult parts several times.

Arrange for a time to read it to the class.

EXPRESS TO VALLEY FORGE

by Earl J. Dias

Characters

(*2 boys, 4 girls, and the narrator*)

NARRATOR

GRANDMA HEATHER, *an old woman*

KATHLEEN, *servant at the Heather Inn*
DEBORAH HEATHER, *an attractive girl of seventeen*
MR. HEATHER, *her father*
MRS. HEATHER, *her mother*
ELIJAH HARRIS, *the stagecoach driver*

NARRATOR: The play you are about to hear takes place late in an afternoon in January, 1778. We are in the kitchen of the Heather Inn in Chester County, Pennsylvania, which is about ten miles from Valley Forge. Grandma Heather is sitting in the rocking chair, knitting. Kathleen, the servant, is taking cups, saucers, plates and cutlery from the cabinet and setting the table. The day is very cold, and Kathleen blows on her fingers to try to warm them up.

KATHLEEN: By all the saints, 'tis cold! This Pennsylvania is a bitter land, if you ask me. Snow and ice and hail and sleet— 'tis enough to chill the Divil himself.

GRANDMA: Now don't be complaining, Kathleen. After all, you've been here only a month. Wait till the spring when everything is fresh and green, and the summer when a cool breeze from the Schuylkill River fans us.

KATHLEEN: Sure, and who'll be wantin' a cool breeze after not havin' a minute all winter when your feet weren't frozen and your whole body didn't feel like an icicle?

GRANDMA (*Chuckling*): You'll feel otherwise when summer comes. Come here, child. Are you really so unhappy here?

KATHLEEN (*Quickly*): Oh, no, ma'am, I wouldn't want to be givin' the wrong impression. Sure, you and Mr. and Mrs. Heather, and that sweet colleen, Deborah, have been kindness itself to me.

GRANDMA: And remember, you're to be a bond servant only for a year. Then you'll be free to do as you wish.

KATHLEEN: And like as not I'll choose to stay here at the Heather Inn, ma'am. 'Tis only that at times I miss the green grass and the peat bogs of old Erin.

GRANDMA: Of course you do. I felt the same way when I came from England years and years before you were born. And now, child, let's hear your lessons.

KATHLEEN: As you will, ma'am. But I do notice that Mr. and Mrs. Heather do not approve of what you say to me. Nor does that Elijah Harris, the stagecoach driver.

GRANDMA (*Nippily*): That's because they're blind fools, Kathleen—afraid to change as the world changes. They close their eyes to what's going on about them. Now, let's hear what you know. What is freedom, child?

KATHLEEN (*Reciting, as though she has memorized the answer*): Freedom, ma'am, is the right to think and act as you believe, provided you do not hamper the freedom of others in doing so.

GRANDMA: Splendid, child, splendid! And now, who is the chief fighter for freedom?

KATHLEEN (*Chuckling*): General George Washington, ma'am —him that is camped with his men, poor souls, not ten miles from here at Valley Forge.

GRANDMA: And against whom is he fighting?

KATHLEEN: The Lobster Backs, ma'am, or the Red Coats, or the British—give 'em what name you wish.

GRANDMA: Don't tempt me, child. And who will win the fight?

KATHLEEN (*Chuckling again*): General George Washington, ma'am—and sure, you've told me that a thousand times.

NARRATOR: Deborah enters. Neither Kathleen nor Grandma sees her.

GRANDMA: And who is the greatest man in the land?

KATHLEEN (*Laughing merrily*): By the good saints, ma'am, the answers to your questions are all the same. Sure, and a parrot could answer them.

DEBORAH (*Loudly*): General George Washington.

NARRATOR: Kathleen leaps to her feet, startled. Grandma picks up her knitting and resumes it hurriedly. Deborah laughs as she comes to the rocker and gives Grandma an affectionate hug, and then goes to the table, where she seats herself with a sigh.

KATHLEEN: Faith, Miss Deborah, and you gave us a start.

GRANDMA: Where have you been, Deborah?

DEBORAH: Out in the stable. Blacksmith Hawkins is mending the wheel of Elijah's stagecoach. Elijah had to stop here to get it done.

GRANDMA: Any passengers? Anybody who travels in such bitter weather either has rocks in his head where his brains ought to be or is up to no good.

DEBORAH: Don't be so suspicious, Grandma.

GRANDMA: I only know what I've seen. The country round about is teeming with spies and nosey critters who look as though they'd slit your throat with pleasure.

DEBORAH: There is just one passenger, and he looks harmless enough. A little, mild-mannered man with a wen on his nose.

GRANDMA: I never did trust people with wens.

KATHLEEN (*Gayly*): And has Elijah proposed to you again, Miss Deborah? Sure, and the man must have a dry throat from asking you so often!

DEBORAH: He proposes every time I see him—and in the same words. I think he wrote the speech and learned it by rote—like an actor in a play.

KATHLEEN: He's a handsome enough man.

GRANDMA: But too old for Deborah—May and December don't suit each other, as you'd know if you'd lived as long as I have. Besides, I don't like his ideas. He has too many friends among the Lobster Backs.

DEBORAH: I nearly forgot, Kathleen. Elijah wants a cup of tea. Will you take it to him in the stable?

KATHLEEN: That I will, Miss Deborah.

NARRATOR: Kathleen takes her cloak from the hook, puts it on and takes a cup to the fireplace and pours tea into it. She speaks a few words and leaves for the stable.

KATHLEEN: Sure, and the poor man will be needin' something hot out in that cold stable.

DEBORAH: Have you ever known a colder winter, Grandma? Abner Hawkins says that General Washington and his men are well-nigh freezing to death at Valley Forge.

GRANDMA: And you've had no word from Nathan Merriman?

DEBORAH (*Sadly*): None at all. Though I know he's still on General Washington's staff.

GRANDMA: And your heart's there with him, isn't it, child?

NARRATOR: Deborah, beginning to feel a chill, rises from the footstool and goes over to the bench. She sits in front of the fireplace and warms her hands as she talks.

DEBORAH: Yes, Grandma. But the war looks so hopeless now. Elijah says that Washington's army will not last out the winter—over half of his men have deserted. Sometimes I think that I'll never see Nathan again—that he's sacrificing himself for a losing cause.

GRANDMA: Don't speak that way, child. Causes aren't lost so easily. Some day you'll be proud that Nathan fought the good fight—and won. General Washington knows what he's doing.

NARRATOR: Mr. and Mrs. Heather enter the room. Both are bundled against the cold. Mr. Heather is cold and grumpy.

MR. HEATHER (*Grumpily*): General Washington! General Washington! That's your tune from morn till night, Mother.

GRANDMA: And a good tune, too.

MRS. HEATHER: A flat-nosed Virginia squire who has brought nothing but death and destruction to Pennsylvania. The sooner he is defeated, the better!

MR. HEATHER: Right! Then some of us will be able to sleep o' nights—and sleep in peace.

GRANDMA (*Angrily*): But not in freedom. Lick King George's boots if your tongue's long enough. *I* won't!

MR. HEATHER (*Impatiently*): Now, Mother, we've spoken enough of this before. In heaven's name, let's have some repose under this roof. Deborah, I saw Elijah in the stable. Why aren't you with him?

GRANDMA: She doesn't want to be—that's why.

MRS. HEATHER: The girl is still mooning over that young scamp, Nathan Merriman, who left his good farm to fight for Washington and his rabble.

DEBORAH: He isn't a scamp. He's doing what he thinks right.

MR. HEATHER: Don't contradict your mother, child. As for Elijah, he's a good, sound man who would make you a respectable, God-fearing husband.

GRANDMA: Hmmph! He's too friendly with the British for my liking.

MR. HEATHER: Oh, Mother, you'll drive us mad with your politics.

GRANDMA: You want waking up—both of you!

MR. HEATHER: That's enough, Mother. As for you, Deborah, you'd do well to think kindly on Elijah's proposal. There are many maids in Pennsylvania who would be happy to have him.

MRS. HEATHER (*Tenderly*): And, after all, child, marriage might help to get a lot of silly notions out of your head. We're thinking only of your welfare.

MR. HEATHER: Come, Martha, we'd best get out of these heavy clothes and rest a bit before supper. The walk from the village was a tiring one. And, Mother, for the sake of peace in this household, forget about your precious General Washington.

GRANDMA: To think that a son of mine would talk like a cloth head. It fair raises my hackles, I can tell you.

DEBORAH: Mother and Father want to return to normal living, Grandma. I suppose we can't blame them for that. They're sick of war and confusion.

GRANDMA: And how do you think Washington and his men feel in the snowdrifts at Valley Forge, with the wind biting like a mad dog?

DEBORAH: I know, Grandma. I know. But sometimes it seems

as though the bloodshed will never end and that Nathan—

GRANDMA: And that Nathan will never return? But he will, child. Have faith. He will.

NARRATOR: Kathleen bursts into the room. She is breathless with excitement and can scarcely wait to speak.

KATHLEEN: Oh, the saints protect us! I've heard the most terrible thing!

DEBORAH: What is it, Kathleen?

KATHLEEN: Sure and there's evil in the world! Evil all around!

GRANDMA: For mercy's sake, child, tell your story!

KATHLEEN (*Getting her breath*): Well, ma'am, I took the tea to Elijah. Faith he was deep in talk, he was, with a stranger.

DEBORAH: That was the stagecoach passenger.

KATHLEEN: They stopped their talk when I brought the tea, and sure it seemed to me they looked a bit guilty. I'd heard them mention the name of General Washington, though.

GRANDMA: Aha!

KATHLEEN: So Elijah drank his tea, and I left, I did—or, at least, he thought so. But I crept behind the stable and listened —there's many a crack in the wall—and I heard the most terrible thing. You wouldn't believe it.

NARRATOR: A very tall, heavy, broad-shouldered man of forty, good-looking enough but rather pompous and with an air of false heartiness, enters the Inn. He turns to Kathleen and speaks.

ELIJAH: Wouldn't believe what, my Irish lass? You look as though you'd seen a ghost or Satan himself.

GRANDMA: Get Elijah a cup of something hot, child.

ELIJAH: More tea. That last was good. It warms the bones on a day as bitter cold as this.

NARRATOR: Kathleen goes to the fireplace, pours tea from the kettle into a cup, and hands it to Elijah. Deborah and Grandma cast exasperated looks at each other as Elijah sits down on a bench and drinks his tea.

ELIJAH: Your hand's shaking, lass. Well, it's cold enough to make a body shiver.

DEBORAH: Where is your passenger, Elijah?

ELIJAH: He has walked over to the Blake farm. He knows old Blake and wants to chat with him. (*Chuckling*) He went alone, I can tell you. I'd not walk a mile in cold such as this.

DEBORAH: Is the wheel repaired?

ELIJAH: Right as rain, and the horses are hitched up. We'll leave when the passenger returns—in an hour or so. There's no particular hurry. I'm so far behind my schedule now that time no longer matters.

DEBORAH: Elijah, do you remember the artist fellow who stayed here in October?

ELIJAH: Aye, a thin rail of a man with eyes that seemed to pop out of his head.

DEBORAH: He painted my portrait while he was here—a miniature he called it.

ELIJAH: Did he now?

DEBORAH: Would you like the picture, Elijah?

GRANDMA: What in the world are—

DEBORAH (*Warningly*): Now, Grandma! Would you like it, Elijah?

ELIJAH: Why, of course I'd like it, lass. Are your feelings softening toward old Elijah? Are you beginning to realize he's not a bad fellow? Does this mean that you and I—

DEBORAH: It might, Elijah.

ELIJAH: Then fetch the picture, lass.

DEBORAH: It's upstairs in Mother's and Father's room. Why don't you get it, Elijah? Mother and Father will be glad to give it to you, for they think highly of you, as you know.

ELIJAH: Do they, now?

DEBORAH: They think that you'd turn any girl's head. And I think they're right. Tell them I said you were to have the miniature.

ELIJAH: And one kiss to seal the bargain.

DEBORAH: Later, Elijah.

ELIJAH: Ah, this has turned into a fine day. I will see you later, lass.

KATHLEEN: Faith, and I thought he'd never go! 'Tis quick I must be now. Elijah and the stranger were talkin'. Tomorrow night a messenger will be ridin' from Valley Forge with the campaign plans for the spring. He'll be ridin' to Philadelphia to deliver the plans to the leaders of the Continental Congress. The stranger, with Elijah's help, will waylay the messenger, get the plans, and turn them over to the British. And the messenger—

GRANDMA (*Impatiently*): Out with it, child.

KATHLEEN: The messenger is like to be killed. And the messenger is to be Nathan Merriman.

DEBORAH (*Gasping*): Nathan! Oh! But how did they know all this?

KATHLEEN: From what I gathered, 'tis Elijah himself who nosed out the information.

GRANDMA: The mealy-mouthed windbag!

DEBORAH: I must do something! The stagecoach is all ready to go.

KATHLEEN: Oh, Miss Deborah, you're not thinkin' of takin' it!

GRANDMA: Of course she is! And I'd like to see Elijah's face when he finds out!

DEBORAH: I'll drive the coach to Valley Forge and warn Nathan!

GRANDMA: Good girl!

KATHLEEN: But the weather's so bitter.

GRANDMA: Not so bitter as Elijah, blast him to blazes, will be.

DEBORAH: If only Elijah stays up there until I'm away.

GRANDMA: He'll stay there. He'll stay there if I have to sit on him—depend on it. And give my love to General Washington.

KATHLEEN: The saints preserve us!

NARRATOR: Kathleen goes to the window and looks out intently. Suddenly the sound of the stagecoach is heard as it gets under way. Kathleen speaks with relief.

KATHLEEN: She's off, thank heaven, and may good St. Patrick guide her on her way.

NARRATOR: The next scene takes place five hours later. Mr. and Mrs. Heather are seated at the table in the kitchen of the inn. Grandma is sitting in her rocker knitting. Kathleen is sitting on the bench before the fireplace, while Elijah paces up and down pompously and nervously. All seem worried except Grandma.

ELIJAH: Five hours now since the minx left! I don't understand how a maid who is supposed to be well brought up and modest could do such a thing.

GRANDMA: Deborah's not a minx, Elijah. You'll favor me by keeping such thoughts to yourself.

MR. HEATHER: Yes, Elijah. I'll not have my daughter slandered. I grant you she may be headstrong and willful at times.

MRS. HEATHER: As she has a right to be. I was myself at her age.

GRANDMA: Well, you're both beginning to sound almost human—for a change.

ELIJAH (*Sarcastically*): Headstrong and willful, indeed. The girl steals my stage—she'll probably ruin the horses—and I'm supposed to smile at her little whim as being merely the pleasant little folly of youth. (*Thoughtfully*) It seems to me that she was unusually pleasant to me this afternoon—I should have been suspicious.

GRANDMA (*Sharply*): No more of that, Elijah.

ELIJAH (*Angrily*): And have I no right to complain? How can I explain all this later? A slip of a girl makes off with my coach! My passenger is angry beyond belief; he has stalked off to the Blake farm calling down curses on my head! To be tricked thus by a girl! I'll be a laughing-stock! And for what earthly reason should she want to drive the coach? It's beyond all understanding.

GRANDMA: Perhaps that great brain of yours just isn't working well tonight, Elijah.

MR. HEATHER: I surmise that you know more about all this than you're telling, Mother.

GRANDMA: I? Why, son, I'm as innocent as a new-born sparrow.

MRS. HEATHER: Will you bring me some tea, Kathleen?

KATHLEEN: Yes, ma'am. Mr. Heather, would you be wantin' some, sir?

MR. HEATHER: No, Kathleen, my stomach is so queasy with this infernal waiting that I'd not trust it with tea or anything else.

ELIJAH: And I'll wager that this Irish lass knows a thing or two.

KATHLEEN (*Innocently*): Me, sir?

ELIJAH: Aye, you've been strangely quiet all the night.

KATHLEEN (*Primly*): 'Tis a servant's place to be seen and not heard, sir.

ELIJAH: No sign of Deborah. Where can she have gone?

MRS. HEATHER: You may as well sit and be comfortable, Elijah. She'll be here when she arrives—not before. There's nothing any of us can do but wait.

ELIJAH: And to think I asked so willful a creature to be my wife, believing she was a quiet, modest young woman who would grace my hearth.

GRANDMA: She never said "yes" that I know of.

MR. HEATHER: Let's not stir up more trouble, Mother. Elijah is beside himself with worry and perhaps doesn't mean what he says. Such criticism of Deborah is not gentlemanly, Elijah. She may have good reason for what she does.

ELIJAH: Reason! To steal my stage from under my nose!

NARRATOR: The sound of the stagecoach is heard in the distance. Elijah rushes to the door and dashes outside. Kathleen and Mr. and Mrs. Heather go to the window and look. Grandma does not seem to care, as she remains in her rocker, knitting and chuckling to herself.

KATHLEEN (*Excitedly*): Faith, and it's Miss Deborah, all right! The saints be praised! Oh, Elijah seems to be tellin' her a thing or two, and she's laughin'.

GRANDMA: Good!

ELIJAH: And now, Miss Deborah, come in here. We'd like the reason for all this!

MRS. HEATHER: Are you all right, child?

DEBORAH (*Gayly*): Yes, Mother, of course.

MR. HEATHER: Now, Deborah, you owe us all an explanation. What whim was it that made you do such a thing?

ELIJAH: Aye, Miss Heather, what whim—

DEBORAH: I'm no longer Miss Heather, Elijah.

MRS. HEATHER: What do you mean, child?

DEBORAH (*Proudly*): I am now Mrs. Nathan Merriman.

MR. HEATHER (*Astonished*): Mrs. Nathan Merriman!

KATHLEEN: Sure, and what a lovely surprise!

ELIJAH: Lovely surprise! Do you mean that you stole my stage only to go to your own wedding?

DEBORAH (*Laughing*): Borrowed, Elijah—not stole. I did, indeed. Nathan and I were married in camp at Valley Forge by Parson Ames who is there with the troops.

MR. HEATHER: You drove on this bitter night to Valley Forge?

DEBORAH: I did, Father.

ELIJAH: So it's Mrs. Nathan Merriman, is it? I won't be needing this miniature of your lovely self, then. As for your marriage, it might not be a healthful one.

DEBORAH (*Coldly*): Indeed?

ELIJAH: Indeed! I know a thing or two concerning Nathan Merriman. Your marriage may be a brief one.

MRS. HEATHER: What do you mean, Elijah?

ELIJAH: Never you mind. Time will tell. And, Mistress Deborah, it's only my regard for your father and mother that prevents me from prosecuting you for stealing my coach.

DEBORAH: Thank you, sir.

ELIJAH: Aye, I know a thing or two about Nathan Merriman. And now I leave you. Good night.

MRS. HEATHER: Well, child, this is a mystery to me. If you wanted Nathan enough to steal a stage and drive ten miles to him, there's nothing left to say.

234 *EXPRESS TO VALLEY FORGE*

DEBORAH: I know I've done the right thing, Mother. Don't you worry.

MR. HEATHER: At least you're back safely. (*Sternly*) I may have more to say about this in the morning.

GRANDMA: I'm sure you will.

MR. HEATHER (*Yawning*): But now it's time all decent folk were in bed. Come, Martha. We must go along to bed.

NARRATOR: Mr. and Mrs. Heather go out. Deborah rushes to Grandma, who hugs her.

GRANDMA: Bravely done, child. Is everything safe now for Nathan?

DEBORAH: Yes, Grandma. The plans will be delivered, but Elijah will never know it.

KATHLEEN: Congratulations, Miss Deborah, on your marriage.

DEBORAH: Isn't it wonderful, Kathleen! Nathan said there was no sense in wasting a good opportunity with Parson Ames on hand.

GRANDMA: Did you see General Washington?

KATHLEEN: Oh, yes, did you see the General?

DEBORAH: Indeed, I did. He attended the wedding ceremony. He's so kind. He called me his little apple-cheeked patriot and said that my ride tonight might prove as important as Paul Revere's ride three years ago. (*Sadly*) But, Grandma, the men are suffering so at Valley Forge. The General tries to seem cheerful though, and he seems to be keeping up the spirits of his men.

GRANDMA: Of course.

DEBORAH: I told the General all about you, Grandma. And he gave me this letter for you.

GRANDMA (*Amazed*): A letter for me from the General?

DEBORAH: Yes, Grandma.

KATHLEEN: Now will wonders never cease! Oh, do read it to us, ma'am!

GRANDMA: "My dear Grandma—"

KATHLEEN: Grandma, indeed. Why, how human the General is!

GRANDMA: "Your granddaughter, a brave girl, has made it known to me what a loyal and steadfast admirer I have in you. Although I am unworthy of such admiration, please believe that it is faith such as yours that gives me strength to go on in the arduous tasks which I consider to be my duty and privilege. So long as such loyal spirits as yours light the way through the darkness, our cause will not be lost, and freedom will be won. Your obedient and grateful servant, George Washington."

KATHLEEN: 'Tis beautiful, that's what it is!

DEBORAH: It's a lovely letter, Grandma.

GRANDMA: He has made a foolish old woman very happy. Kathleen, sit here. It's not too late for our lessons. Now, let's begin. What is freedom, child?

KATHLEEN: Freedom, ma'am, is the right to think and act as you believe, provided that you do not hamper the freedom of others in doing so.

GRANDMA: And who is the greatest fighter for freedom?

KATHLEEN: General George Washington, ma'am.

GRANDMA: And now—and I want you to answer too, Deborah—who is the finest man in the land?

KATHLEEN *and* DEBORAH: General George Washington!

NARRATOR: Everyone laughs happily. Kathleen and Deborah hug Grandma affectionately as they repeat their answer. Grandma nods with pleasure.

GRANDMA: General George Washington—the finest man in America!

THE END

Scheherazade

Scheherazade is a famous princess of legend and fairy tale. This play is a bit different from some other stories you may have read about her. Read the entire play to yourself and be prepared to answer the following questions:

Why did the Sultan have his wives killed?
How many wives had he had beheaded?
How long did he allow them to live?
Why do you think Scheherazade offered to marry the Sultan?

Be sure you can pronounce these words:

Scheherazade — Sheh-heh-rah-zod
Schahriah — Shah-rī-ah
Dinazade — Din-nah-zod

Ask your teacher for help if necessary.

Remember to use your voice to express fear, surprise, delight, etc.

If you are the Sultan, be very sure to talk as you believe a Sultan would. Stand tall and give power and dignity to your voice.

Work in this play to come in with your part right on time. Long pauses, nudges, sleepy forgetful people, will spoil the play for the people who are listening. Remember, they have no books! *By your reading* you make this play interesting or dull to the listener.

With your chairman decide who should take the various parts.

Read your part over to yourself until you understand where you come in and what you say.

Practice reading the play together. After each reading, discuss together how it could be improved.

Check these things:

1. Did you read smoothly?
2. Did you make your voice fit the character?
3. Did you come in on time?
4. Did you make the play sound interesting and exciting?

Tell your teacher when you are ready to read to the class.

SCHEHERAZADE

by May Lynch

Characters

(3 boys, 7 girls, and the narrator)
NARRATOR
SCHEHERAZADE, *the new queen*
SCHAHRIAH, *the sultan*
DINAZADE, *sister of Scheherazade*
ROYAL COOK
PAGE
EXECUTIONER
SEAMSTRESS
NUTMEG ⎫
POPPYSEED ⎬ *maids*
LOTUS PETAL ⎭

NARRATOR: This play takes place long, long ago. The setting is the throne room of the Sultan's palace. Two maids, Nutmeg and Poppyseed, are dusting the throne as another maid, Lotus Petal, enters.

LOTUS PETAL: Nutmeg! Poppyseed! Nutmeg! Poppyseed! Oh, there you are. I hope your work is all finished. Are you ready to greet the new queen?

POPPYSEED: Yes, Lotus Petal, we are trying to memorize her name.

NUTMEG: I have it down in my mind now. Scheherazade. (*Slowly*) Sche-he-ra-zade.

POPPYSEED: I'll never learn it, Lotus Petal. Let me try—Sche-heard-a-what?

NUTMEG: No, no. Listen. Sche-he-ra-zade—zod—zod. Think of this—"I am zod when Lotus Petal catches me napping instead of dusting."

POPPYSEED: Well, I am zod. Every day I must learn a new name. Each day the name is harder.

NUTMEG: Queens, queens, queens! Every day there is a new one on the throne. Let me see—I think today makes 435 queens.

POPPYSEED: Sche-he-ra-zade. Sche-herazade. Poor thing. She will die just as the others have died. Chop, chop, chop, and off rolls her pretty little head.

NUTMEG: The royal executioner has already worn out several hatchets. They say he really has an ax to grind.

POPPYSEED: Lotus Petal, you have been around here so long. Don't you think our grand and supreme ruler, commander-in-chief of twenty-one kingdoms (*Pause*), is a bit—well—strange?

LOTUS PETAL: Shhhhh! Never say that! The walls have ears and keyholes have big, big eyes.

POPPYSEED: Say "yes," Lotus Petal, or I shall think I am the one who is crazy.

LOTUS PETAL (*Whispers*): One might say (*Pause*), one might say (*Pause*) he is eccentric.

NUTMEG: Eccentric!

LOTUS PETAL: Shhhhh!

NUTMEG: Eccentric! Off with her head! Eccentric!

SEAMSTRESS: Needles and pins, needles and pins, when the Sultan marries, the trouble begins.

LOTUS PETAL: What's the trouble, Royal Seamstress?

SEAMSTRESS: Trouble? Trouble? How would you like to make

a wedding dress every day for 435 days? I can't see straight.

NUTMEG: Our Sultan is only eccentric.

POPPYSEED: He's a wicked, mean old man.

NUTMEG: He's a bad old man, all right.

LOTUS PETAL: When you are as old as I, Poppyseed and Nutmeg, you will find there are reasons for everything.

POPPYSEED: Reasons for everything? Then explain his theory of decapitation.

NUTMEG: That means chopping off somebody's head.

LOTUS PETAL: I know, I know.

POPPYSEED: Go ahead and explain it, Lotus Petal.

LOTUS PETAL: Well, His Majesty, the grand and supreme ruler and commander-in-chief of twenty-one kingdoms, was once a happy man. He was a handsome, young prince in the days of my mother, Fig Blossom. However, he married a wicked young woman who treated him ever so badly, and because of this harsh treatment, he hates women!

NUTMEG: Really? All women?

LOTUS PETAL: "All women are evil," said the unhappy, once-happy prince, and he decided that no woman would ever be able to make him unhappy again. So he thought of this plan.

POPPYSEED: What plan?

LOTUS PETAL: Every day wedding bells would ring out, to be heard far and wide in the kingdom.

NUTMEG: How romantic.

LOTUS PETAL: But every day he would choose a different bride. Then the day after the wedding, the bride would have to appear before the Royal Court Advisor.

NUTMEG: What for?

LOTUS PETAL: To be beheaded royally, of course. All the brides are daughters of nobles.

POPPYSEED: But (*Slowly*) Sche-he-ra-zade is the daughter of the Court Advisor!

LOTUS PETAL: Alas, all the nobles' daughters have been used up.

NUTMEG: How many women are there in the kingdom?

LOTUS PETAL: If the Court Advisor fails to have the queen beheaded, he himself will be beheaded. Ah, greetings to you, Cook. Are you baking another wedding cake?

COOK: Lotus Petal, you must come help me. I'm having trouble with the wedding cake makers. They're all going on strike. They say they are sick of making wedding cakes. Can't you lend me some of your maids to mix the icing?

NUTMEG: Let us help, Lotus Petal. We love to lick the bowls.

LOTUS PETAL: Very well, if you are sure the dusting is done.

COOK: Have you heard the news? The new queen is the daughter of the Court Advisor—and the second cook's brother knows the page who heard that she volunteered to marry the Sultan!

POPPYSEED: She must be a sorceress! How exciting! Only a witch would dare to marry our (*Whispers*) eccentric Sultan.

NUTMEG: The Court Advisor has another daughter. That makes 436. Who will be next?

NARRATOR: Later the same day the Sultan and Scheherazade enter the throne room. The Page announces them to the court attendants.

PAGE: Make way for His Majesty, Schahriah, supreme ruler and commander-in-chief of twenty-one kingdoms. Make way for Her Majesty, Scheherazade, royal bride of His Majesty, grand and supreme ruler of twenty-one kingdoms. Hail to the Sultan! Hail to his beautiful bride!

SULTAN: Ah, my dear, you are by far the most beautiful woman I have ever seen. No wonder our royal subjects stare and stare at you. They have never seen such a fair queen.

SCHEHERAZADE: Surely, my husband exaggerates.

SULTAN (*Aside*): What a beauty! How sad that she must leave this world.

NARRATOR: The Sultan presents Scheherazade with a chest of beautiful jewelry, saying—

SULTAN: Some trinkets for my bride.

SCHEHERAZADE: How lovely! I've heard of such wonderful gems, but I've never seen any like these!

NARRATOR: The Queen holds the gems to the light. As she looks at them, she begins to weep.

SULTAN (*Concerned*): Why do you weep, my precious one? These are for you to wear. Pray do not weep tears that are bigger than these diamonds.

SCHEHERAZADE: I weep, dear husband, because I am homesick for my dear little sister, Dinazade. We have never been separated before.

SULTAN: Page! Page! Dispatch a royal messenger and bring back the second daughter of the Court Advisor. My bride must be happy—(*He sighs*) for a little while.

NARRATOR: The Royal Cook enters and bows before the Sultan.

COOK: The royal wedding cake is prepared, Your Royal Highness, but I fear that there will be none tomorrow. The royal kitchen is on strike.

SULTAN: On strike? How silly! Why are they striking?

COOK: They are tired of making wedding cakes, Your Highness. Today was the four-hundred-and-thirty-fifth. They want to make doughnuts or pies or tarts or something different.

SCHEHERAZADE: Tarts! Tarts! I'd love some tarts! Let's have tarts tomorrow and doughnuts next day and pie the day after that!

NARRATOR: The Sultan stares straight ahead while the attendants begin to whisper and shake their heads sadly. They are concerned for Scheherazade.

SULTAN: Very well—er—tarts! Make tarts!

PAGE (*Announcing*): Make way for the daughter of the Royal Court Advisor and sister to the royal bride, Dinazade.

NARRATOR: Dinazade enters. When she sees her sister, the child runs to her and kisses her fondly.

SCHEHERAZADE: Dear little sister, I was beginning to think we would never see each other.

DINAZADE: I thought we'd never put our heads together again.

SCHEHERAZADE: Dear husband, before we depart for our marriage supper, may I take some moments of your time? I'd like to tell my little sister a story. I usually do at bedtime.

SULTAN: Of course, of course, but isn't she big for bedtime stories?

SCHEHERAZADE: None are too old, and none are too young. Come, little one, sit at my feet, and I shall begin.

Once upon a time there was a fisherman who was too poor to get food for his wife and sons. The waters would yield no fish, and because he did not want the gods to think him greedy, he would cast his net only four times. His sons argued this point, but the fisherman wanted to please the gods. However, one day he was about ready to go home, when there appeared on his line a copper vessel. On it was the seal of Solomon. He opened it quickly with his knife, and out came a genie. "Prepare to die," said the genie. "You may be granted one favor before you die." "Well," said the fisherman, "I want you to answer one question." "Anything," said the genie. "Were you really in this vessel?" asked the man. "Of course," said the genie. "I don't believe it. You must prove it. Let me see you get back into the vessel." So, of course, the genie—

Dinazade! Oh, my precious little sister, you are already asleep. I'll have to finish the tale another time. (*She yawns.*) I'm tired and sleepy, myself.

SULTAN: Oh, dear, just when the story was getting interesting. You don't suppose the genie got back into the vessel, do you? Scheherazade! Wake up! Oh, dear, I'll have to wait until tomorrow to hear how the fisherman makes out.

PAGE: But, sir, you are committed to leave early in the morning for the twelfth kingdom inspection.

SULTAN: So? I'll hear the end of the story tomorrow night.

PAGE: Is not the royal queen to be beheaded?

SULTAN: Summon the Court Advisor and Royal Executioner. Her death must be postponed.

NARRATOR: And now it is one month later. The Sultan and Scheherazade are in the throne room, alone.

SCHEHERAZADE: And so, Aladdin married the princess and took her to live in the palace the genie of the lamp had given him.

NARRATOR: The Page enters and bows before the Sultan.

SULTAN: Page, haven't I told you never, never to interrupt me when I am listening to the stories of Scheherazade? You have done so six times this month.

PAGE: Sir, there is trouble in the nineteenth and twentieth kingdoms. They have sent for you.

SULTAN: Tell them to settle their own troubles. My place is at the side of my wife.

NARRATOR: The Royal Cook enters and approaches the Sultan fearfully.

COOK: Your Royal Highness—

SULTAN: Be off! How shall I find out what happened to Aladdin?

COOK: Your Highness, the kitchen help is on strike again.

SULTAN: Again? Why?

COOK: They claim that everyone else in the palace is allowed to listen to the stories of the queen but they are always cooking, and so they never hear about Ali Baba or the Enchanted Horse or—or—

SULTAN: Hm—how do you know about these tales? Who has been carrying tales?

COOK: Your Highness, I listened at the keyhole. My specialty was always wedding cakes, but lately, I have had nothing to do.

NARRATOR: Nutmeg and Poppyseed come into the room. They bow low before the Sultan.

NUTMEG: It's partly our fault, your Royal Highness. Since the arrival of our worthy and lovely queen, we have had nothing to dust. We've been sitting here with the rest of the court listening to these marvelous stories.

POPPYSEED: She must know a thousand and one of them, your

Royal Highness. We love to hear them, and we wanted everyone to hear them—

NUTMEG: So we told the Royal Cook to listen at the royal key-hole.

POPPYSEED: We didn't think you'd mind. You have become so kind, and such a wonderful ruler. Everyone in the whole kingdom loves you now.

NARRATOR: Bowing as he advances, the Royal Executioner comes into the throne room.

EXECUTIONER: I am the Royal Executioner, Your Highness. I've thrown away my royal hatchet and have made a beautiful garden where the queens used to be beheaded. Anybody in the kingdom will help me dig and plant and carry sod because they are so happy about the change in policy around here.

NARRATOR: A woman enters carrying two beautiful robes. She is the Court Seamstress. She, too, speaks to the Sultan.

SEAMSTRESS: I'm the Royal Seamstress, Your Highness. Since the new queen has been telling stories, we've been able to get all the palace mending done. That hasn't happened in years because we were always stitching wedding dresses. You've made everyone so happy, Your Royal Highness, that we've fashioned new robes for you both.

DINAZADE: Come, come, sister. Tell us the rest of the story or we shall never get on to the next one.

SULTAN: First I must make a proclamation. I hereby make my promise and give my sacred word that there shall be no more beheadings, anywhere in the twenty-one kingdoms. We shall live always in peace and happiness as we have done since Scheherazade came to the throne. She is wise and good and has melted a wicked old heart.

ALL: Hail to the Sultan, Schahriah! Hail to the beautiful Scheherazade!

THE END

The First Cat on Mars

This is an imaginative story which attempts to describe life as it will be when we can move through space and visit other planets at will.

Read the entire play to yourself and find the answers to the following:

1. Why did Bigger bring a cat on board?
2. How long was the trip to Mars?
3. Why was the space ship going to Mars?
4. List two things that were different on this flight from the way they would be on a flight we could take today.
5. Why did Bigger become fond of the cat?

Now choose parts.

Read your part to yourself. Be sure you know every word. Ask for help if you need it.

Practice reading the play together.

Check yourself on these points:

1. Does your voice show anger, fear, surprise?
2. Do you come in with your part *right on time?*
3. Do you read smoothly and easily so that you sound as if you were really talking to someone?

If you are sure you are doing well, ask the teacher for the tape recorder. Read the play and get it on tape. Play the tape to your group. You can listen to yourself and find out how you need to improve.

Practice again.

Now read to the tape recorder. Ask the teacher if you may play the tape to the class.

THE FIRST CAT ON MARS

by James Macpherson Harper

Characters

(10 boys and the narrator)

NARRATOR
1ST PILOT, *the pilot of the rocket ship*
2ND PILOT, *his assistant*
COOKIE, *the chef*
CAL, *the timekeeper (his real name is Calendar)*
DOC, *a veterinarian*
SKIPPER, *the ship's captain*
TIMER
YOUNGER
TOM
BIGGER

NARRATOR: This play takes place some time in the future in a control room of a rocket ship bound for Mars. The voices of the crew can be heard preparing for take-off.

YOUNGER: Cast off all lines.

1ST PILOT: Thirty seconds till take-off.

2ND PILOT: Hey! Watch out for that boom down there! All ready? O.K., then, remove all gantries!

SKIPPER: All stations report!

TOM: Station one secure!

CAL: Station two secure!

1ST PILOT: Station five secure!

COOKIE: Station three secure!

YOUNGER: Station six secure!

2ND PILOT: Station eight secure!

BIGGER: Station four secure!

Doc: Medical Station secure!

Tom: Station seven secure!

Skipper: Close all hatches! (*Pause*) All crew members, strap yourselves in! . . . (*Pause*) . . . Timer, begin the count-down!

Timer: Seven seconds . . . six seconds . . . five seconds . . . four seconds . . . three seconds . . . two seconds . . . one second . . . zero seconds. . . .

Narrator: There is a tremendous noise as the rocket ship blasts off. Finally, all is under control, and the members of the crew begin to talk together.

2nd Pilot: So you can see that if any meteors get in our path, the alarm will go off while they are miles away. Then the automatic pilot will change our course to avoid a collision.

Younger: But I thought that there was very little danger of hitting anything, way out here in space.

2nd Pilot: It only seems that way. Come over here! Now you can see many more stars and planets that you can't see on Earth because of all the layers of clouds and dust. What you can't see from here are the millions of meteors and asteroids that are ahead of us. If we hit a swarm of meteors on this trip, we'll be dodging all over the place to avoid them.

Younger: But, with an automatic pilot, what's the use of worrying?

2nd Pilot: Plenty of use—just one of those little chunks could rip a hole in our hull so big that we'd blow apart, because there is a lot of pressure in here and none out there. So, we still have to be on guard all the time, even though there hasn't been an accident for a long time. Hey, Doc, how's the kitten today?

Doc: Tinker is just fine, aren't you, Tinker?

Younger: Gee, to see all those cows and pigs and chickens and even a kitten, on this ship, makes me wonder what's going on.

Tom: Well, you'll get used to hauling a lot of different things, after you've been riding the rockets awhile. The miners up on Mars are going to need all the things we take to them.

2ND PILOT: Yeah, and if any more colonists go up, they'll need lots more food.

YOUNGER: But why don't the cows give any milk? Or the chickens any eggs?

TOM: Well, in the first place, they're all very young, so you can't expect any eggs or milk. And then, they were all given injections before we left that would cause all the food they eat to be used up, so we have to carry less food for them. It's something like the medicine they take back on Earth for liver trouble, only we give the injections to slow them down, not to pep them up.

DOC: Boy, I wish we could bring them out of it for awhile. I could sure use a real fried egg for a change, instead of getting powdered eggs, powdered milk, powdered fruit, powdered cereals, and powdered vegetables, all the time.

TOM: Yeah, it's a wonder they haven't figured out some way they could give us powdered knives, forks, and spoons.

2ND PILOT: Or maybe even a dehydrated cook?

COOKIE: Aw, I do the best I can with all that powdered food.

2ND PILOT: Cookie, you cook like a rocket engineer—everything all burnt out!

COOKIE: Oh, yeah? Well, you pilot this thing like a short-order cook—everything half-done and on top of each other!

2ND PILOT: Cheer up! It could be worse!

CAL: Just think, boys, only 204 more days till we can sink our teeth in a real Martian steak-—ahhh!

BIGGER: Well, here's old Calendar Cal himself! I thought you'd be back there giving all our water supply to your precious posies!

CAL: Don't make fun of those seedlings, Bigger. They're going to make big changes in the farming up there.

YOUNGER: Gee whiz, can't they even raise their own seedlings?

CAL: Well, with these new varieties, their crops will be larger, and they can feed more people. Then we'll take more colonists up, so they can mine more minerals and smelt more metals for us to carry back to earth. And without some of those tough metals in the hull of this baby, we wouldn't be as we are. Why, six or seven years ago, meteors the size of a pea could rip us wide open—now they hardly make a dent.

BIGGER: Oh, sure, now it takes only one the size of a peanut to tear us apart. That's what I call real progress!

SKIPPER: Glad you men brought the subject up. We're approaching the danger zone now, so we'll have several Emergency Drills in the next few days.

BIGGER: Aw, Skipper, there hasn't been a ship hit by a large meteor in three years.

SKIPPER: Well, Bigger, up till now, our detection screens have been working perfectly, and the Emergency Pilot is ready to throw us into a new course in a split-second, but if we should enter a swarm of meteors too dense for our computing machines to handle, or if our machinery should stop for a second, the Emergency Drills could mean life-or-death to all of us! Any questions? Very well, then, get the cat out of the way, and everyone to his Emergency Station! Doc, you get your first-aid equipment set up. The drill will begin in two minutes.

NARRATOR: Bigger doesn't get ready immediately. He delivers a speech to nobody in particular. Listen.

BIGGER: Join the Space-Force, boys. Fill up on de-e-e-licious, de-e-e-hydrated delicacies; see last year's movies; take 258-day, one-way trips to Mars . . . straight up; see all the stars and planets, up real close; make friends with all kinds of meteors; count 'em as they go past; see all the . . .

SKIPPER: Bigger!

BIGGER: Yes, sir!

SKIPPER: Now hear this! We will run a series of three simulated emergencies. From the second I announce the location of each supposed hit, your stations will be timed by control instruments, and you should have each torn compartment blocked-off and pressurized within two seconds. The hull crew should have a temporary patch in place within fifteen seconds of the time they leave the pressure chamber. Hull crew, double-check your suits. The alarm bell will ring in thirty seconds for the first drill!

NARRATOR: The next scene takes place when the men have been on board for some days. The First Pilot is at the controls. Doc and Younger are playing with Tinker, the pet cat. Cal is counting the days on the calendar as Bigger comes in.

CAL: Get your Christmas shopping done early, boys . . . only 199 more days till we set her down on beautiful, barren Mars.

BIGGER: Yeah, join the Space-Force, boys! If you have the mentality of a child of three, and are a perfect physical specimen—having one perfect eye; one perfect arm; and one perfectly healthy lung, Uncle Pluto and Aunt Venus want you! So you can learn to go through meteor drills in half the time it would take a normal, three-headed person. If you have these qualifications, and have never finished kindergarten, you may some day command your own rocket ship!

DOC: Why, Bigger, with all those qualifications, why aren't you commanding this bucket?

CAL: Yeah, Bigger could run this ship all by himself, with only Tinker to take the orders and run through all the emergency drills for him.

COOKIE: I can see him training the cat to run the ship and telling her, "Wake me up at half-past 257 days, and I'll do the landing."

BIGGER: At least I could teach her to cook better than you do!

COOKIE: Oh, yeah? If I know you, you'd be cooking "cat steaks" for yourself, before you even got close to Mars!

BIGGER: Well, she's my cat, isn't she?

DOC: Hey, Bigger, you're not going to sell Tinker when we get there, are you?

BIGGER: I'd like to know why I shouldn't!

DOC: Well, she's a quiet little mascot and full of fun. I'd like to see her go along with us on some more trips.

BIGGER: Oh, yeah? Some of the colonists up there would pay

anything to own the very first housecat on Mars . . . and I aim to make them really pay for this one.

COOKIE: How about the regulations?

BIGGER: It's all legal! They say that each rocket crew may have a small mascot of some sort . . . but they don't say you can't take one up and come back without it! I figure that in the next few trips, with more kittens, I can make a nice pile of money! (*Pause*) Well boys, I have to check our oxygen supply, before Skipper checks on me . . . Stay happy!

CAL: Bigger, if you knock over any more of my plants, while you're fooling around back there, I'll make you happy!

1ST PILOT: I thought it was funny when Bigger offered to buy a mascot for the ship. But I suppose you find one like him on every ship.

NARRATOR: Alarms ring suddenly in short bursts. Panel lights flash. The First Pilot works frantically at the controls. Then everything is quiet. The Skipper enters, followed by the Second Pilot.

SKIPPER: Everything O.K. here? Good. We came through in pretty good shape. Get that station yet?

2ND PILOT: Yes, sir. We're in contact with Luna Station. You can go ahead now, sir.

SKIPPER: Hello, Luna Station, hello, Luna Station. This is U.S. Space Force Freighter 74-D. At 1300 hours and thirty-seven point five minutes, on the fifty-ninth day of our scheduled run, we encountered a large swarm of meteors. We were traveling in assigned orbit, at 25,000 meters per second. Most of the swarm was passed through in thirteen point five seconds. We suffered three small rips in the outer hull, one large tear in the port fin, and numerous dents. No casualties or injuries. Cargo uninjured and intact. We are back on orbit. End of report from U.S.F.F. 74-D.

YOUNGER: Boy, that was some swarm of meteors, wasn't it?

BIGGER: Wait'll you've been on this run awhile longer. Why, I remember one time when we were out of fuel, out of oxygen, and out of food, and we were still millions of miles away from Mars!

YOUNGER: Gee! What happened?

CAL: Don't let him catch you with that old chestnut, kid. We were back on Earth, hadn't taken off yet, hadn't loaded any fuel, food or oxygen; how could we get to Mars?

BIGGER: Aw, you guys spoil everything! I had him believing all of it!

TOM: Hey! Have any of you guys seen Tinker?

CAL: I thought you had put her in her harness.

TOM: Cookie says she was looking sort of sick, so he took her into the galley. When he turned around later, she was gone! We both looked all over for her.

YOUNGER: If she's sick, we'd better find her . . . maybe she's dying, or hurt real bad!

BIGGER: If you guys have lost her, you're going to pay me every cent I could have made by selling her.

TOM: Hold onto your teeth, Bigger! I don't think she stepped outside for a breath of fresh vacuum . . . she's around, some place!

CAL: Yeah, Bigger, maybe she put on one of our space suits and went for a walk around the block.

COOKIE: Did you find her yet?

CAL: Take it easy, Cookie, we'll find her soon enough.

YOUNGER: Was she very sick? Do you think she's dying some place? Where did you last see her?

COOKIE: Hold off, Younger. Give me a chance to answer, will you? She looked pretty sick to me, so I took her into the galley to give her some bicarb of soda, but when I turned around, she was gone!

BIGGER: How could you lose that cat?

CAL: I thought you didn't like the cat, Bigger. Every time I've seen you near her, your eyes showed dollar signs, instead of pupils!

SKIPPER: Let's stop the squabbling! We'll divide the ship up and hunt for her. Cal, you take the crew's quarters; Tom, you can take the animals' compartment; Cookie will check the galley, again; Bigger will look through the cargo; I'll check on the engine room; Younger and Doc can bring whatever first-aid equipment we might need! Everyone take off, now, and really comb the ship!

NARRATOR: All leave except the Second Pilot, who takes over the controls. The others come in and out carrying medicine and first-aid kits. Younger adds a pair of crutches to the pile of equipment.

SKIPPER: Any luck?

CAL: No, sir!

COOKIE: I looked everywhere . . . not a trace of so much as a whisker!

CAL: Boy, it looks as if Doc expects a major operation. Here's aspirin, mouth wash, castor oil, iodine, and even a bottle of cough syrup! Now what in heck is he going to use cough syrup for?

COOKIE: If he can't find anything else wrong with her, maybe he plans to give Tinker a cough! Any luck, Tom?

TOM: Not a bit of it! I'm almost ready to believe in ghosts!

SKIPPER: Say, Doc, just what are the crutches for?

DOC: Younger, old man, I don't think we'll need them . . . for a kitten!

CAL: Yeah, Younger! Don't you think they're a bit too short for her?

SKIPPER: Now that we've covered all the places where Tinker could be hiding, I guess we . . . wait a minute! Where's Bigger?

CAL: He was back in the cargo hold. She could hide in a thousand places, back there among all those seedlings of mine! I'd better go help him!

NARRATOR: At last Bigger returns carrying Tinker. The crew watches anxiously while Doc examines the kitten.

CAL: How is she, Doc?

TOM: What's wrong with her, Doc?

YOUNGER: Is she going to get well?

SKIPPER: Hold on, and let Doc make his examination!

DOC: Take it all back!

YOUNGER: What for, Doc?

DOC: Never mind! Just put it all away again!

COOKIE: What do you mean? Is—is—she beyond all hope?

DOC: No! I guess she'll live awhile longer.

CAL: You mean she's crippled?

DOC: I mean there's not a doggone thing wrong with her!

NARRATOR: Everyone grins and relaxes, happy to know the kitten is safe.

TOM: Boy, that's a relief! I thought sure she was a goner!

COOKIE: She certainly looks better than she did awhile ago!

CAL: How did she look when you found her, Bigger?

BIGGER: I guess your plants and seedlings did the trick, Cal. She chewed up about a dozen of them, back there!

TOM: I'll be doggoned! I've heard of dogs eating grass when they were sick, but never cats!

COOKIE: Well, you can still make your big pile of money, when we get to Mars, Bigger . . . she's still alive!

BIGGER: No, I . . . I don't think I'll sell her, after all.

CAL: Well, what happened to you? Did you eat some of my seedlings, too?

BIGGER: No . . . I . . . not exactly! Commander, I . . . after the meteors hit us, I forgot to check the oxygen valves, and they were loosened by the jolts we took! I just now tightened everything, but the reserve supply of oxygen is . . . gone! There'll be enough to get us there, but that's all! Tinker here was chewing on the seedlings right next to the valves when I found her, and then I noticed the red warning light was on, and . . . and . . . that's it!

SKIPPER: I don't have to tell you men how serious this could be. It's like a lot of other things in our lives . . . we must all do our own jobs, or we won't live to brag about it! Bigger, do you know that the regulations state that such an offense as this may be punished by the death of the person who endangers the mission or lives of the crew?

BIGGER: Yes, sir! All I can say is—I'm sorry it happened! I guess I must have been too excited about the meteors hitting us. I'd never been on a ship that was hit before! But, that's no excuse. I guess I deserve anything you say!

CAL: Skipper, I know this is serious—but couldn't you change the punishment? After all, Bigger caught it before any great damage was done.

SKIPPER: As Bigger himself says, there is no excuse.

DOC: Excuse me for interfering, Skipper, but don't the regulations say—that is, couldn't you—

SKIPPER: If you're trying to say the regulations state that the punishment is up to me, that's perfectly correct.

CAL: I think we've all learned a big lesson from this, Skipper.

SKIPPER: Maybe it was a good thing for us all to learn a lesson so cheaply from one man's forgetfulness. In this case, it was Bigger who "goofed off"—it could have been any one of us.

CAL: That's right.

SKIPPER: However, Bigger did commit a serious offense. But in view of the unusual confusion caused by the meteors, Bigger will be demoted to the grade of Rookie and will lose half of this trip's pay. Do you feel this punishment is too harsh, Bigger?

BIGGER: No, sir! Thank you, sir! If it hadn't been for Tinker, I probably wouldn't have checked the valves until too late! You know, I guess I have never realized how wonderful a mascot really can be, until a few minutes ago!

TOM: Tinker, old gal, it looks as if you'll still be the first cat on Mars, all right, but I think those colonists up there will be darn lucky even to get a good long look at you . . . every three years!

THE END

A Hat for Mother

Read this play to yourself. As you read, think about the following questions.

1. Why were the girls making a hat instead of buying one?
2. What did each girl contribute?
3. How did Mrs. Langley help to make the project successful?

With the help of your chairman, choose people for the different parts. Read your part over to yourself two or three times. Be sure you know every word. Remember to read very smoothly just as you would talk.

Try to use your voice to express different feelings. Take turns trying the lines below.

With surprise: "I *am* surprised, but what for? Is it my *birthday?*"

Playfully: "I just got it on. *Don't you dare* try to take it off."

Forcefully: "Bonnie! *Stop that nonsense.* It *can't* be better than the one I have on."

Eagerly: "She's coming up the steps. (*Pause*) She's on the porch. (*Pause*) She's coming in the door."

Pleading: "Oh! Mother, *do* open it. This suspense is *awful*."

Now read the play aloud. Help each other with voices, difficult words, and phrases. Practice two or three times until you are ready to read the play to your class.

A HAT FOR MOTHER

by Marguerite Kreger Phillips

Characters

(6 girls and the narrator)

NARRATOR

MRS. ROGER LANGLEY, *the mother*

JILL, *a teen-ager*

BONNIE, *age twelve*

LOIS
LOLA } *twins, age ten*

CINDY, *the youngest daughter*

NARRATOR: The play you are about to hear takes place late one afternoon in May. Lois and Lola are busy dusting and mopping. They are hurrying to get the house spic and span before Mother comes home.

LOLA: Why don't you take that rag off your head, Lois? You stop every half second to tie it. How can you get the dusting done?

LOIS: You just tend to your part of the work, Lola, and I'll take care of mine. Mother will be home from the office before we're ready if we don't hurry up.

LOLA: She can't do that. Jill has to get here with the hat.

LOIS: Oh! I hope Mother will like it.

LOLA (*Startled*): Why shouldn't she like it? We put enough things together and Jill is doing the trimming.

LOIS: That's just it. Did we put too many things together?

LOLA: We did the best we could with what money we had.

LOIS: I'm just hoping the rayon I gave Jill for the crown will be enough.

LOLA: Now you have me worrying. I dyed that blue ribbon myself, but I followed the directions my art teacher gave me.

LOIS: Jill passed judgment on everything we contributed, and her Home Ec teacher considers her an "A" student, a judge of what is good style even if she is only fourteen. Now, empty that wastebasket and stop making me nervous about Mother's hat. It just has to turn out beautiful!

LOLA: If you're finished with the mop, why don't you put it away? By the way, what about supper?

LOIS: It has to be warmed up. We want to give Mother her hat first, then we can all enjoy our meal. If we had to sit and worry about whether she was going to like the hat, we wouldn't be able to eat a thing.

LOLA: I would! I'm hungry now.

LOIS: Oh, you!

NARRATOR: Just at this moment, the door opens and Cindy comes running in with a large package.

CINDY: Look what they left at our door. A package for Mom.

LOIS: What is it?

CINDY: A package. Can't you see?

LOIS: And I can read. It's for Mother.

CINDY: That's what I said.

LOIS: Cindy, it has the word "Paris" on it.

LOLA: Did I hear someone say "Paris"?

CINDY: You sure did. Does Mom know somebody in Paris?

LOIS: I don't think so—she never told us about anybody.

LOLA: You mean the stamps are French? That looks like John Tyler on those stamps. He was no Frenchman.

LOIS: Ahem! Ahem! The family philatelist speaks!

LOLA: You have eyes. Use them.

LOIS: I hate to admit it, but you're right.

LOLA (*A bit boastfully*): Naturally—I know my stamps. Those are ten-cent stamps and they have the picture of John Tyler on them.

CINDY: Why does the box say "Paris," then?

Lois (*Spelling aloud*): P-a-r-i-s. And what's this? M-i-l-l-i-n—
Oh dear, the rest of the word is rubbed out.

Lola: Let's wait for Mother to figure it out.

Lois: I have to put this mop away.

Lola: I wish Jill would come.

Cindy: And what do I do with this package?

Lois: Dump it on the chair, and let's all hope it is something nice for Mother.

Cindy: She'll have enough to make her happy when she sees the hat we've made. She won't need anything else.

Lois (*Pointedly*): Jill really did all the trimming.

Cindy: How could she trim it if I didn't furnish those bluejay feathers?

Lois (*A bit grudgingly*): Jill did say they were perfect.

Lola: Bonnie should be coming soon. Put this duster away with the mop, like a pal.

Narrator: Lois takes the duster and the mop and places them in the closet. Just as she closes the closet door, Bonnie rushes in all out of breath.

Bonnie: Oh dear, am I late? I hope Mother isn't home yet.

Cindy: You're late, but Mother isn't here.

Bonnie: Where is it? I don't see the hat.

Lola: For the simple reason that Jill hasn't brought it yet.

Bonnie: I'll simply swoon if my roses don't look right.

Lola: That would be a big help, especially when it's your turn to get supper! Lois and I want the surprise first, then eats.

Bonnie: That's O.K. I just have to turn on the oven and set the things in to warm. Mother got everything ready before she left this morning. Oh—what's that package on the chair?

Lois: Just a package for Mother.

Bonnie (*Instantly excited*): For Mother?

Cindy: And it's from Paris.

Bonnie: Paris? I wonder what it can be.

Lois: Oh, Bonnie, put it down. Go wash and take a look at the food. We don't want you out in the kitchen when Mother gets here.

BONNIE: Hmm, that word "Paris" isn't part of the postmark.

LOLA: How about the food? The package won't run away.

BONNIE: You're too young to understand the significance of "Paris," but I guess I can wait.

NARRATOR: At last Bonnie decides to go into the kitchen and prepare some food. Just after she leaves, Jill comes in with a large hatbox. She places it on the table, opens it slowly and takes out a beautiful blue hat. Bonnie comes back into the living room when she hears the girls talking.

BONNIE: Oh, Jill, you're home! Let me see the hat. Oh, those roses are sweet. Now, if it just suits Mother.

LOLA: My ribbon looks new!

JILL: And see what a lovely crown that blue rayon made, Lois.

LOIS (*Warmly*): Jill, it's your artistic work that makes the hat what it is. Your fingers did it.

BONNIE: She's right, Jill, we couldn't have managed it alone. I'll be back in two seconds. I still have to put the vegetables in to warm.

JILL: Now, where shall we have it when Mother gets here?

LOLA: How about right in the middle of that table, but inside the box so she has to dive for it.

JILL: Fine!

CINDY: And when Mom shows up, we'll all shout "Surprise!" We'll give her our surprise first, then show her the other package.

JILL (*Surprised*): What other package?

LOIS (*Indifferently*): The package on that chair.

JILL: When did this come?

LOIS: A little while ago.

JILL: It doesn't weigh much.

BONNIE: Take a look at the words near the postmark.

JILL: Paris?

LOIS: And see that other word? (*Spells it out*) M-i-l-l-i-n—

BONNIE (*Anxiously*): Jill, that could be the beginning of the word millinery.

JILL (*Gasps*): Millinery? You mean this could be a hat?

CINDY: Don't let Mom see this package if it's a hat—at least until she has a chance to look at the one we made her.

JILL: Mother wouldn't send away for a hat. She has to watch her budget too closely with five of us to support.

BONNIE (*Near tears*): And the one we made is so beautiful.

JILL (*Sighs deeply*): Still we'll have to tell her about this package.

CINDY (*Bravely*): I know my mother. She won't even look at it until she's seen what's in that box on the table.

LOLA: Go see if she's coming.

BONNIE: Oh, I do want Mother to have beautiful things and if that's a hat from Paris—

LOIS (*Cutting in*): How could it be a hat from Paris?

CINDY: Look—there's Mother. She's coming up the steps. (*Pause*) She's on the porch. (*Pause*) She's coming in the door.

JILL: Ready, everybody. Let's all get over in back of the table.

ALL (*Shouting*): Surprise! Surprise, Mother!

MRS. LANGLEY: I *am* surprised, but what for? Is it my birthday?

LOLA: No! But it will soon be Mother's Day.

JILL: The surprise is in the box.

LOIS: And over on that chair is another package that came for you by mail.

MRS. LANGLEY: For me?

CINDY: Shall I get it for you?

MRS. LANGLEY: I don't remember ordering anything. Oh, let it wait. Your surprise is what I'm interested in.

JILL: Maybe that package is important.

MRS. LANGLEY: Nothing is more important than what you girls have in that box.

NARRATOR: Mrs. Langley moves over to the table and carefully lifts the hat from the box. Holding it in front of her, she looks at it with delight and then speaks.

MRS. LANGLEY: Oh! A hat! Isn't it beautiful? Those feathers—

those roses—it's all just perfect. I'm so thrilled, I'm absolutely weak.

LOLA: There, Mother, sit down.

MRS. LANGLEY: Just see how perfectly that ribbon blends with these feathers. And the roses are darling. How did you ever do this? How could you, with the little allowance I'm able to give you?

LOIS: You have smart children!

CINDY: Smart? We're *super!*

JILL: Do you really like it, Mother?

MRS. LANGLEY: I love it. Now, you put it on me.

BONNIE: I'll get you a mirror.

CINDY: I never thought it would turn out that pretty.

LOIS: You forget that the pretty face under the hat helps.

MRS. LANGLEY: Don't spoil me, children.

LOLA (*Very solemnly*): Now, you'd better look at the other package.

MRS. LANGLEY: I suppose so.

BONNIE: Mother, the back looks beautiful.

MRS. LANGLEY: Why, this hat does things for me!

JILL: Now, shall I take the hat off?

MRS. LANGLEY (*Playfully*): Don't you dare try to take it off. I just got it on.

LOIS: Here's the package that came for you. It has the word "Paris" on it.

MRS. LANGLEY (*Gasps*): Oh, no!

JILL: What's wrong, Mother?

MRS. LANGLEY: I'm all right . . . just a little startled.

JILL: You act as if you know what's in the package.

MRS. LANGLEY: But I don't need what's in that package, if it's what I think it is. How is dinner coming, Bonnie?

BONNIE: Mother, you're trying to put us off.

MRS. LANGLEY: I'm not. I'm perfectly content with your surprise, and I don't need what's in that package.

BONNIE (*Tragically*): I knew it! I knew it! It's a hat. And if it's a hat from Paris, you're afraid you'll hurt our feelings—

MRS. LANGLEY (*Cutting in*): Bonnie! Stop that nonsense. No hat could be better than the one I have on. Now, I guess I have to tell you how I know what's in that package.

LOIS: It's postmarked Cleveland, Ohio. I can just make it out.

MRS. LANGLEY: Yes, I know.

LOLA: You know?

JILL: Oh, Mother, do open it. This suspense is awful.

MRS. LANGLEY: First I must tell you something, something that will surprise you and make me feel very foolish.

LOIS: Why, Mother!

CINDY: I don't know what you mean, Mom, but you're tops with me.

MRS. LANGLEY: I entered a contest about two months ago—

JILL (*Interrupting*): And this is a prize?

MRS. LANGLEY: I'm afraid so.

CINDY: Hurrah! My mother won a prize!

LOIS: What's wrong with winning a prize, Mother? You don't look a bit happy about it. If you won it, it's yours. What kind of daughters do you think you have? We'll all be proud of you.

MRS. LANGLEY: Even if the prize is a hat?

GIRLS: Even if it's a hat!

MRS. LANGLEY: What darlings you are.

JILL: What did you do to win a prize?

MRS. LANGLEY: I had to write some poetry.

BONNIE: Poetry? My very own mother, a poet!

MRS. LANGLEY: Not good poetry, I'm afraid. That's why I'm embarrassed. It was really only a jingle.

CINDY: All poetry jingles.

MRS. LANGLEY: Promise you won't laugh at me. Laugh at the jingle if you wish, but not at me.

JILL: Shouldn't you open the package first?

MRS. LANGLEY: No. When I entered the contest, I specified the third prize and that was a hat from Paris.

JILL: From Paris!

CINDY: I still like the one we made.

MRS. LANGLEY: Good for you, Cindy. This is the work of all of you—I have faith in it.

CINDY: I pulled those feathers out of a bird.

BONNIE: Cindy! Did you have to tell that?

CINDY: It didn't hurt the bird. The bird was dead.

MRS. LANGLEY (*Laughs gaily*): And the rest of you worked equally as hard, I am sure.

CINDY: Jill worked the hardest. She put it together.

MRS. LANGLEY: And it is the most becoming hat I've ever had.

JILL: Oh, Mother, we'll try not to be jealous if it turns out that you like the hat you won better than ours.

LOIS: How about the poetry?

BONNIE: You should have told us you were a poet.

MRS. LANGLEY: You won't call me a poet when you hear it, but it had to be something silly about a hat. (*Clears her throat*)

> Can it be the birds I hear
> When you walk down the street?
> Or flowers of the early spring
>   I smell as you pass by?
> No! 'tis just that hat
>   Above your brow
> Suggests these things to me
>   I vow!

NARRATOR: They all laugh at Mrs. Langley's poetry, then set to work to open the package. Mother pulls out a flat oddly-shaped hat which resembles a bag. She holds it out in her hand, and speaks to the children.

MRS. LANGLEY: I'll appreciate having you master-minds tell me just what this is supposed to be.

BONNIE: Mother, you know very well it's a hat.

JILL: Of course it's a hat.

BONNIE: It has to be. That's what the prize was.

MRS. LANGLEY: Yes, the third prize was to be a hat from Paris.

BONNIE: And a millinery firm wouldn't give a hat for a prize that wasn't a hat.

JILL: I'll have to admit I can't tell front from back.

CINDY: Let me put it on. Now, what does it look like above my brow?

MRS. LANGLEY: Not a hat, I vow!

JILL: Mother, you should give it a chance. Try it on.

MRS. LANGLEY: I wouldn't be seen under it. I have the hat I like right on my head, and there it's going to stay! Bonnie, when do we eat?

THE END

The Mechanical Man

This is a play about a mechanical man that was used by a teacher to help some boys and girls learn something very important.

Read the play to yourself. Ask for help on any words you cannot pronounce or do not understand.

What was the trick that Mr. Lake played on the children?

How do you think a mechanical voice would sound? Would it be smooth and flowing? Would it be slow and deliberate?

Take turns trying some of the mechanical man's lines.

"It is evident that you are quite fond of Toasted Corn Curlies because you ate them for breakfast this morning."

"The successful candidate in next week's election will be—Joe Halliday."

"Have you students registered for the class election?"

"It would be a poor election if everyone wanted to—but no one made any effort to—*vote!*"

Choose the person who sounded most like a mechanical man for that part.

Choose the other parts.

Study your part by yourself.

Practice reading the play aloud.

Remember:

1. Speak naturally but clearly.
2. Make your voice show feeling—surprise, timidity, impatience, etc.
3. Come in on time with your part. *Be alert*—don't wait for a nudge from a friend.

If there are places where you feel some extra work is needed, practice them.

Now try the whole play again.

When you are ready, have your chairman arrange for a time to read the play to the entire class.

THE MECHANICAL MAN

by John Murray

Characters

(6 boys, 6 girls, and the narrator)

NARRATOR

MR. LAKE, *the science teacher at Lincoln Junior High School*

THE MECHANICAL MAN

TOM
JACK
BILL
LARRY
MARY
ANN } *students at Lincoln Junior High School*
BETTY
ALICE
FLO
DEBBIE

NARRATOR: The play you are about to hear opens in the office of Mr. Lake, a science teacher at Lincoln Junior High School. Betty, Ann, Mary, Tom, and Jack, students of Mr. Lake, are in the office. Betty and Ann study the control panel board located on a table. Betty starts to press one of the buttons but Ann stops her.

ANN: You'd better not touch anything, Betty. Mr. Lake is terribly particular about his inventions.

JACK: Has he been inventing things again, Ann?

ANN: I don't know, Jack. He asked us all to come here after school to see a big surprise.

BETTY: We can be sure that his idea of a "surprise" will be some new contraption.

TOM: He sounded pretty mysterious to me.

JACK: Mr. Lake is like that, Tom. He knew that if he didn't give his surprise a big build-up, we'd probably be at football practice.

MARY: I hope he makes this surprise good. I promised Mother I'd be home early today.

TOM: Leave it to Mr. Lake, Mary. He won't let us down.

NARRATOR: Bill, Larry, Alice, Flo, and Debbie enter the office, carrying books.

JACK: Hey! It looks like Old Home Week. What are you doing here?

BILL: Mr. Lake asked us to come to his office after school.

ALICE: Yes, he said something about a surprise.

MARY: You, too?

LARRY: Mr. Lake has come up with some pretty good ideas. I suppose he wants to show us a new invention.

FLO: Why should he pick us, Larry? We're certainly not his prize pupils.

LARRY: It beats me, Flo, but I'm pretty excited about the whole thing.

JACK: I suppose you had to miss football practice today, too, Bill.

BILL: I told Coach I'd be a little late. I'd rather see Mr. Lake's invention anyway.

DEBBIE: Mr. Lake certainly seemed excited when he asked us to report here.

ANN: I wish he'd get here, Debbie. This suspense is terrific. What's the matter, Alice? You look worried.

ALICE: I'm not exactly worried, but Mr. Lake acted so strangely. Why didn't he invite the entire science class?

BILL: This is a coincidence!

TOM: What do you mean?

BILL: Don't you remember when we all met like this—almost one year ago?

JACK: I don't get it.

MARY: We've met at school a hundred times.

BILL: Oh, I know that, but we were on a special committee last year. All of us!

BETTY (*Thoughtfully*): Why, yes, we were the campaign chairmen for last year's school election.

LARRY: What has last year's election got to do with it?

BILL: I don't know, but it certainly is pretty funny that the same group should be called together again.

ALICE: And Mr. Lake is the chairman of the Teacher-Student election board this year.

TOM: It doesn't make sense to me. Class elections will be held next week. It's too late for Mr. Lake to organize another new campaign board.

FLO: I wasn't even planning to register for the election this year.

DEBBIE: Neither was I.

JACK: I wasn't going to vote, either. We did our share last year to get Jeff Kennedy elected class president and everyone knows he's as good as elected this year, too.

ALICE: Jeff's been a good class president. He's taken an interest in all the school projects, and he's done a lot for the class.

BILL: Yes, you can't beat Kennedy.

LARRY: I don't understand why Joe Halliday's even bothering to run against Jeff. He doesn't stand a chance.

MARY: Well, Joe is all right, but I don't think he'd ever be a successful class president.

FLO: Poor Joe! I guess he realizes he's licked already. He has certainly done everything to get votes, though.

DEBBIE: Yes, his committee held several big rallies.

FLO: We needn't worry. Jeff will still carry a majority.

TOM: I suppose we should have registered for the election. It doesn't seem right that none of us is even going to bother to vote.

JACK: Jeff Kennedy is popular enough. Our votes won't matter.

MARY: That's how I feel, too. We did our share last year. Let someone else vote now.

ALICE: I was planning to register, but I've been so busy every day after school that I almost missed the deadline.

FLO: Miss Clayton says tomorrow is the last day she'll accept registrations.

TOM: Well, not finding time to register sounds like a pretty weak excuse to me.

ALICE: You're not planning to vote, either. I guess none of us is going to vote this year.

LARRY: Oh, cut it out! We're arguing about nothing.

JACK: Yes, we still don't know what Mr. Lake wants.

NARRATOR: Mr. Lake comes into the office and joins the boys and girls.

MR. LAKE: Hello. I'm glad that everyone could make it.

BILL: Wild horses couldn't keep us away, Mr. Lake. We're excited.

MR. LAKE: I guess I'm excited, too. I've stumbled onto something that I think you might find very interesting.

DEBBIE: Are you sure you called the right students? We don't know too much about inventions.

MR. LAKE: I think you will appreciate this one.

JACK: I hope you invented a three-day school week!

MR. LAKE: It's more important than that.

ALICE: What is it, Mr. Lake? I'm so excited I could scream.

MR. LAKE: Just a minute.

NARRATOR: Mr. Lake leaves the group of students and walks to the work table. He sits at the table and begins to adjust all the dials at the control panel. He becomes absorbed in his work and forgets about the students for a moment.

FLO: What is that machine, Betty?

BETTY (*Hushed tone*): I think it's a remote control panel.

MARY: Oh, I've heard of those things. You can control a radio in another room by pressing a button. What is the panel used for?

NARRATOR: Mr. Lake continues to adjust the dials. Then, apparently satisfied, he stands up.

MR. LAKE: There!

DEBBIE: I—I didn't notice anything.

MR. LAKE: You will. I think you all will be really amazed.

NARRATOR: Mr. Lake smiles and points toward the closet. The pupils stare expectantly at the closet door.

ALICE: Someone's inside the closet.

BILL: Yes, I heard it, too.

LARRY: It sounds as though someone is moving around in there.

DEBBIE: That's impossible. Why, it—it's a closet. No one could have been in there all that time.

NARRATOR: The students hear a scuffling sound which grows louder and louder. Then the closet door is thrown open, and a mechanical man appears in the doorway. With slow, automatic steps, he enters the room. The students back away from him.

DEBBIE: I'm frightened!

FLO: I can't believe it!

ALICE: It's incredible!

LARRY: It can't be true! I've read about this stuff—but it can't be true!

MR. LAKE: I'm very proud of my mechanical man!

BETTY: He—it's almost real. It looked at me! It stared at me!

BILL (*Slowly*): A mechanical man!

MR. LAKE: I worked on the automaton for quite some time. It's my greatest invention. Wouldn't you like to study it a little closer?

ANN: I'm afraid to go near it!

MR. LAKE: Oh, it won't harm you. Mortimer wouldn't hurt a fly.

MARY: Mortimer?

MR. LAKE: Yes, I had to call my invention something. I thought Mortimer sounded scholarly. Look!

NARRATOR: Mr. Lake steps behind the mechanical man and presses a button. Immediately, a slow, raspy voice is heard.

MECHANICAL MAN: I am very glad that you could come here to see me this afternoon.

JACK: It— It talks!

MR. LAKE: Yes. Electronic control is wonderful. Mortimer can walk—and talk—and think!

TOM: Think?

MR. LAKE: Oh, yes. Mortimer has an electrical nervous system comparable to the finest brain.

ALICE: How does it work?

MR. LAKE: That's an interesting question. It's a little difficult to explain, but I assure you that Mortimer comes up with the right answer every time.

BILL: The right answer?

MR. LAKE: Yes. Mortimer must first receive a problem reduced to a mathematical symbol. Every object is represented by a numeral. In turn, he reacts to a similar number and the answer is—there! It's like making a recording of one's voice.

TOM: Can the machine answer anything?

MR. LAKE: Mortimer hasn't let me down yet.

LARRY: Oh, Mr. Lake! In a minute you'll tell me Mortimer knows what I had for breakfast this morning.

MR. LAKE: I'll not make any promises, but I'm glad you asked the question. I think that Mortimer can help us out.

LARRY: Impossible!

MR. LAKE: We'll see.

NARRATOR: Mr. Lake goes to the mechanical man and presses several buttons. Larry watches uncomfortably.

MR. LAKE: I've put the question to Mortimer. Now, we'll learn something.

MECHANICAL MAN: Larry! Larry Thompson!

LARRY: Why, he's calling my name!

MECHANICAL MAN: I wish that you had asked me a more important question. I'm annoyed by these little things.

LARRY: He's talking to me!

MECHANICAL MAN: It is evident that you are quite fond of Toasted Corn Curlies because you ate them for breakfast this morning.

LARRY: What?

MECHANICAL MAN: You will eat Toasted Corn Curlies every morning for the rest of the week!

MR. LAKE: Did that answer your question?

LARRY (*Slowly*): The machine knew.

ANN: It's still impossible. I—I won't believe it. No machine can do that!

MR. LAKE: You saw Mortimer in action.

BETTY: It's the strangest thing I ever saw.

MR. LAKE: Would you like another demonstration?

FLO: It's uncanny.

MR. LAKE: The machine can answer any question.

DEBBIE: I'd be afraid to ask it anything.

ALICE: How many people know about the mechanical man?

MR. LAKE: There aren't too many. I haven't perfected Mortimer yet.

LARRY: Do you mean it will get better?

MR. LAKE: Oh, yes.

BILL: I never want to see that day. The mechanical man knows too much already.

JACK: Well, I think that Mortimer is great. Can you imagine what a boon he'll be to the world?

MR. LAKE: I think he'll give great service to everyone.

JACK: Nothing will stop him. We'll have the right answer for everything—disease, poverty, wars. Don't you think the machine is great, Tom?

TOM (*Slowly*): Yes, but there are things that people must find out for themselves. Can Mortimer really foretell the future?

MR. LAKE: Why, yes. It's really as easy as telling the past. I can present the question and Mortimer will do the rest.

BILL: That should be interesting, but what can we ask him about the future? After all, we wouldn't know whether he was giving us the right answer.

MR. LAKE (*Suddenly*): I have it! Let's ask him about next week's school election.

DEBBIE: That's a great idea. Everyone knows that Jeff Kennedy has the election all sewed up.

FLO: Yes, if Mortimer mentions Jeff's name, we'll really know he's on the beam.

NARRATOR: Once more Mr. Lake adjusts the buttons on the mechanical man.

MR. LAKE: We'll have the name of the successful candidate shortly.

JACK: I can tell you that answer already.

ALICE: But Mortimer is only a machine.

MECHANICAL MAN: The successful candidate in next week's election will be—Joe Halliday!

JACK: Joe Halliday?

ANN: That's ridiculous. He doesn't stand a chance.

FLO: Something must be wrong with the machine.

MECHANICAL MAN: The successful candidate in next week's election will be—Joe Halliday!

JACK: The laugh's on Mortimer. That can't possibly be right. Everyone knows that Jeff Kennedy will win the election.

DEBBIE: Everyone is going to vote for Jeff.

MECHANICAL MAN: Are you students planning to vote for Jeff Kennedy?

DEBBIE (*Frightened*): Oh, it spoke to me!

MECHANICAL MAN: Have you students registered for the class election?

JACK: We weren't planning to vote next week.

FLO: Everyone knew that Jeff would win easily without our few votes.

MECHANICAL MAN: If no one votes for Jeff Kennedy, then Joe Halliday will win the election.

ANN: Joe would make a terrible president.

Tom: All the things that Jeff has worked for will be lost if Joe gets in.

Debbie: I certainly wouldn't want to see Joe Halliday president of our class.

Mechanical Man: The successful candidate in next week's election will be—Joe Halliday!

Mr. Lake: I'm afraid that Mortimer has given his prediction.

Tom: It may be a wonderful machine, but I still don't believe it.

Jack: How can Joe Halliday possibly win?

Mr. Lake: He's conducted quite a campaign and I suppose that Jeff's supporters are over-confident.

Debbie: Mortimer had a good point. He said that if no one voted for Jeff, he couldn't hope to win.

Flo: I never thought of that.

Ann: Neither did I.

Alice: Oh, how can one vote matter?

Mr. Lake: Well, the strength of the voter is a powerful weapon. There have been many cases where *one* vote decided an election.

Alice: But certainly everyone doesn't have to vote in every election.

Mr. Lake: If everyone felt like that, we wouldn't have very fair politics. Votes could be bought—unscrupulous men could always be elected to office, and there would be little we could do to stop them.

Ann: We all voted last year.

Mr. Lake: Yes, but taking an interest in politics for one year isn't enough. We have to study the politicians' platforms every year, and make sure that we are electing the best possible person for the job.

Betty: You make it sound terribly serious, Mr. Lake. After all, it is only a school election.

Mr. Lake: Maybe Mortimer will have something to say about that.

Mechanical Man: Good government begins in schools, towns,

communities and small cities. If we take no interest in our own little government, how can we hope to have a good federal government?

LARRY: He has something there!

MECHANICAL MAN: Some people think that it is not necessary to vote in the "little" elections. They will vote in a Presidential year, but very few can name their councilmen, assemblymen and direct lawmakers.

ALICE (*Apologetically*): I was going to vote—really I was—but I've been so busy that I almost forgot to register.

MECHANICAL MAN: It would be a poor election if everyone wanted to—but no one made any effort to—*vote!*

MR. LAKE: I think Mortimer is right. Women fought for many years to win the right to vote. It's your duty to exercise that right. Then we'll never have to fear the danger of bad government. Did anyone else have a reason for not voting? (*Pause*) Then I think that Mortimer has said enough for one day.

NARRATOR: Going in back of Mortimer, Mr. Lake makes a final adjustment of the controls. The mechanical man returns to the closet, and the door closes.

FLO: I'm terribly mystified—and terribly ashamed!

ALICE: I don't know whatever happened to make us think that our votes didn't matter.

BILL: It took a mechanical man to put us on the right track.

ALICE: I'm certainly going to take time to register for this election. I wonder whether Miss Clayton is still in her homeroom.

MR. LAKE: I think you'll find her there.

BILL: Wait for me, Alice. It's about time I registered, too.

FLO: Same here.

DEBBIE: I second the motion.

MR. LAKE: I think I've won some voters for the election.

BILL: You? Mortimer should take the credit.

MR. LAKE: I think we were both responsible.

ANN: I don't understand. How did you know we weren't planning to vote?

MR. LAKE: Miss Clayton spoke to me about it. She noticed that your names were missing from the registration lists, and she also knew that you were very active last year.

FLO: Is that why you called us here?

MR. LAKE: Yes, I thought that if I gave you a gentle reminder, you would be willing to vote next week.

TOM: I still don't get it. Wasn't this Mortimer business on the level?

MR. LAKE: Well, Mortimer is a fine mechanical man. He'll do everything I request at the push of a button.

ANN: He was able to forecast the future, and tell us about the past.

MR. LAKE: Oh, a mechanical man can't do all that! I must confess I guaranteed Miss Clayton that you would vote.

DEBBIE: But the mechanical man spoke. He—he answered our questions.

MR. LAKE: Mortimer has a fine electrical system. When I pressed a series of buttons, the current started a series of recordings which made him speak. It was similar to—a juke box!

MARY: A juke box?

MR. LAKE: Yes. Mortimer actually can't speak at all!

BETTY: Well, I never—

LARRY: Did you make those recordings beforehand? I thought there was something familiar about Mortimer's voice.

MR. LAKE: I'm the guilty person.

LARRY: But how did you arrange that act about my breakfast? Mortimer—or you—said that I had Toasted Corn Curlies, and you hit the nail on the head!

MR. LAKE: Well, that was prearranged. I had the good fortune to meet your mother at the grocery store yesterday. She bought two boxes of Corn Curlies and said that she could serve you nothing else because you needed twenty-five Corn Curlies box-tops to get a new football.

LARRY: I am saving the tops.

MR. LAKE: With all those Corn Curlies around your house, it was a good chance that you would eat them this morning and every morning for a long time to come!

LARRY: And I walked right into the trap!

MR. LAKE: It wasn't a trap. I knew that my little speech couldn't convince any of you to vote, and I realized that Mortimer was a better persuader.

LARRY: He certainly did a good job.

ALICE: We were all very foolish and we're glad that you and Mortimer showed us up.

DEBBIE: Come on, gang. Maybe if we hurry to Miss Clayton's we can still register.

MR. LAKE: I'll come along, too. I want to see Miss Clayton's face when I walk in with all these potential voters.

ANN (*Sadly*): Oh, dear!

FLO: What's the matter?

ANN: Oh, it's nothing. I'm terribly disappointed in Mortimer, though. I'm sorry that he can't do our thinking for us.

FLO: What a terrible thing to say! I certainly don't want a machine to do my thinking for me.

ANN: Oh, not all the time, but I have a terrific algebra assignment tonight and I could certainly use some help!

MR. LAKE: That's your problem. A mechanical man can do many wonderful things, but he'll never be able to take away the rights of man. He'll never speak by his own power—and he'll never think!

NARRATOR: Mr. Lake and the students go out. Then the closet door slowly opens again. The mechanical man, walking in robot fashion, appears. He walks to the center of the room, glances cautiously to the right and left. Let us listen to his final words.

MECHANICAL MAN: I may be just a mechanical man, but I know it's everybody's duty to vote!

THE END

Robin Hood Tricks the Sheriff

Legends about Robin Hood have been part of stories, plays, poems, and songs for centuries. These legends are supposedly based on fact and have been handed down from generation to generation.

What was it that made Robin Hood popular even though he was an outlaw?

What would we mean if we said he was a colorful character?

Read the play to yourself. Be prepared to give two reasons why he was a most unusual outlaw.

Practice the following line. Each time you read it, make different words important.

Well *done*, Robin! *You* are always kind to the poor.
Well done, Robin! You are *always* kind to the poor.
Well done, Robin! You are always *kind* to the poor.
Well done, Robin! You are *always* kind to the *poor*.

Each time you make a different word stand out, you change the meaning a little.

Assign parts. Practice your part to yourself. Decide which words should stand out to make your part have meaning.

Read the play out loud.

Remember to:

1. Speak distinctly.
2. Try to sound like the character you are supposed to be.
3. Come in quickly with your part.
4. Use your voice to show meaning.
5. Pay attention to the punctuation.

When your group is ready, make arrangements with your teacher to read your play to the class.

ROBIN HOOD TRICKS THE SHERIFF

by Eva Jacob

Characters

(15 boys, 4 girls, and the narrator)

NARRATOR

ROBIN HOOD, *the leader of a group of outlaws*

LITTLE JOHN, *Robin Hood's right-hand man*

FRIAR TUCK
SCARLET
GILBERT — *Outlaws*
WILL STUTELEY — *in*
MICHAEL — *Robin Hood's*
MUCH — *band*
KET THE TROW
HOB O' THE HILL

JOAN
SIBBIE — *peasant maids*
BETTY
MEG

SHERIFF OF NOTTINGHAM, *Robin Hood's enemy*

FOUR SOLDIERS

NARRATOR: This play takes place long ago, in the days of Robin Hood. It is early morning. In a glade in Sherwood Forest, Robin Hood's men are busy at their morning tasks. Ket, Hob, and Much are placing kindling wood in the stone fireplace. Little John, Will Stuteley, and Michael are trimming their arrows while Friar Tuck looks over their shoulders. Robin Hood comes into the glade.

ROBIN HOOD: Good morrow to you, merry men!

OUTLAWS: Good morrow, Robin!

WILL STUTELEY: Tell us, Robin, where have you been?

ROBIN: I just brought a good fat deer to the poor woodcutter at the edge of the greenwood.

FRIAR TUCK: Well done, Robin! You are always kind to the poor.

NARRATOR: Scarlet and Gilbert enter from left, quarreling.

GILBERT: I am still a better bowman than you are, Scarlet.

SCARLET: Nay, Gilbert, I am better. I beat you today, with my trusty bow.

GILBERT: But my trusty bow won yesterday!

SCARLET: And my trusty bow won the day before that!

GILBERT: Robin, which one of us is better?

SCARLET: My head against a leaden farthing—I won today!

GILBERT: But my arrow split the mark yesterday!

NARRATOR: Robin raises his hand trying vainly to silence them while the other outlaws grin and nudge each other.

SCARLET: My arrow won the day before that—twice it split the mark! And the wind was against me, too!

ROBIN: Peace, you saucy varlets! Must you make us all deaf with your foolish noise? You are both good bowmen.

MUCH: And Robin Hood's the best bowman of us all!

OUTLAWS: Hurrah for Robin Hood!
Let every good bowman now join in a song:

> Robin Hood's men are we.
> We hunt and we roam in the woods all day long,
> Roam in the woods so free.
> We love to work and we love to play,
> We hunt and sing the whole long day,
> We eat and drink;
> Our life is gay,
> We're outlaws brave and free!

NARRATOR: At the end of the song, Little John motions for silence.

LITTLE JOHN: Hark! I hear footsteps in yonder leaves!

WILL: They're coming this way!

MICHAEL: Now I hear them, too!

NARRATOR: Some peasant maids come running into the glade.

JOAN: Where's Robin Hood?

SIBBIE: Quick—there's danger!

NARRATOR: The outlaws, now alert, move toward the maids. Robin steps forward.

ROBIN: I am Robin Hood. What is the matter?

BETTY: The Sheriff of Nottingham is hunting for you!

MEG: He's in Sherwood Forest this very moment!

SIBBIE: With soldiers—dozens of them!

NARRATOR: The outlaws glance at each other, look to the right and left, and feel for their weapons.

JOAN: The Sheriff searched our house, trying to find you.

BETTY: He hit my grandmother when she wouldn't tell where you were hiding!

ROBIN (*Indignantly*): The Sheriff shall pay for this!

FRIAR: Hitting a helpless old woman—that scoundrel!

JOAN: And he's hunting for you, Robin! He's coming closer all the time.

MUCH: What shall we do?

LITTLE JOHN: The Sheriff's men outnumber us.

MICHAEL: We must not be captured—let's run and hide!

WILL: Yes, let's hide in the rushes near the bog!

ROBIN: Stay! I have a better plan.

GILBERT: What is your plan, Robin?

ROBIN: Wait and see. Ket, bring me that old beggar's cloak we've been keeping.

KET: You mean that tattered old piece of rag?

ROBIN: Yes. Bring it to me. And Hob, bring me an old stave.

HOB: Yes, sir!

SIBBIE: And what should we do, Robin?

BETTY: There isn't time to run home now! The Sheriff's men will find us!

ROBIN: Fear not. My men will bring you to a safe hiding place.

SCARLET: Aye, that we will. You'll be hidden where the bushes grow thick as a castle wall.

KET: Here's your cloak, Robin! Faith, 'tis an ugly thing!

MUCH (*Curiously*): What are you going to do with it, Robin?

ROBIN: Why, I'll just put it on, that's what I'll do.

KET: Let me help you, sir.

NARRATOR: As Ket puts a cloak around Robin's shoulders, Hob enters with a stave. He hands it to Robin. Robin stoops and takes a few hobbling steps, like an old man, while the outlaws and maids watch him curiously.

MEG: Why Robin, you look just like an old beggar!

ROBIN: Right you are, lassie! The Sheriff will never recognize me dressed like this.

FRIAR: Why Robin, are you going to beg pennies of the Sheriff?

ROBIN: Not exactly. I think I shall invite the Sheriff to dine with us tonight.

MUCH: By my troth, Robin, he'll be a welcome guest!

LITTLE JOHN: A very welcome guest—I'd like to carve him up for the crows!

ROBIN: You men must hide in these trees and await my signal. Hurry now and hide!

NARRATOR: The outlaws and girls go out. Robin, hobbling like an old man, cups his hand to his ear to listen.

ROBIN: Aha! I think I hear the Sheriff coming. That villain— I'll make him pay for his cruelty!

NARRATOR: The outlaws reappear, each carrying a leafy tree branch. They hold the branches in front of them so that they are hidden behind the foliage.

ROBIN: I'll make that Sheriff sorry he ever came hunting for Robin Hood!

NARRATOR: The Sheriff enters, carrying a wooden stave. He is followed by soldiers, one of whom carries a bag of gold. The outlaws are hidden by the foliage, and the soldiers cannot see them.

SHERIFF: Halt! Who are you, ragged fellow?

ROBIN (*In a quavering voice*): Alas, I am just a poor old beggar.

SHERIFF (*Disdainfully*): You're an old bundle of rags, that's what you are! What are you doing here?

ROBIN: Alas and alack! I've been robbed! That villain took my last penny!

SHERIFF: What villain?

ROBIN (*Sadly*): That rascal—Robin Hood.

1ST SOLDIER: Robin Hood!

ROBIN (*Playing dumb*): Yes . . . alas . . . my last penny.

SHERIFF: Harken, beggar—do you know where Robin Hood is hiding?

ROBIN: Why, yes. He's not far away, that rascal—no, he's not far away at all.

SHERIFF: Lead us to him!

ROBIN: Certainly, dear Sheriff, but what will you give me if I lead you to Robin Hood?

SHERIFF: I shall reward you handsomely. I'll give you a bag of gold. But you must take us to the outlaw.

ROBIN: Fear not, good Sheriff. I'll lead you straight to Robin Hood. Follow me.

SHERIFF: When I catch that villain, I'll hang him from the tallest tree in Nottingham!

NARRATOR: Scarlet, who is hidden by the trees, hoots like an owl.

SHERIFF: What was that?

2ND SOLDIER: Evil spirits!

3RD SOLDIER: I smell witches in the air!

4TH SOLDIER (*Sniffing*): By my sword, I smell them, too!

ROBIN: Why, that's just an owl! You're not *afraid*, are you?

SOLDIERS: Afraid? Of course we're not afraid!

SHERIFF: Lead on, beggar. But mind you, no tricks! Just wait till I catch that rascal! Just wait till I get my hands on him!

NARRATOR: Little John gives a weird laugh from behind the trees.

1ST SOLDIER: This place is bewitched!

2ND SOLDIER: I—I don't like this forest!

3RD SOLDIER: Let's go back!

4TH SOLDIER: Yes, let's run before it's too late!

SHERIFF: Cowards! We will not give up the chase! Beggar, if you're trying to trick me, I'll beat you black and blue.

ROBIN: Peace, Sheriff. Surely you're not afraid of a few witches.

SHERIFF: Witches! Of c-course I'm not afraid! I'm the bravest officer of the King! L-lead on.

NARRATOR: The Sheriff and soldiers begin to tiptoe fearfully. Little John gives another laugh which is louder and longer than before. The soldiers flee from the strange laughter. As they run, one of them drops the bag of gold.

SHERIFF: Come back, you deserters! You lily-livered cowards, come back!

ROBIN: Let them go, good Sheriff. I don't think they really want to find Robin Hood.

SHERIFF: You wretch! You tattered old knave! You're trying to trick me—that's what you're doing! I'll break my stave on your shoulders, I'll beat you from here to Nottingham.

ROBIN: Gently, Sheriff! That temper ill becomes an officer of the King!

NARRATOR: Robin deftly sidesteps the Sheriff and blows his whistle. The outlaws step out and surround the Sheriff.

SHERIFF: Unhand me, you varlets!

LITTLE JOHN: Nay, Sheriff, we have you now! Robin, shall I finish him off?

ROBIN (*Genially*): Oh, no, Little John. The Sheriff is our guest. Welcome to Sherwood Forest! Robin Hood, at your service. Lend us your sword for a while, good Sheriff.

SHERIFF (*Furious*): You false rogue! You villain! How could I let you trick me this way?

MICHAEL: Calm yourself, good Sheriff. You'll feel much better after dinner.

SHERIFF: Dinner! How dare you?

LITTLE JOHN: We've roasted one of the King's finest deer for you, Sheriff. You'll eat nothing but the best! Do sit down.

SHERIFF (*Sputtering*): I will not eat! I will not sit down!

NARRATOR: The outlaws are in a playful mood. Little John pushes the Sheriff, who tumbles over Michael. Suddenly the Sheriff finds himself sitting down.

ROBIN: I'm right glad you decided to sit down, good Sheriff. Of course you will eat with us. We are famous for our hospitality.

HOB: I'll bring on the venison!

KET: I'll pour us a tankard of hearty ale!

WILL: And I'll bring the brave peasant maids to join us.

ROBIN: Come gather 'round, my merry men, and join the Sheriff at dinner.

NARRATOR: The outlaws sit down beside Robin and the Sheriff. Friar Tuck picks up the bag of gold dropped by the soldier and brings it to Robin.

FRIAR: Look, Robin! I found this bag lying near yonder tree. It doesn't sound like goose feathers. Now what could be in it?

SHERIFF: You knave! That's my gold! Thieves! Villains! Robbers!

ROBIN (*Courteously*): Oh, no, dear Sheriff. We never steal. But we do love to invite guests like yourself to dine with us.

FRIAR TUCK: And our meals, I'll grant, are rather costly.

ROBIN: For instance, the venison you eat tonight will cost you exactly one bag of gold—which you promised me anyway.

LITTLE JOHN: 'Tis only fair, good Sheriff. After all, the beggar did lead you to Robin Hood!

SHERIFF: I'll make you sorry for this, you thieving rascal! You'll pay for this outrage!

ROBIN: Save your breath to cool your dinner, Sheriff. At this moment, you're paying, not I.

NARRATOR: Will enters with the maids.

MICHAEL: Here are the lassies! Come sit down and watch the Sheriff eat!

ROBIN: Thank you, dear Sheriff, for your thoughtful gift. We will give this bag of gold to these gentle maids to take home to their families.

JOAN: Thank you, good Robin. And thank you, Sheriff.

ROBIN: Now fall to, my friends—here's venison! A hearty good appetite to thee, sir Sheriff! Let's all make merry!

OUTLAWS:
Hail, hail, we're outlaws free!
Hunt in cap and feather,
Sing in sunny weather,
Hail, hail, we're outlaws free—
Robin Hood's bold men are we!

THE END